Praise for **David Sr**

"*Utterly in command of the obscure primary sources, David Smart has crafted a compelling biography of climbing's great misunderstood genius. . . . It's a dazzling achievement.*"

—David Roberts, author of *Limits of the Known*

". . . *a nuanced and elegant biography of Emilio Comici, a climber who was immersed in the simmering ideological tension of eastern Italy between the two Great Wars, and who cared deeply about the aesthetics of climbing.*"

—Bernadette McDonald, author of *Art of Freedom*

". . . *one of the most important mountain biographers of our time. He's proven, once again, that he's a master of meticulous research, expert at unweaving a myth from a man, and uniquely able to offer insight in how time, and place, and mountains themselves, all work to shape the character of a mountain life.*"

—Geoff Powter, author of *Inner Ranges*

"*Emilio Comici was one of the most important mountaineers of the Sixth Grade years and a lover of climbing aesthetics, and yet no complete and exhaustive biography of him had been written before now. With this new book David Smart has filled a void in the history of mountaineering.*"

—Mirella Tenderini, author of *The Duke of Abruzzi*

"*Much of the book made me think of the closing song from the musical Hamilton; I kept imagining Comici, who was so concerned about greatness and about how other climbers viewed him, singing the lines: 'Let me tell you what I wish I'd known | When I was young and dreamed of glory | You have no control | Who lives, who dies, who tells your story?' I think Comici would be pleased with David Smart for telling his story so well.*"

—Alex Honnold

"David Smart's immensely knowledgeable and beautifully written biography of Emilio Comici establishes the Italian climber as one of the leading alpinists of the 20th century. . . . one of the best climbing biographies I have ever read."
—Maurice Isserman, author of *Continental Divide*

"Smart's brilliance is equally even-handed as both biographer and cultural historian. A long-awaited and absolutely essential book."
—David Stevenson, author of *Warnings Against Myself*

"David Smart writes with the authority of a top investigative journalist and the skills of a dramatist who brings the rivalries and romances of history alive on a vertiginous stage."
—John Porter, author of *One Day as a Tiger*

"The finest biography of an adventure figure I have ever found."
—John Long, author of *The Stonemasters*

"Smart . . . has intricately woven stories of Preuss' life and accomplishments with vivid illustrations of the times and the rising middle class in the outdoors into a magnificent biography."
—*The Suburban Mountaineer*

". . . a skillfully written and meticulously researched book."
—*Climber Magazine UK*

". . . an intriguing dive into the [Preuss'] life and accomplishments."
—*Revelstoke Mountaineer*

Royal Robbins

The American Climber

David Smart

Foreword by John Long

MOUNTAINEERS
BOOKS

MOUNTAINEERS BOOKS is dedicated
to the exploration, preservation, and enjoyment
of outdoor and wilderness areas.

1001 SW Klickitat Way, Suite 201, Seattle, WA 98134
800-553-4453, www.mountaineersbooks.org

Printed in China

Distributed in the United Kingdom by Cordee, www.cordee.co.uk

26 25 24 23   1 2 3 4 5

Copyeditor: Matt Samet
Design and layout: Melissa McFeeters
Cartographer: Bart Wright and Melissa McFeeters
Cover photograph: *Royal Robbins in Yosemite Valley, 1961* (Photo by Tom Frost, courtesy of
NACHA)

Library of Congress Cataloging-in-Publication Data
Names: Chaundy-Smart, David, 1962- author.
Title: Royal Robbins : the American climber / David Smart ; Foreword by John Long.
Description: Seattle, WA : Mountaineers Books, 2023. | Includes bibliographical references.
| Summary: "Definitive biography of one of America's most influential outdoor figures"—
Provided by publisher.
Identifiers: LCCN 2022056397 (print) | LCCN 2022056398 (ebook) | ISBN 9781680516586
(paperback) | ISBN 9781680516593 (epub)
Subjects: LCSH: Robbins, Royal. | Mountaineers—Ohio—Biography. | Mountaineering—
United States. | Rock climbing—United States.
Classification: LCC GV199.92.R62 S63 2023 (print) | LCC GV199.92.R62 (ebook) | DDC
796.522/30973—dc23/eng/20221214
LC record available at https://lccn.loc.gov/2022056397
LC ebook record available at https://lccn.loc.gov/2022056398

Mountaineers Books titles may be purchased for corporate, educational, or other
promotional sales, and our authors are available for a wide range of events. For information
on special discounts or booking an author, contact our customer service at 800-553-4453 or
mbooks@mountaineersbooks.org.

Printed on FSC®-certified materials

ISBN (paperback): 978-1-68051-658-6
ISBN (ebook): 978-1-68051-659-3

An independent nonprofit publisher since 1960

For Elizabeth, Tamara, and Damon

One must have heroes, which is to say, one must create them. And they become real through our envy, our devotion. It is we who give them their majesty, their power, which we ourselves could never possess. And in turn, they give some back. But they are mortal, these heroes, just as we are.

—James Salter

Contents

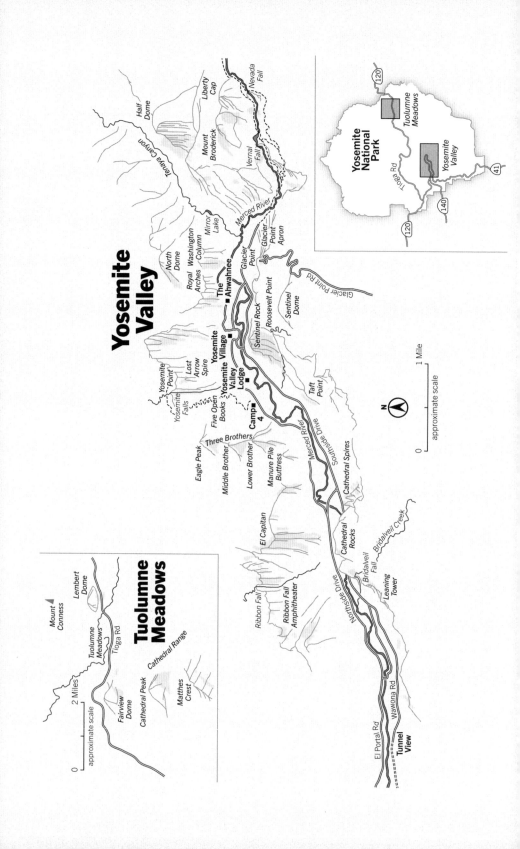

Foreword

When I was a sophomore in high school and wannabe rock star, I'd often wander through the Backpacker Shop, in Claremont, California, eyeing all the rock gear I couldn't afford just yet, wondering how I'd ever learn how to use it once I could. That's when I saw the poster for Mountain Paraphernalia, featuring a trim Royal Robbins—manicured beard, creased knickers and red knicker socks, a white hat that I equated, for some reason, with British Formula One drivers—pasted on a vertical rock face what appeared like a mile off the deck. I still remember the rush of seeing that photo: As I imagined myself on that rock face, my heart redlined and I had to brace myself against the wall of the shop. I wanted to be Royal Robbins so badly I could have screamed.

Royal Robbins (1935–2017) marched point for the Yosemite Pioneers during the "Golden Age" of American rock climbing—the 1950s and '60s, when the Valley's granite walls were first ascended. Several factors conspire to make him a historical figure.

First, the venue for Robbins's most notable ascents: Yosemite Valley, crown jewel of the National Park Service, with over three million annual visitors. Immortalized by John Muir and the early paintings of Albert Bierstadt and Thomas Moran, by photographer Carleton Watkins, and later, Ansel Adams, whose words and images burned Yosemite into world consciousness. Then the iconic granite monoliths like El Capitan and Half Dome, which, along with the waterfalls, are Yosemite's main attractions. The thought of climbing those walls strikes terror in the hearts of tourists who gape up from the meadows, enveloped in a timeless awe, wondering what sorts of mad people dare such heights. And finally, the era, when an entire generation chased the "last unknowns." The 1950s and '60s saw space exploration go from sending a dog into orbit (1957) to landing a man on the moon (1969). Meanwhile, on Earth, Tenzing Norgay and Edmund Hillary summited Everest (1953). In 1957, Robbins, Jerry Gallwas, and Mike Sherrick bagged the first ascent of the *Regular Northwest Face* of Half Dome. The following year, mighty El Capitan fell to Warren Harding, Wayne Merry, George Whitmore, and Rich Calderwood.

These two ascents, arguably the first genuine "big walls" climbed in the United States, thrust Yosemite to the forefront of rock climbing and kick-started the adventure-sports movement. Even more than what they did, Robbins and the Yosemite Pioneers are legends for what they began, namely the ever-growing outdoor-recreation market. Yet in today's age of fleeting Instagram "stars" and a splintered climbing community in which distinction hinges on our differences, even Robbins—titan that he was—is known mostly as a historical footnote. Who looks back these days? It's always been that way.

· · · · ·

When I first stumbled into the Valley as a seventeen-year-old nobody in the early '70s, I knew and cared little about Robbins the person (I would later work for the man, if only briefly). I only wanted to bag the giant rocks Robbins and the Yosemite Pioneers had packed into the pipe dreams of all of us wannabe rock stars. Only later, when I could view my Yosemite experience in a wider context, did I appreciate the gravity of the past and how even the greatest among us, then and now, are still orbiting Royal Robbins.

The warp and weft of Robbins's life is lyrically described by David Smart, as only a skilled biographer can do. But over the decades, since I first tracked Robbins's footsteps, his sway over me has reached far beyond the granite walls we shared in common.

Robbins's early years were the trainwreck that often breeds felons and drunks. Luckily for "RR," he found climbing, a way out of his hardscrabble youth, and he threw himself at the rock with abandon. As his climbs got harder, so increased the commitment, risk, and fear. Perhaps during his second ascent of the North Face of the Sentinel (he and his partners were still teenagers) in 1953, or four years later, on the first ascent of the *Regular Northwest Face* of Half Dome, Robbins realized the great truth that Viktor Frankl had discovered during his captivity in Nazi concentration camps. As Frankl wrote in *Man's Search for Meaning*, which details his ordeal, when a person has a reason to live, they can face almost any travail.

Such an approach, commonly born from trials by fire, goes directly against our instinctual response to avoid pain and seek pleasure and security. Problem is, we all have an expiration date, which leaves us wondering what anything *means*. Since our aversion to suffering runs so deep, few come to know, as an existential fact, that purpose and meaning accrue from facing difficulties, all while exploring what we can *bring* to the adventure. Not easy. Life happens. Dreams unravel. Friends and family drop away as we hurtle toward the vanishing point.

And that's where Royal's legacy has paid the richest dividends. Learning that we are strangely saved by meeting life on its own terms, embracing the whole catastrophe, and discovering what grit and passion we can muster for the task. Remembering that, in any set of circumstances, no matter how grave, we can follow Robbins's example and choose our own way. Anything less leaves us underutilized.

There are Rubicons that Robbins likely never crossed, which Smart brings into sharp, sometimes painful focus. A thorny aloofness plagued the man, which he escaped—if ever—only within his nuclear family. Nobody gets it all. But there's every sign that Robbins lived and died by his own lights, choosing his own way, often the path of greatest resistance, to explore and confirm who he was and what he had. That's why he's Royal Robbins. That's why he marched point, opening the route for the rest of us to follow. That's why his story is not solely for the outdoor crowd, but for all of humanity.

John Long
March 2023

A Note
on Sources

This book was written after extensive research. I reviewed Royal's own writings—both published and unpublished, including journals—existing publications like the *American Alpine Journal* and *Summit*, correspondence between Royal and his peers, and extensive interviews with Royal's family and friends. Unless noted otherwise, in all cases where someone "said" something, the quoted material comes directly from an interview I conducted. In all cases where someone "wrote" something, the source is either cited in the body text or, in cases where further clarification was needed, there is a citation in Notes.

1

Ride the Trail in Style

A MAN IN A WHITE HAT has been making his way up the 3,000-foot granite face of El Capitan for five days—a wall no one has ever climbed alone. The *Muir Wall* had been ascended a few years earlier by men he knows, men driven into a state of ascetic reverie on the first ascent by the difficulty and isolation, men who could live on ten raisins a day.

His means of ascent is pitons hammered into cracks. Where he is at the moment, the crack is thin and leaning, tucked away in a stone corner—a dihedral. He stretches up toward a section that looks wider, and stuffs a tiny piton into the crack. As he reaches for his hammer, he utters a stream of puns and quotes from Emerson, Tolkien, and the French existentialists. He belts out songs as they float to the surface of his consciousness. Listening like a piano tuner for the right note when steel meshes with granite, he taps on the piton, sweating even though it's 50 degrees and windy.

The piton doesn't ring true, but he has no choice. He clips a webbing etrier to it, feeds a foot of rope through the thin prusik sling he uses to shorten his rope, and stands up in it. The piton tears free with a tiny grinding whine and he falls into the 2,500 feet of space below. Before he has time to think, he smashes into the rock, the rope tied around his waist crushing his belly. His heart hammers against his ribcage. He hates falling but always forces himself to keep climbing until he does.

Checking to see that he is still wearing his hat, he straightens his glasses and looks up to where his piton tore free. His friends say that through those black plastic spectacles, he sees the wall differently than they do. He refers to himself as an unstoppable demon, a glutton for rock, but now he faces a problem. He cannot make a piton work where others have. El Capitan is a stadium, and he is its star. People who know his views, who look up to him, are watching from the meadow below; it would be the same at any cliff in the US, France, or the United Kingdom. He is their champion—a legend.

The only option is to drill a hole and place a bolt, a practice he abhors. A paint salesman and high school dropout, he sees things when he looks up that few have contemplated—his own death, potential climbing routes where others see only blank stone. He sees the rock as something whose beauty will persist long after climbers have gone. A bolt would besmirch it, a mark of human shame because his friends have climbed past here without it. But there is no one to rescue him—no way off but up.

· · · · ·

In the early morning of February 3, 1935, Mason County, West Virginia, lay under weeks of snowfall. The temperature in the silent streets of Point Pleasant was minus 15 degrees Fahrenheit. In the rented second floor of a small house on the outskirts, twenty-year-old Beulah Bowen was in the midst of a protracted, painful labor.

"It's a pity," said one of the midwives, "she has to die so young." But the scars on Beulah's torso from a childhood accident with a gas heater showed her resilience. She would survive her labor, as would the child.

Beulah named her son Royal Shannon Robbins, after her husband, who went by Shannon. Royal later described his given name as "a lower-class Irish ploy," but his father came from a brood of unusually named progeny, including brothers Loring and Marvel and sister Wenotah. Royal's paternal grandfather, John Robbins, was a stonemason who knew the textures and smells of granite and discovered how it cooperated with his chisel. He is most remembered for the poetic act of carving his own tombstone. Stone offered the poor an outlet for the pharaonic urge to leave traces, to come to terms with the brevity and uncertainty of life.

Shannon's name was likely borrowed from a popular schoolbook author, and he hoped to be a writer like his namesake, but his folk were Appalachian workers who could write little more than their own names, instead passing down detailed family trees and oral history. Shannon left school at six, and learned to write by cribbing from books. When he wasn't reading, he liked to fight, and became the state welterweight boxing champion.

Early in 1934, Shannon sauntered into the drugstore where Beulah worked in Gallipolis, on the Ohio side of the eponymous river. He was two years older than her and did odd jobs at a garage, but she was intrigued by his manners, movie-star moustache, and sad smile. The attraction was mutual, and they married in the minister's house on July 3.

Shannon was a poor excuse of a husband. He drank to excess, smashed the furniture in fits of rage, and had affairs. He threatened to burn Beulah's clothes if she followed him to one of his lovers' houses and made up stories about a twin brother who had been killed in a brawl—and whose assailants he claimed to have murdered. Worse, he seemed to believe his own lies. After two years of marriage, Beulah decided that she and Royal had a better chance of surviving without Shannon, so she threw him out.

The following January, the Ohio River flooded the streets of Point Pleasant, and many people drowned or died of hypothermia. "The water rose nearly to the second story," Royal wrote in his journal, "where my mother waited in terror, holding me tight. My father was elsewhere, he was often elsewhere." Beulah, whom Royal described as "radiant in her purity and innocence," was his refuge, guarding him from the cold, dark waters.

· · · · ·

Beulah met James "Jimmy" Lee Chandler the next year, and they fell in love. Soon Royal and his mother moved to Chandler's hometown of Mansfield, Ohio. When they married, Beulah took his last name and used it for the rest of her life. Chandler changed Royal's name to Jimmy Chandler, because he thought Royal sounded too "high-falutin'," and he wanted Royal to seem like his son. And although Royal's father was legally entitled to object, no one knew his whereabouts.

Chandler soon proved little better than his predecessor. Employers fired him after a few days because he was argumentative and often drunk.

The family lived off the wages Beulah made at a drugstore. One evening when Royal was five he refused to go to bed, and Chandler whipped his bare buttocks with his belt until they bled. Royal claimed to have "asked for" the punishment, as if to take back agency from Chandler; to avoid further beatings, Royal accepted Chandler's fantasy that he was his father.

For his own protection, Beulah sent Royal to live at Roy and Leoda Probst's foster home for children. When he wet his bed, the foster-home matrons held his face beneath the showerhead until he was half-drowned. Without state oversight or even restrictions on punishment, they repeated the torture with impunity, but without results.

Standing under the showerhead, Royal's pride and shame collided, and he discovered an unshakeable inner composure. He began to pity the matrons who sought to break him by such feeble means. The emotional and physical blows of his childhood would be offset by an uncanny sense of invulnerability.

In 1940, it became clear that the US would soon be participating in the Second World War. Shannon Robbins and Jimmy Chandler filled out their draft cards. Beulah lost some hours at the drugstore because cosmetic sales had dwindled, and wartime work to replace her wages was slow to come to Mansfield. Jimmy's older brother, William, had moved to Los Angeles with his wife, Velma, and owned a gas station on La Brea Avenue. Beulah and Jimmy decided to try their luck out in California, where every month the promise of wartime work drew thousands of hopeful survivors of the Great Depression.

Their first stop was a clapboard rental near Pier Avenue in Hermosa Beach, steps from the roaring Pacific, the first and only thing Royal loved about the town. The ocean's enormity offered shelter to a boy who longed to escape an environment mismanaged by petty adults. He learned to let the currents carry him out and wash him back onto the beach, indulging a forbidden impulse to surrender, half-terrified, to the immeasurable power of nature.

The birth of Royal's half-sister, Helen Penelope Chandler (Penny), on September 15, 1941, inspired Jimmy to spend a few days looking for work, but he soon found his new responsibility tiresome and retired to the bar.

Royal became profoundly protective of Penny, and remained so throughout his life.

The sense of a world under threat from above was palpable in Los Angeles. Searchlights combed the night skies for Japanese aircraft. Hundreds of Japanese balloons carrying incendiary devices drifted across the Pacific and landed on the West Coast. Bubble-gum cards depicted the silhouettes of enemy aircraft. Comic books, chewing gum, and toys reflected an obsession with flight. America's most powerful hero, Superman, could fly without an aircraft, and in Royal's daydreams, so could he.

As he wrote in *My Life: To Be Brave*, "Looking down, I could see houses here, trees there, and rivers, and roads. . . . My dream-flying could occur only by dint of great effort. . . . I flew not by grace or skill, but by pure force of will. I flew because I *would*." In this fantasy, his inner discipline, the resolve that defeated abuse and shame, overcame the limitations of his body, even of gravity itself.

A boy with such an intense interior life was powerless against the attractions of the movies. When he was six, his favorite serial, featuring Nyoka the Jungle Girl, hit the screens. Nyoka Gordon, a crack shot, equestrian, rock climber, and judo expert, wore khaki shorts, a blouse with cartridge tubes sewn over the bust, and pistol holsters. Her sidekick, an obvious surrogate for boy movie-goers, had a pet shoulder-monkey and wore a similar uniform. Episodes usually climaxed with Nyoka and her scantily clad nemesis, Vultura, locked in hand-to hand combat while Vultura's gorilla sidekick joined in or gesticulated on the sidelines.

Thoughts of Nyoka haunted Royal. One night he dreamt Beulah was being attacked by Vultura's gorilla and woke up in a panic. He climbed out his window and convinced the neighbors to call the police to check on her.

When the family moved to West Hollywood, Royal became a regular patron at the westerns-only venue of the Hitching Post at Hollywood and Vine. On the silver screen, the heroic western landscape, with its mountains and colossal sandstone walls, inspired character contests between heroes who slept right on the desert sand next to their campfires. Dale Evans, Royal's second movie crush after Nyoka, wore six shooters, rode horses, and preferred the open range to domestic life. She was also the first outdoorsperson in Royal's life who didn't just ride the trail, but did it with style—a philosophy declared in the refrain to her signature song.

· · · · ·

In 1942, the Chandlers couldn't make rent and moved to a trailer park in Redondo Beach, a few miles south. Kids welcomed Royal by shooting him in the back of the neck with an air rifle. Royal tried to prove his worth by standing behind a sign while a boy shot it with a bow and arrow. He stuck his head out at the last moment to show off, and the arrow struck him above the nose. The scar never went away.

Despite his bravado, a certain sadness pervaded Royal's mien during those years. In a 1942 photograph, he salutes the camera in a costume uniform with a Sam Browne belt, looking worried and unsure. Royal rarely smiled in boyhood photos, unless he was with Beulah.

In 1944, the Chandlers again could no longer make rent and moved in with Jimmy's brother, William, William's wife, Velma, and their children. The contrast between Jimmy's struggling family and his brother's happy home drove Jimmy to drink even more. Arguments between Beulah and Jimmy became frequent and violent. One day, Jimmy called Royal a sissy after a girl beat him in an impromptu footrace. "Being called a Sissy," wrote Royal, who as an adult never lost his respect for the athletic abilities of women, "was the worst thing in my life." Royal was no weakling, but neither was he especially fast or strong. He saw his body's failure, however, as just another limitation to overcome. His willfulness supplied him with a desperate kind of hope.

Through her retail job, Beulah eventually made enough money to rent a house on the impoverished streets between the Hollywood movie lots where America's dreams (and nightmares) were forged. Royal described their little house on Seward Avenue as "decent," although their sleep was often interrupted by the bells at Fire Station 51, just across the street. It was a small price for the opportunity to hang around the station, playing horseshoes and comparing the firemen to the two fathers in Royal's life.

Kids in the family's new neighborhood played dangerous games. Royal destroyed his bicycle in a crash with another boy, stepped on a nail in an abandoned warehouse, battled kids from other streets on vacant lots, and trespassed through backyards not, as he recalled, "to get to Santa Monica Boulevard, but to make the journey *interesting*." Beulah thought Royal needed more structure, and in 1944 she enrolled him in Wolf Cubs. The rules and ceremonies of the weekly meetings disheartened him. After he tried unsuccessfully to get a girl to notice him by wearing his Cub uniform, he quit.

Beulah often asked Royal to go down to Davy Jones's Locker, a bar, and tell his stepfather to come home. When Jimmy ran out of drinking money, he would ask Beulah for a few dollars. Denied his liquor money, he became loud, sometimes even violent. One evening in 1945, Royal awoke to hear Jimmy and Beulah fighting. When his mother cried out, "Jim, put down that knife," Royal climbed out his window and ran to the Technicolor plant half a block away. By the time the police arrived with Royal in the patrol car, Beulah had escaped to the fire station and Jimmy had fled.

Although Beulah then banned Jimmy from her life, he returned one night when Royal was alone. He produced a knife, not to threaten Royal, but to cut off his own finger to prove he had changed. "Jimmy," Beulah would tell Royal, "was at his worst on Seward Avenue." He left with all his fingers, and soon after ended up in a mental health facility. A few years later, he died in a bar fight.

In the summer of 1945, America defeated Japan. Beulah called Royal into her room and told him things he half-remembered but had suppressed to make peace with Jimmy. For the first time in years, she spoke the name she had given Royal at birth. Beulah told Royal that his biological father, Shannon, had been a hunter, writer, and professional boxer. She told her son that now he could use his father's name.

"I instantly knew I wanted to be like my father," Royal said. "I didn't want my step-father's name. I could slough it off like a snake sloughs its skin." A proud son with a real father, Royal informally added "Junior" to his name when signing some of his letters.

Soon after, however, a less joyous reminder of life back in Mason County arrived at Seward Avenue. Royal's grandparents came to stay, in search of work. However, his grandmother's enthusiasm for corporal punishment didn't sit well with the unmonitored home life Royal had enjoyed. He fled to a Salvation Army warehouse where he hid out for a few days reading used comic books. He'd run away to "measure his importance" to adults, but his grandparents, homesick for West Virginia, were soon gone anyway. Beulah proposed a visit with his father, who she hoped would straighten the boy out.

Shannon, however, had neither thrived nor changed his ways. His letters to Royal described wrestling with an octopus so large it capsized his boat, pulling a four-hundred-pound halibut out of the Aleutian Sea, and various incredible feats in the ring and on the baseball diamond. Royal, a ten-year-old survivor of an abusive stepfather, longed to reunite with his true father. Shannon, however, had left out a few key autobiographical facts.

After the divorce, Shannon had drifted north to Detroit. By April 1940, he was a resident at the Eloise Psychiatric Hospital in Nankin, Michigan. The next spring, he volunteered for the West Virginia National Guard at Fort Benjamin Harrison in Indianapolis. On March 22, 1942, Shannon's unit shipped from Seattle to Kodiak Island to help defend Alaska against Japanese invasion. Shannon, in correspondence with Beulah, claimed he'd been a tugboat captain during his service and his boat had been washed onto a reef. Immobilized by injuries, he lay on the beach for three days before he was rescued. In mid-October 1944, he was discharged. He took a room in the decrepit Milner Hotel in Detroit, drank, and lived off his veteran's benefits.

After what must have been a frightening solitary cross-country trip, the idealistic son who had taken his father's name found Shannon in what he called a "shabby, dark and cheerless" room. Royal hungered for his father's approval and made the most of any small compliment Shannon offered him, but mostly, he found his father strange and insecure. Shannon said he had crawled through the backseat of a car that blocked him at an intersection to show the driver that no one was going to get in his way. Royal thought the story made his father sound like a fool. Nonetheless, Royal wrote his father regularly for a year after he returned to Los Angeles. Shannon responded occasionally with letters, in the margins of which he sometimes scribbled notes begging Beulah to take him back.

· · · · ·

One scorching early summer afternoon, after a dip in the pool at the local YMCA, Royal discovered a sign-up sheet for a free, weeklong camp near Bear Lake in the San Bernardino National Forest. He signed up right away.

Royal's love for camp was undeniable, unexpected, and irreversible. Seduced by the treasure hunts, hikes, singsongs, clean air, and pine trees, he wrote Beulah to tell her he didn't want to come home. "The days go very slow here," he wrote, "and that's what is good about it."

But camp came to an end. Back in Los Angeles, Royal could access his beloved outdoors only by hitching rides in strangers' cars or hopping on the Santa Monica Boulevard streetcar to reach the sand cliffs of the Pacific Palisades, the beach, and the ocean. Summer vacation eventually ended, and the freedom of the seaside and memories of camp made school seem suffocating and joyless.

His spelling was poor and arithmetic baffled him, and by the time he enrolled in Vine Street Elementary in Hollywood, he had already left three schools before he could make friends or get to know the teachers. Stymied by conventional learning, Royal took his intellectual curiosity to the public library. Later in life, Royal told novelist James Salter that as a boy he read "mostly dog stories," which was partly true. His favorite writer, Albert Payson Terhune, pitted the heroic, purebred dogs of his novels against villainous, larcenous, racially stereotyped mongrels.

Royal also enjoyed Mary O'Hara's *My Friend Flicka*, the saga of a boy's unrequitable love for a wild horse, and Felix Salten's *Bambi, A Life in the Woods*, with its absentee father who comes through for his son in the end. In another favorite, Ann Sewell's *Black Beauty*, articulate and emotionally complex horses survive the savage treatment of brutish humans. As a victim of physical abuse, Royal empathized. He venerated heroes, but did not emulate them. In class, he threw paper airplanes, spoke out of turn, and once lit a fire in a wastepaper basket. His marks plummeted. It was the era of corporal punishment, and he was often punished, but rarely corrected.

After class, Royal wandered the neighborhood with his friends Steve Smith, Tom Akawie, and Royal Slagle (the only other Royal that Robbins would ever meet). They graduated from hitching rides on streetcars to jumping on the mile-long, Union Pacific trains lurching out of town, bound for unknown destinations. When the novelty of riding the rails wore off, Royal suggested jumping from the roof of one train onto another headed in the opposite direction. When he tried it, he slipped and almost fell beneath the cars to a grisly death. "I had done something special," he wrote, "something very daring, and this gave me a secret satisfaction."

As a serial hitchhiker, Royal was occasionally assaulted or propositioned for sex by male drivers. Hitchhiking could lead to a charge of juvenile delinquency, but molestors were rarely prosecuted in California. "I had to take risks," Royal said. "Child molesters were just one of the dangers we daily faced on the streets of L.A."

In 1947, twelve-year-old Royal enrolled in Thomas Starr King Junior High School, where he continued to struggle. Royal hoped his potential was perhaps undiscovered, but a school intelligence test revealed no hidden gifts. Physically assaulted by other students twice, he did not strike back. He could abide suffering and risk, but he lacked his father's inclination toward violence.

A gangly, awkward teenager, he floundered in school and stewed in dark thoughts about the future. In spring of 1947, however, he received an invitation to return to the YMCA Camp at Bear Lake—an experience that would alter the direction of his life.

2

Anarchy and Aimlessness

CAMP PROMISED A NEW START in the clean air of the Sierra woods. In 1947, however, there was a fifty-dollar fee. Some of Royal's friends signed up, but Beulah couldn't afford it. "I had to go," Royal said, "and I wasn't going to take no for an answer," not even from the almighty. He dropped out of Sunday school, he wrote, "turned [his] back on God, and became the Devil's disciple."

Royal decided to get his camp fees by robbery. He accosted a man on Las Palmas Avenue in broad daylight with a toy pistol. The victim laughed, gave him a dollar bill, and walked on. Royal gave up on going to camp, but not on crime. In late 1947, twelve-year-old Royal, Steve King, and Royal Slagle began to slit bedroom window screens with a nail and grab any purses or wallets within reach. Royal sometimes crawled inside and crept across the room in search of other loot, even if he could hear his victims talking in the hallway.

"We were no run-of-the-mill burglars," Royal wrote. "We might not have realized it, but money was a secondary goal." They broke the law for the thrills. The police reacted to a scourge of similar "Boy Burglars" with heightened vigilance, and many of these gangs, including Royal's, were eventually caught in the act. Royal felt insulted when the police didn't believe he was the leader, but he became less sanguine when he was delivered to the Los Angeles Central Juvenile Hall in Boyle Heights, with its mildewed walls and rusting window bars.

He was put in a uniform, forced to do military-style exercises in the yard, and slept in a dormitory with inmates who had committed violent crimes. Sexual and physical assaults were common at the center. The open toilets exposed a vulnerability about nudity exacerbated by his history of abuse. He "avoided looking at those using the toilets," he wrote in his autobiography, and "avoided the eyes of those waiting." Three days later, Beulah convinced the judge Royal was a good boy who would never offend again. Steve Smith was also released. Royal Slagle's parents chose to leave him in the juvenile justice system.

Beulah could no longer afford the rent for Seward Avenue, and the family moved back to William and Velma Chandler's on Commonwealth Avenue. Royal became a paperboy, selling the liberal-leaning *Herald Express* and the conservative-leaning *Los Angeles Daily News,* depending on the customer's views, at the corner of Santa Monica Boulevard and Vermont Avenue.

After a few months, Beulah saved enough to move out and rent a series of small houses, first on Griffith Park Avenue, then Mohawk, and finally on Hyperion. In Griffith Park, Royal discovered that climbing on the crumbling conglomerate of Bee Rock was as thrilling as burglary, without the risk of jail. In January 1948, on the suggestion of his scrambling partner Homer—William Chandler's nephew—Royal joined Troop 127 of the Boy Scouts of America.

The police department sponsored the troop to give boys an alternative to petty crime. Scoutmaster Phil Bailey was a beat cop, a veteran, and, for Royal, a sorely needed father figure. Bailey dubbed his Scouts "the Rainbow Troop," to emphasize the group's racial inclusiveness.

The Boy Scouts, per their handbook, emphasized fighting "everything unclean," in an era when Biblical concepts of sexual and moral cleanliness still resonated. "Scout's Honor" emphasized self-respect, playing by the rules, and an abhorrence of cheats; to "be prepared" was to harden yourself for the outdoor life. *The Boy Scout Handbook's* claim that being good at baseball didn't make you a good outdoorsperson offered hope to boys like

Royal, who were always picked last for teams. Royal wrote that Scouting kept him "from drowning in a sea of anarchy and aimlessness."

Scouts gave Royal free access to outdoor activities ranging from bike rides and hikes to weeklong hiking trips in the hills above Los Angeles. The more time Royal spent outdoors, the more he hungered for it. Truancy broke with Scout philosophy, but Royal couldn't help himself. He skipped school to hitchhike to the San Gabriel Mountains, fifty miles north of Los Angeles. Alone in the canyons, he hiked and explored, becoming stronger and more self-reliant. His troop leaders praised his growing confidence, but they might have been more circumspect had they known he'd gained some of it during school hours.

In 1949, Scoutmaster Bailey took a few scouts to Yosemite to assess its potential for a troop camping trip. The park was about a five-hour trip from Los Angeles, the farthest Royal had traveled since visiting his father in Detroit. Royal's eyes were drawn to the 3,000-foot-tall, mile-long wall that dominated the Valley. That was El Capitan, Bailey told him. It would never be climbed.

Royal, like many Scouts, listened to Clem Glass's *Scoutmaster of the Air* program on KFI Los Angeles. Glass had founded the High Sierra Patrol, an annual, multiday hike in the mountains. Although Royal had been a Scout for less than a year and didn't qualify, Bailey used his influence to get him on the trip. In a photograph taken during the High Sierra Patrol outing in Yosemite, Bailey, in full uniform, beams at his convert to the straight and narrow. Royal looks ecstatic in his uniform, although he only had a single merit badge on his sleeve.

Royal was pleased when the leaders weighed the packs and his was the lightest. At night, he wished he had brought an extra blanket, but he didn't complain and slept on the ground next to the campfire. On their first day, invigorated by the alpine terrain, Royal swapped packs with a boy with an oversized pack, selflessly carrying the heavier load for the rest of the trip.

On their second day, Royal had his first glimpse of the granite tooth of Fin Dome. When two of the leaders announced they would lead four boys to the summit, Royal volunteered, describing his urge to scale it as "instinctive." The regular route up the west face of Fin Dome can be climbed without a rope, but the Scout leaders chose a more direct, technical line up the face. The climbers roped together, but they had no pitons, carabiners, or secure belays.

"Blessed with a degree of agility," Royal wrote, "I clambered like a monkey up the short rock steps . . . the movements came naturally, as if climbing was in my blood. I was at ease with the steepness and exposure."

On the summit, wrote Royal, they sat "wolfing the food down," and "surveyed our domain, like kings." In this moment of pure, almost religious joy, Royal Robbins became a climber. The sport would haunt his every step. Attempts to put anything else ahead of climbing would fail. He joyfully subjected himself to its risks and demands. On his ecstatic, unroped descent of Fin Dome, he wrote that he "felt superior" to his companions and descended in a series of leaps, only slowing down after he nearly fell to his death.

A single climb had rendered powerless the negative influences in Royal's life: adult authority, an unstable home life, school. After he returned to Los Angeles, he stole manila ropes from a trucking yard to use on his own adventures. He scrounged money to buy three pitons and a carabiner from an army surplus store. At the library, he checked out Kenneth Henderson's *Handbook of North American Mountaineering,* which had been written to teach the American military basic climbing techniques. Few climbers ever read a sentence with more interest and intention than Royal brought to Henderson's proposition that "the use of pitons opens up many interesting possibilities."

Royal continued to skip school for the San Gabriels, but now he scoured them for cliffs. Potential rope partners bold enough to skip school were scarce. Kids rarely tagged along with him twice. Mostly, he climbed on his own.

· · · · ·

In October of 1949, Royal made the first ascent of 600-foot-high Mount Williamson Rock. On a steep lieback near the top, he hammered in a piton, passed the rope through the eye, and tied both ends to his waist. The forces of a fall would crush his abdomen and possibly kill him, but if he made it, he could pull the rope up from above.

With a partner, the climb would have been straightforward. But as a solo, it quickly and unexpectedly became a serious adventure. Most could not survive, let alone flourish, in this world where simple things became so suddenly weighty and unyielding, but Royal did so with creativity and style. On a second visit to Mount Williamson Rock with Tom Akawie (who would go on to become a notable artist), Royal chose a harder climb. The logic of competition, if only against himself, had already begun to inform Royal's route choices. He was now a climber.

Royal's penultimate Scouting adventure was Troop 127's journey to the National Jamboree in Valley Forge, Pennsylvania, in 1950. On the return trip, the Troop's bus suffered numerous mechanical breakdowns, but Royal caused one of the longest delays when he and a few others snuck off into the South Dakota Badlands. They returned, hours after the scheduled departure time, to angry and worried Scoutmasters. For Royal, the freedom of those few hours in the wild was worth the reprimands.

In September 1950, Royal began ninth grade at John Marshall High School with a predictable lack of enthusiasm. "Royal wasn't unpopular and he wasn't isolated, but some of the teachers got mad at him," said Bill Derr, his closest school friend. "One time we threw a transom rod out the window and it just missed the gardener. Another time, he was supposed to give a talk about rock climbing, and after a few words, went to the back of the class, tied into a rope that I hid in my desk and I lowered him out the window. The vice principal didn't like that." Few realized that when Royal wasn't playing the high-spirited prankster he was scribbling messages of self-loathing in his notebooks.

In the midst of this turmoil, Royal came upon James Ramsey Ullman's 1941 book, *High Conquest*. It was a discovery of monumental significance. "It is the ultimate wisdom of the mountains that a man is never more a man than when he is striving for what is beyond his grasp," Ullman wrote in a passage Royal memorized, "and that there is no conquest worth the winning save that over his own weakness, ignorance, and fear." Ullman concluded his book with the suggestion that it is "not the victory, but the game itself that matters." "I was a sucker," Royal later wrote for the *Alpine Journal*, "for heroic prose like that."

In November 1950, Royal made his first visit to a cliff in the Los
Angeles suburb of Chatsworth that he'd spotted from the roof of a train.
The climbers' bolts Royal found on Stoney Point's sandstone boulders
rendered the area's graffiti and broken glass all but invisible to him. Real
climbers scaled these rocks, and so would he.

One day out at Stoney, after he ripped out a piton an inner voice had
told him not to trust, he fell to the ground and broke his arm. As Royal
moped around the house in a cast, he concluded that nothing made him
as happy as climbing. He decided that in the future, he would always listen
to his inner voice—the broken arm would be his last climbing injury for
more than a half a century.

Royal was back at Stoney Point before his cast was removed. A group
of climbers, the first he had ever met, were toproping on a steep-sided
twenty-foot-high boulder. He overcame his shyness to ask who they were.
Ellen Wilts looked the part of a climber and introduced herself and told
him they were from the Rock Climbing Section (RCS) of the Los Angeles
Chapter of the Sierra Club. Lean and fit, Wilts asked Royal to join them.
Royal would later write that his new friends were "the best people I had
ever met." A few weeks later he went to his first Sierra Club meeting.

The Los Angeles RCS was one of the most vibrant rock climbing communities in North America. On occasion, there were more than 125 rock
climbers at Sierra Club events at Stoney Point alone. Presentations by
experts like Chuck Wilts, John Mendenhall, and Glen Dawson were the
highlight of evening meetings. "This was more like it," Royal said, "why
talk about anything else?"

The RCS produced the monthly *Mugelnoos* newsletter to announce
upcoming events, report on climbs, and relay local climbing and skiing
gossip. Royal read every issue cover to cover; soon, the leaders and legends of California climbing were more familiar and important to him than
baseball stars were to his peers. In an age when young men looked up to
the superficial machismo of Dean Martin and Frank Sinatra, Royal thrilled
to Clarence King's 1872 volume *Mountaineering in the Sierra Nevada* and
John Muir's 1894 *The Mountains of California*.

Even the Sierra Club could not satisfy Royal's hunger for the outdoors.
Royal joined Derr's Scout troop for an ascent of 10,834-foot Mount San

Jacinto from the north, a rugged 8,000-foot scramble. On the descent, Royal snuck away to climb a twenty-foot-high cliff. The leader chastised him, and he never again went on another Boy Scout excursion.

Royal and a friend hitchhiked to Yosemite. "Luckily, we couldn't get off the ground in the Valley," said Royal in an interview. The rangers recommended that they instead check out Ostrander Lake—in the park south of the Valley proper—and so "we camped up there and climbed around the cliffs, which are more hospitable than the fierce things that rise out of the Valley." His first climbing trip to Yosemite had been a modest success.

At Stoney Point in the spring of 1951, Royal met Frank Hoover, Fred Martin, and Don Wilson. The three college freshmen had met as summer interns at the Natural History Museum of Los Angeles County the year before and began backpacking and climbing together. Wilson's professor, Chuck Wilts, Ellen's husband, encouraged them to join the RCS.

Hoover was a Los Angeles City College student and an amusing source of dirty limericks, but only a moderately talented climber. Martin had graduated from Huntington Beach High School and was attending the California Institute of Technology in Pasadena to study physics. Wilson, who studied biology at the University of Southern California, was the trio's unofficial leader. At eighteen, he was also the oldest of the three. In a 1951 photograph, he is festooned with ropes, and carabiners hang from the belt loops of his jeans. He wears a baseball cap with an upturned bill. Long, muscular arms hang from his T-shirt sleeves, and a cigarette stuck between his fingers makes him look like the neighborhood tough guy.

That hot summer, hits like "Aba Daba Honeymoon" by Debbie Reynolds and "Come On-A My House" by Rosemary Clooney dominated the airwaves, but Wilson, who had seen his first opera at twelve, tuned in to classical music programs. Royal was a quick convert. "I liked its precision and control," he wrote, "and I liked the grand sweep of the romantic symphonies. When I listened to them, it was like being in the mountains." His sister, Penny, complained that Royal considered himself superior to her because of his musical preferences, and she was right.

Inspired by his new friends' literary tastes, Royal devoured the cheap American paperback translations of Jean-Paul Sartre and Albert Camus, and declared himself an existentialist. Camus and Sartre diverge on many points, but the basic notion that the autonomous individual is the center of all meaningful change in life resonated with his personal experience. Royal also picked up French guide and resistance fighter Roger Frison-Roche's *First on the Rope*, the bleak tale of a young Chamonix man's struggle to become a guide. "It's only when you've been injured," wrote Frison-Roche, "or weakened in some way, that you can really appreciate being alive."

Wilson and Royal were the most competitive climbers in their group. Royal annoyed Wilson with his critiques of other climbers' performances, and Wilson nettled Royal by finishing his sentences for him and questioning his motives. Because he was the only member of the group with a car, Wilson also decided when and where they went climbing.

Royal tried to learn to drive in Bill Derr's nearly derelict 1937 LaSalle Coupe. "I tried to teach him by making him drive close to other cars," said Derr. "I called out the distances as he got closer," but Royal had a frightening lack of talent for steering. Without a license, Royal was confined to the passenger seat in Wilson's car. His need to prove that he could drive overwhelmed his judgment, and one night he stole Beulah's newly acquired Buick and drove it seventy miles north to Lancaster and back. His relationship with motor vehicles would remain a dangerous one.

· · · · ·

In the summer of 1951, Royal visited the domes of Kings Canyon in the southern Sierra for his first backcountry climbs as part of an RCS trip. On the drive, Roy Gorin, an ex-naval officer and a stickler for rules, warned Royal that if he didn't change his course and obey the club rules, he could be injured or worse. Royal was surprised that his penchant for leading hard climbs was against the club rules.

As at all RCS climbs, the rope teams had been decided in advance. Royal was to climb with John Mendenhall, a deeply experienced climber who had introduced technical climbing to California before World War II. "Mendenhall was easy-going and happy to mentor the greenest member of the RCS," Royal later wrote to the Mendenhalls's daughter, Valerie. "John was my mentor and my hero—I wanted to be just like him." Two weeks later, Royal made his first RCS trip to Tahquitz Rock, with Wilson and Hoover. At Lunch Rock, the staging area beneath the main face, Royal eagerly tried to pick out routes up the wall as Gorin read out climbing teams from his clipboard.

Royal's first climb was *Fingertip Traverse* (5.4), led by Gorin's friend George Harr, to whom Royal referred in his autobiography as "very much a rule follower and enforcer." Harr, however, bent the rules, letting Royal lead the crux. Royal ditched Harr after their first route and climbed two more routes with Wilson and Hoover, earning him a reprimand from Gorin.

Royal also got another chance to rope up with his hero, John Mendenhall. They didn't climb hard, but Royal loved being with Mendenhall, who told him about climbing *Open Book*, the hardest route at Tahquitz. Mendenhall speculated that at great difficulty, the second pitch could be free climbed, planting the seed of ambition in a young man who hungered to prove himself.

On an August trip to Pacifico Mountain, Royal climbed with Chuck Wilts for the first time, and with Ray van Aken, an engineer at the Naval Air Weapons Station China Lake in the Mojave Desert; both men were impressed by Royal's enthusiasm. That day, however, he overheard Gorin speculate that he climbed so aggressively that he wouldn't live past twenty. Instead of taking Gorin's concerns seriously, Royal decided that upstaging Gorin was his destiny. In Royal's mind, he already climbed in a world where his peerlessness actuated history.

The RCS took Royal along on their Labor Day ascent of Mount Williamson (14,380 feet), the second-highest mountain in the Sierra Nevada, yet he found himself disappointed by the easy climbing. One of his favorite writers, Clarence King, had described the peak as a featureless pillar of granite in his account of the first ascent in 1864. Royal learned that day that even legends must sometimes be doubted. He decided to try to climb, and to speak of climbing, in a way that would make him beyond reproach.

In September 1951, Royal began tenth grade with a new level of confidence and self-expressiveness. "Unlike must [sic] people think, Mountianeering [sic] is not a sport for muscle men," he wrote in an essay, "it is complex and interesting, and a challenge to the agility, strength and endurance of a man, but also requires more intelligence [sic] than any out-door [sic] sport." The teacher crossed out the spelling errors and gave Royal a B, his highest mark ever. Another essay, "What I Did Last Summer," records Royal's climbs with the dispassionate technical detail of a guide-book author, as if his teacher had asked for simple route descriptions.

Derr and Royal hitchhiked to Mount Williamson Rock in October, because Derr's LaSalle was broken again. A few miles from their usual drop-off point, they were picked up by Lynn Newcomb, the owner of Mount Waterman, the only private lift resort in the San Gabriels. Newcomb had a soft spot for mountain-loving kids and offered Derr and Royal jobs on the hills once ski season started in December. Royal had tried skiing as a Boy Scout and sprained his ankle, but the offer of a job renewed his interest.

Skiing was a growing industry, catering to Angelenos who wanted to escape the heat and pollution for the snow-covered mountains. When the season's first snow fell in the San Gabriels, the *Los Angeles Times* ski columnist, Ethel Van de Grift, would gush, "It's snowing! IT'S SNOWING!" At Van de Grift's call, the members of ski clubs like the Edelweiss and San Gorgonio headed for the Angeles National Forest, home of Mount Waterman, nearby Kratka Ridge, and a half dozen other resorts.

In early December, Royal and Derr started their part-time jobs at Mount Waterman. Royal worked on a tow rope at the top of the mountain. Apart from a brief adventure searching for a lost snowplow on the Angeles Crest Highway, Royal showed little interest in skiing off-piste, which required more equipment, offered no paycheck, and unlike resort skiing and climb-ing, involved hours of dull, repetitive movement.

Royal's job offered plenty of opportunities to ski. Through emulation, practice, and a humility he only occasionally showed on the rock, Royal became a ski racer on the Southwestern Division Junior team. "He was self-taught," said Dick Dorworth, a top junior ski racer in the 1950s, "more of a mental than a natural skier, but determined and hard-working."

In 1951, Beulah moved the family to a ground-floor duplex on Berkeley Avenue in the pleasant, lower-middle-class neighbourhood of Silver Lake. Royal's main contributions to the decor were the skis he leaned against the living-room wall and the finger stains over the front doorjamb from doing pull-ups, his only concession to training. Beulah provided a safe and comfortable home, but in grade twelve, the contrast between the joy Royal felt in the mountains and the misery he felt in school came to a head, and he decided to drop out. To his surprise, Bill Derr, who was a good student, had been thinking the same thing. They quit at the same time.

"Dunno why," said Derr. "I was just bored of it, I guess."

Beulah was disappointed, but Royal was seventeen and she couldn't stop him. Royal was relieved to free himself of what he called a giant load of "mental rubbish."

. . . . .

In early May 1952, Royal tried to toprope a smooth, twenty-foot-high wall at Pacifico Mountain, but kept falling off the last moves. He decided to fall only when the rock spat him off, and he made it. From then on he climbed until he fell, whether he was leading or toproping. It was a powerful psychological breakthrough, made possible partly by the tensile strength of the nylon ropes that had replaced hemp lines. Royal's friends adopted the "fail falling" credo, and when Frank Hoover took an eighty-foot fall at Tahquitz, they joked about joining the "80–100 club."

One day, on the way to Santa Monica Beach from a half-hearted snow-climbing session in the San Gabriels, Wilson, Royal, Derr, and Slagle spotted a vertical, 100-foot-high pillar of dirt separated from the Pacific Palisades by erosion. Cars gathered while Royal chopped footholds up the pillar, pounding snow pitons into the dirt for protection. When he reached the summit, a police officer with a bullhorn ordered him down, changed his mind, then told him to wait for the fire department. When the fire engine arrived, he was out of reach of their ladder. Taking advantage of the hullabaloo, Royal rappelled down, out of sight, on the other side. The police warned them not to try the stunt again. Royal named the feature Palisade Pinnacle. Wilson and Hoover made the only other known ascent, on a foggy night to avoid detection, before it collapsed in the mid-1950s.

Wilson flouted RCS rules and the state drinking age to introduce Royal to beer, which became his only concession to teenage indulgences. Royal's friends discussed dating, but he remained inexperienced and mostly uninterested. Climbing surpassed other pastimes, but when he later wrote of "virgin rock" and "stripping [an] unclimbed tower of its virginity," he hinted at hidden longings.

Royal made his first serious climbing trip to Yosemite on Memorial Day weekend, under the watchful eye of Roy Gorin. They were based in Camp 4, a primitive, unregulated campsite popular with visitors on a budget and surrounded by excellent boulders for climbers to play on.

The park rangers were sympathetic to the tourists who loved bear feedings and the Firefall, a spectacle in which park workers pushed a giant bonfire off Glacier Point Apron, but they were suspicious of climbers. Qualified climbing leaders were registered with the park service by the Sierra Club and American Alpine Club (AAC). Rangers enforced a registration system and, on occasion in a display of petty authority, would arbitrarily block climbers' plans.

That weekend, a ranger saw Royal and a friend bouldering and told them they had to register first. "It didn't sound right to us," Royal wrote, "so we went and spoke to the park superintendent." The ranger, it turned out, had made up the rule on a whim.

At that time in Yosemite, there were only a few dozen established routes. The vertical, 1,600-foot-high North Face of Sentinel Rock (usually referred to as the Sentinel) had been climbed in 1950 by San Francisco climber Allen Steck and Swiss-American John Salathé. That same year, Salathé had climbed the 1,500-foot *Lost Arrow Chimney* with San Francisco climber Ax Nelson. Neither route had been repeated. The only floor-to-rim route accessible to most climbers was the *Royal Arches,* a 2,000-foot-long, mostly easy slab.

The 400-foot route up Higher Cathedral Spire was Royal's first Valley climb. Gorin told Royal he had to lead the crux pitch, a tricky piece of routefinding with an unlikely traverse. Royal asked around for advice on how he would know when to start the traverse. "You just climb as high as you can," said Harr, "then traverse."

Gorin belayed silently as Royal missed the traverse and climbed straight up until he was level with the belay ledge. Gorin flailed away seconding but eventually reached the belay. He wrote in the summit register that the *Robbins Variation* was not recommended. In a photograph, Royal grins mischievously as he rappels the route. He had made a first ascent—albeit a trivial one—on his very first Yosemite climb.

Royal also spent hours on the Camp 4 boulders. The hardest problem there was a first ascent by Steck, who'd scaled the North Face of the Cima Grande and the Northwest Face of the Civetta in the Italian Dolomites, two of the hardest walls in Europe. He was nine years older than Royal, a veteran of World War II, erudite, fluent in German, and an alpinist as well as a rock climber. He was also the unofficial dean of Northern California climbers.

"We didn't know any of the Northern California climbers," said Royal, who recognized them by their European-style Tyrolean hats. His climbing friends wore baseball caps. "They were . . . how do you say it, presences." Royal watched as some of the crew attempted the Steck problem and failed—before climbing it twice himself without falling. Nine years passed before it was repeated, even by Royal. In high school, Royal had rejected competitive sports, but in climbing, he knew he could excel.

"What have you guys got around here worth climbing?" Royal asked Steck when they met for the first time later that day. Steck wasn't impressed. The legend of Royal's arrogance, his sense of personal destiny, was born. For now, however, regulations kept Royal's wings clipped in Yosemite. By comparison, two weeks later, he climbed four new routes at Tahquitz in a single weekend.

On the Fourth of July weekend in 1952, Royal made his first alpine climbs on an RCS trip to the Palisades in the Sierra. A natural on rock, he was awkward in crampons and awed by the icy bergschrund. On North Palisade, he slipped on a snow slope and Gorin caught him. Snow climbing would remain Royal's weakest mountain skill—perhaps unsurprising for a climber from sunny Southern California, where the daytime temperature rarely dropped below 70 degrees during climbing season.

From mid-July to late September in 1952, Derr and Royal worked for the US Forest Service as firefighters in McCloud, a small California town twenty miles south of the Oregon border. Their camp was close to Mount Shasta, which Royal, who spent the summer pining for Tahquitz, described as "a slag heap." Weeks of rain kept the woods too damp for forest fires. Derr and Royal shirked work to speed down logging roads in

Derr's LaSalle. "We got the foreman to build us a berm with a grader," said Derr, "and tried to roll the car, but couldn't quite get it to flip over." In late September, fire season ended. The car was destroyed and they hitchhiked home.

On the last trip of the season to Tahquitz, the Los Angeles RCS was joined by the members of the newly formed San Diego Chapter. At the campfire on Saturday night, Royal met San Diegans Barbara Lilley (nicknamed Bobbie), Gary Hemming, Jerry Gallwas, and George Schlief. Royal became fast friends with Gallwas and Hemming, who were both within a year of Royal's age. Though Gallwas was a college student, he lacked Wilson's intellectual hubris or Royal's brashness. Hemming, meanwhile, was a freshman at San Diego State University and, like Royal, aspired to be a great climber. Gallwas later said Hemming was "very bright, fearless, or foolish when it came to safe climbing practices, and a fun climbing companion."

Royal liked the San Diego crew, and without yet knowing it, shared a background with them: Hemming's father was an inveterate gambler, and Gallwas's father, like Royal's, was a heavy, habitual drinker. All three came from single-parent homes with absent fathers.

On Sunday, Wilts, Wilson, and the Mendenhalls made the first ascent of *Super Pooper*, one of the first climbs at Tahquitz to avoid prominent crack systems and link thin, steep, discontinuous features. Royal was impressed and a little jealous. With the ascent of *Super Pooper*, Wilson had become the best climber in Royal's growing circle. Wilson's competitiveness on the rock, however, unlike Royal's, was limited by the demands of his academic career. Climbing harder than others was Royal's only way to prove himself.

Royal met Gallwas again at Pacifico the next week. "I took the RCS membership safety test," said Gallwas, "and watched Royal do a 6th class of about 25 or 30 feet and was so taken that I repeated the pitch that afternoon. It was sort of a bonding experience for both of us." Royal's next route put him at the forefront of the California climbing scene.

The 490-foot-long *Open Book* at Tahquitz had first been climbed by Mendenhall and Harry Sutherland in 1947, and remained unrepeated. The smooth, vertical corner offered solid cracks on the first pitch, which

Mendenhall had free climbed, but the second pitch was mostly too wide for pitons. Mendenhall aided it by pounding sections of two-by-fours into the crack. The crack could be free climbed, but it would be hard to protect.

On a bright October day in 1952, Wilson and Royal stood beneath the *Open Book*. Wilson had just turned eighteen; Royal was seventeen. They had about two years of climbing experience between them. They also had what Royal called "a secret weapon . . . . youthful attitude."

Royal led the strenuous but well-protected first pitch. Wilson declined the crux lead on the second pitch, but Royal was eager to try it. The two wooden wedges from the first ascent had dried and shrunk, but Royal hammered them deeper into the crack and used them as protection. He squirmed upward with an elbow on one side of the crack and a hand on the other. At the crux, he risked a fifty-foot fall.

When a grade system was developed a few years later, the *Open Book* was graded 5.9, the most difficult grade on the free-climbing scale at that time. The route was also dangerous. There were comparable climbs in the United Kingdom and on Saxon sandstone in East Germany, but in California, the *Open Book* was revolutionary, and in the eyes of some, irresponsibly dangerous.

· · · · ·

Royal's obvious next step would be a major climb in Yosemite, but he still wasn't on the park's approved list of leaders. Young climbers chafed at the restrictions; in particular, the freestanding plinth of the Lost Arrow Tip became a lightning rod for youthful aspirations barred by bureaucracy.

Adults like Gorin were granted permission to scale it, but when Gallwas wrote to the park for permission, superintendent John Preston responded: "Not only is the Lost Arrow climb a dangerous one, but it is considered something of a show or a stunt." Gallwas replied, "The desire to make that particular climb has been with me for five years, and I find it rather difficult to banish the thought from my mind."

To climb the Lost Arrow Tip, Royal and Wilson needed a registered leader, and so they teamed up with Barbara Lilley, who was on the park's list. Gary Hemming would travel to Yosemite with them, but had his own climbing plans.

Wilson photographed his companions at Wawona Tunnel lookout. Royal described Lilley, who was six years older than him, as "attractively feminine, even when dressed in flannel shirts and cargo pants." Hemming looks like a movie hoodlum as he squints through his bangs. Royal, in the middle, looks serious under an army surplus sunhat propped up by his large ears. He has grown into a man. His eyes are narrowed and focused, his expression steely. His shoulders are broad, his hands big and relaxed. Usually, he was a scrupulous dresser, but his shirt is misbuttoned. Behind him, the Leaning Tower, Sentinel, Half Dome, El Capitan—the rock walls that will define his life—shine in the autumn sunlight.

Gorin and Wilts had made the second ascent of the Lost Arrow Tip in 1951 and praised the climb for its difficulty and dizzying exposure. Royal's bruising apprenticeship on dubious rock around Los Angeles made him especially proficient at placing pitons in poor cracks, and he surged up the hard aid that had slowed previous parties. Gorin and Wilts had taken fifteen hours. Royal, Wilson, and Lilley reached the summit in eight and a half. Fantasies of flight had foreshadowed Royal's moment alone on the summit. He imagined himself as a winged predator and gazed downward at the insect-like cars and people on the Valley floor.

Lilley had to be back at her job in San Diego the next morning, Royal was on the breakfast shift as a dishwasher in Los Angeles, and Wilson had a morning lecture. A weary, grimy band piled into Lilley's car for the long nighttime drive home.

An hour later, Royal fell asleep at the wheel. The car smashed into a canyon wall and bounced into the middle of the road. They were uninjured, and a passing driver sent a tow truck from Oakhurst. They spent the night in the wrecked vehicle at the garage; in the morning, Royal paid to have it towed to Los Angeles for repairs, which he covered out of his dishwasher's wages. Wilson was furious and claimed that the accident wouldn't have happened had he been driving.

The more conservative members of the RCS began to warm up to Wilson. Some even attributed the successes on the *Open Book* and the Lost Arrow to Wilson's controlling influence on Royal. The RCS made Wilson the first trip leader from Royal's group, and on their November excursion to the quartz monzonite domes of Joshua Tree, entrusted him with a group of beginners. That weekend, Royal overheard Gorin tell other climbers that Royal took too many risks. The next day, Royal was fifty feet up a climb when Gorin walked by with the group of neophytes and told Royal to clip a bolt.

"No need to. It's easy," Royal replied.

Gorin told him he should clip it in case he got vertigo. The same accusation had been leveled against Pierre Servettaz, the protagonist in Royal's favorite climbing novel, *First on the Rope*.

"After 3,000 feet of exposure on the Lost Arrow?" said Royal. "It's not a problem."

Perhaps the comment reminded Gorin that Royal had halved his time on the Lost Arrow Tip.

"Clip in to that bolt!" said Gorin.

Royal clipped it, but after Gorin moved on, unclipped it again. Higher up, when he found a fixed piton, he skipped that as well, muttering, "Screw you, Gorin."

3
Rotten Lucky Bastards

IN DECEMBER 1952, ROYAL QUIT his job at the diner and returned to Kratka Ridge. Every morning, before the tow opened, Royal improved his skiing. The giant slalom favored Royal's strengths—bravery and speed—over quick reaction time. At his first race that year, the *Los Angeles Times* reported that "the proudest moms and dads" cheered from the sidelines. Beulah, unlike the middle-class parents of her son's rivals, had to work that day.

Southwestern junior national champion Kenny Lloyd crashed on the first run, and the second round was cancelled due to a lack of time. Royal, likely the only entrant who had taught himself to ski while working the tow ropes, won by default. On February 9, 1953, six days after Royal's nineteenth birthday, Lloyd won the Grand Slalom at Edelweiss, near Lake Tahoe. Royal came in a respectable fifth. Royal was regularly outclassed by Southwestern juniors like Lloyd, the brother and sister duo of Jewel and Bobby Kinmont, and Dick Dorworth, but his enthusiasm and guts soon crowded Beulah's shelves with trophies, mostly for second and third place.

Royal gained a place at the 1954 Junior Nationals in Alta, Utah, at the end of March. Dorworth shared a room with him. "He had a bizarre, low-key sense of humor," said Dorworth, "but he was also so serious. Our coach wanted everyone to go out and bootpack the course to make it faster."

The young racers shirked the dull, foot-numbing task—"but Royal," said Dorworth, "always told everyone that he had done his two cents' worth and gone out bootpacking." At Alta, Royal hurt his shoulder in a fall, an injury that dogged him into the first months of climbing season. His results didn't allow him to move forward to the next level of competition.

In mid-May, Royal opened his Tahquitz season with a first ascent. "Royal was leading the overhang at the top of what became *Upper Royal's Arch*," said Gallwas, who looked on as Chuck Wilts belayed. "A handhold broke, sending him in a 360-degree backflip nicely belayed by Chuck, and Royal just brushed himself off and reached for a different handhold." He lived by the "fail falling" motto early on. Royal also repeated his free ascent of Mendenhall's *Open Book*. Leading the crux had terrified him less than a year earlier, but now, said Gallwas, Royal had "no hesitation, just smooth moves as he climbed what was a big deal at the time."

At 10:45 p.m., Pacific Standard Time on Friday, May 29, 1953, New Zealander Edmund Hillary and Sherpa Tenzing Norgay reached the summit of Mount Everest. At that moment, Royal was squeezed between Hemming and climbing packs in the backseat of Lilley's car, creeping up the steep switchbacks of Highway 42 toward Yosemite. The ascent of Everest broke a global barrier in climbing, but for Royal and his friends, the most important breakthrough that weekend was that San Francisco climber and lawyer Richard Leonard had convinced the park to declare an unofficial moratorium on listing qualified leaders. Royal finally had unrestricted access to Yosemite's walls, and he was about to meet Gallwas in Camp 4 to enjoy it. For their first climb in this new era, Royal and Gallwas chose Yosemite Point Buttress, a 1,400-foot-high prow a few hundred feet from Lost Arrow Spire. Steck had made several attempts before succeeding in 1952 with fellow San Franciscan Bob Swift, and the climb was both technically difficult and unrepeated.

Royal got into Yosemite a couple of hours before dawn and napped until Gallwas arrived from San Diego. They ate breakfast in Yosemite Lodge, packed their gear, and were ready to go by 10 a.m.

Gallwas, tired from his overnight drive, fell asleep while belaying, and their pack jammed as they hauled it up narrow chimneys; by late afternoon, they had only reached the Pedestal, a ledge 400 feet from the top.

They had planned to do the route in a day, one-upping Steck and Swift, but "looking at the headwall," said Gallwas, "we decided to spend the night." That night it rained, recalled Gallwas, "and gave us a lesson about planning when climbing."

They reached the rim in the late afternoon of the next day. The discomforts of the climb were outweighed by a new sense of confidence, and they agreed to attempt an even harder climb, the second ascent of Sentinel Rock's North Face.

Back in Camp 4, Wilson saw Gallwas and Royal staring at the Sentinel with binoculars, and Gallwas invited Wilson to come along. Wilson started to brag about the pending Sentinel climb right away. "Apparently, [Wilson] approached [Steck] in the wrong way," wrote Royal, "and he came off as a smart aleck, a presumptuous kid who would be out of his depth on the Sentinel."

But they weren't. Wilson free climbed a roof that became known as the Wilson Overhang. At the 1,000-foot mark, Royal avoided aid climbing by wriggling up a claustrophobic chimney later dubbed the Narrows. They reached the top in two days, less than half the time for the first ascent.

At Tahquitz on June 20, Royal made the first free ascent of *The Innominate*, later graded 5.10, with Gallwas. The overhanging and technical second pitch took climbing at Tahquitz into a new gymnastic realm. Royal climbed free, without falls or previous practice, past six aid pitons. He didn't know it, but even by the early 1950s, he was one of the best free climbers in the world, and his friends were barely less skilled. Yet when George Harr wrote in the *Mugelnoos* that aid had been eliminated from *The Innominate* by "guess who?" Royal took the omission of his name as a slight, stewing over how he would answer Harr's snub with climbs so difficult that it would be impossible to omit his name in the future.

The August 13, 1953, issue of *Mugelnoos* published a new system of grading rock climbs invented by Wilts, Wilson, and Royal, and it became one of the most influential documents in the history of American climbing. The new system had four grades for unroped climbing. The fifth grade, reserved for free climbing, and the sixth, for aid climbing, were subdivided into decimal grades from zero to nine. The first California climb harder than 5.9 was graded 5.10, not 6.1, because it was a free climb. The decimal-point value of 5.10 is the same value as 5.1, and 5.11 is only a shade higher, but these were problems for the future.

The *Mugelnoos* listed Tahquitz's thirty-four established climbs by grade. The two 5.9s, *Open Book* and *The Innominate*, were both first free climbed by Royal. Some climbers were impressed; others agreed with James Ramsey Ullman's complaint that grade systems were "aiding and abetting this suicidal insanity . . . competition, literally to the death." There were complaints that the whole exercise had served only to demonstrate the young upstart's ascendancy. The article, after all, finally identified him as the "you know who" behind the first free ascent of *The Innominate*. Royal, for his part, agreed that the system would encourage competition. That's what he wanted.

The frantic pace of trips to Tahquitz and Pacifico continued through the summer. That season, Royal Slagle almost killed Robbins and his friends when he fell asleep at the wheel and wrecked his car; soon thereafter, he disappeared from the climbing scene and into a life of crime.

That winter, Royal returned to the tow rope at Kratka Ridge, but with less enthusiasm than in previous years. In the spring of 1954, after a few days digging ditches, he took a job at Taylor Railyard, carrying heavy sacks through the haze of exhaust and the din of locomotives until the other laborers took pity on him and carried part of his quota. Out in the wider world, when the task wasn't climbing, there seemed to be something frail about Royal.

While he moped around the house on weekends, trying to recover enough strength to face another week at the railyard, other young climbers came to the fore. On a rare occasion when Royal overcame his exhaustion enough to go to Tahquitz, he made the first ascent of *The Blank*, with Gallwas.

That June, Joe Fitschen, a 19-year-old climber from Los Angeles, slipped and tumbled down the cliffs below the descent trail at Tahquitz. Royal had only met Fitschen in passing at Stoney Point, but he heard that his mother wanted to visit him in the hospital in Hemet. Royal, who was sensitive to the predicaments of mothers, borrowed a car and drove her to Hemet.

Fitschen had seen Royal at Stoney Point. He thought Royal and Wilson "looked like they had come out the high school auto shop," their hair long and combed back in ducktails. Still, Royal's visit came at an opportune time in Fitschen's life. Fitschen was still unsure about climbing. He'd come to the sport through his mother, who had taken refuge from a failed marriage on Sierra Club outings. He was uncertain about his life as a frat pledge and student at Occidental College in Eagle Rock, California. Intellectually restless, physically active, and sexually frustrated, Fitschen had found the main outlet for his inmost feelings in jazz. But now, Royal's visit was a tacit invitation to friendship with the crew of hard, young climbers.

When Fitschen recovered, he threw himself into climbing and became a weekday regular at Royal's house. They listened to classical music, drank beer, and talked about D. H. Lawrence's erotic novels and the Anglo-Californian Aldous Huxley, who expounded on the subjects of higher consciousness, sexuality, and Eastern philosophy. Royal had a hip new friend, expanding literary tastes, and a freshly sprouted goatee, but he worried about his future and looked in a decidedly more mainstream direction for answers. "I, at that time, had a low opinion of the business world," Royal wrote in an unpublished essay. "But banks were different. Bankers were honorable and honest and upstanding. And that's what I wanted to be." A career in banking also seemed like a good way to make amends for his years as a juvenile delinquent.

In January 1955, Royal got a job in the bookkeeping department of the Union Bank. He also took his supervisor's advice and earned his high school diploma at night school. Jerry Carrico was the only long-term friend Royal made at the bank. They were both junior employees, although Carrico was a college graduate with higher goals in finance. Carrico taught Royal to play chess. The game was competitive, intellectual, easy to transport, and inexpensive—and for Royal it became a lifelong obsession. He restricted his Huxley discussions to the evenings and climbing to weekends, and by all appearances, he was about to launch an average American adulthood.

That changed, however, on an RCS trip in October 1954, when Royal met Warren John Harding.

. . . . .

Harding was thirty years old, an adult as far as Royal and his teenage friends were concerned, although he lived in Sacramento with his mother and two sisters. Whereas Royal was surrounded by young men who reviled or mourned their absent fathers, Harding had followed his father into his career as a highway road surveyor. Harding had hiked and fished. When he was old enough to drive, he raced sports cars. Like Royal, he saw risky behaviors as proof of mental freedom and character. His heroes included Alfonso de Portago, not because of his pedigree as a Spanish nobleman but because, at seventeen, he flew an airplane under the London Bridge on a dare.

In 1953, Harding discovered climbing in the Tetons in Wyoming. Like Royal, he was smitten. In his first couple seasons, he made the first ascents of Middle Cathedral Rock's 2,000-foot North Buttress and its 1,200-foot East Buttress, as well as the second ascent of the *Lost Arrow Chimney*.

Climbing was a sport of clubs and cliques, but Harding wasn't a joiner and climbed with whoever was available. In October 1954, while he worked on the roads in San Diego, he cold-called Jerry Gallwas and convinced him to bring him on the RCS trip to Tahquitz.

Gaunt, unshaven, and clad in black jeans and a black T-shirt with cut-off sleeves, Harding met Royal for the first time at Lunch Rock that weekend. Harding spoke with "a dark intensity" Royal liked. When Royal suggested that they try a new route, Harding leapt to his feet like a boxer coming out of his corner. Royal pointed out a thin crack. Harding squinted at it, "arms akimbo," wrote Royal; he "instantly felt [he] had chosen a strong partner." Up on the climb, when one of his anchor pitons popped out, Harding laughed and said he was out of practice. Royal, half-terrified and half-impressed, climbed on.

At the campfire that night, Harding told self-deprecating stories of misadventures on the rock and at the racetrack. The myth was born that he enjoyed surrounding himself with enamored women. Harding claimed that his Jaguar had been painted purple at the request of a former girl-friend who had been crowned Miss Puerto Rico in 1935.

Royal and Frank Hoover drank Harding's red wine that night, although not in the same volume as Harding. Red wine tasted good warm, was more potent than beer, and soon became Royal's favorite drink. Gorin reminded Hoover, the official trip leader, that alcohol was banned from Sierra Club trips, but Hoover was already drunk, proving, in Harding's opinion, that booze was allowed. Harding struck Royal that night as a "libertine" who was at once "diabolical," a "breath of fresh air," and, in any mood, "riveting."

Harding wasn't the only iconoclastic climber Royal would come to know. That autumn, Don Wilson introduced Royal to Mark Powell, who had been an overweight, cigarette-smoking, 24-year-old before he picked up climbing. Inspired by a Yosemite climb with Gallwas, he lost weight, quit smoking, and moved into Camp 4. A few months later, he was a broke social misfit, but he was also one of the best free climbers in California.

Royal, however, climbed only on weekends. At the Ski Club Alpine he made friends with John Ahern, who had helped create the Matterhorn attraction at Disneyland in Anaheim, and film editor Lionel (Lin) Ephraim and taught them to climb. But their priorities remained their careers—an outlook that held true for Robbins until, no longer able to compartmentalize climbing in his life, he gave in to the siren song of Yosemite's Half Dome, in particular its looming, vertical, 2,000-foot Northwest Face.

Local carpenter George Anderson had first climbed the severed pluton of rock that was Yosemite's highest point in 1875. Adventurous tourists could scale a ladder of railway ties and wire handrails to the unearthly granite summit. John Salathé and Ax Nelson had climbed the South Face, but the Northwest Face remained unexplored. Postcard photographs by Ansel Adams caught the wall in a light that picked out ledges and cracks forming an almost continuous line up the left side of the face. Climbers took note, and the dark wall became the next object of their dreams.

In 1954, the first party to try it rappelled after a couple of pitches. Hemming and a few others obsessed and made plans, but no one attempted it. Mark Powell had graded climbs by their commitment level, from I to VI. The hardest multiday climbs in Yosemite, the *Steck-Salathé* and the *Lost Arrow Chimney*, were grade V. The Northwest Face of Half Dome was slated to become the first grade VI, Yosemite's biggest prize.

The third week of June 1955, Royal emerged from the bank to attempt the wall with Harding, Gallwas, and Wilson. Big wall climbing was frightening, slow, laborious, and physically uncomfortable. The climbers' basketball shoes were easily crushed by cracks and by prolonged standing in their etriers—aid-climbing ladders made of thin rope. The rack of pitons

weighed fifteen pounds. Leaders got up however they could, using a combination of free and aid climbing. The second climber did each pitch on
toprope or by ascending the rope using prusik loops, and reclipped a rope
for the third climber. Before the third climber began, they waited for their
partners to haul the bag hand over hand. Finally, the leader belayed the
third climber up to the stance as they cleaned the pitons and unsnagged
the haulbag.

After two days of these labors, the foursome was only 450 feet off the
ground. On the morning of the second day, Wilson counseled retreat;
Gallwas, who had calculated that at their present pace they would run out
of water before reaching the summit, agreed. Harding and Royal objected
that there was enough food and water for a couple more days, even if they
eventually had to retreat. Both Royal and Harding believed that, if necessary, they could traverse off the wall two-thirds of the way up, a prospect
that did not offer much solace to the rest of the team.

Royal finally conceded to descend, leaving Harding no choice but to
go along.

"We crept away from there like whipped curs," Royal wrote, "with our
tails between our legs," Gallwas said. "I think Warren made the decision
there and then that any second attempt for him on Half Dome would be
without Don in the party." But it wasn't just Harding who wanted to whit-
tle down the team.

On the descent, an exhausted Gallwas placed a rappel piton Royal
pulled out with his hand. Royal muttered that they would improve
Gallwas's technique and return—a comment he did not share with the
others. Royal apparently wanted to drop Wilson, who had added to the
tensions in their relationship by initiating the retreat on Half Dome. He
also wanted to cut Harding, perhaps because neither he nor Harding could
accept anything but the senior position on a climbing team.

At Mirror Lake, they passed a woman who claimed she could see them
on the face, the vanguard of the army of onlookers who would have their
own role in the story of Yosemite big wall climbing. After a shower, the
team posed for a photograph. Harding in his black jeans, T-shirt, and
pomaded hair, stands to the side. His folded arms make him look fed-up.
Wilson, a couple of steps apart on the opposite side of the group, looks

tense. In the center are Royal and Gallwas. Royal, in his glasses, a clean, tailored shirt, and the basketball shoes he climbed in, holds his left wrist in his right hand. He looks thoughtful and relaxed. Gallwas makes the same gesture, as if this was a secret sign of their solidarity. Only he and Royal would return to make another attempt.

On the way out of the Valley, Royal craned out the passenger-side window for a glimpse of the dark north wall of Middle Cathedral Rock. He commented that although Harding's party had climbed the North Buttress, the North Face remained unclimbed.

"Oh Robbins, just leave it alone," snapped Wilson. "Don't tear down what they did. You're always doing that."

Royal hadn't thought of himself as heartlessly competitive or apt to belittle others. He felt sucker-punched, like he was back on the basketball court in junior high. He had had his disagreements with Wilson, but he had looked up to him too, and emulated his tastes. Royal decided that Wilson saw him only as "a kind of useful monkey, eager to scamper up any climbing problem"—only reinforcing Royal's decision to leave Wilson out of his future Half Dome plans.

Meanwhile Harding, unlike his younger friends, was immune to the tensions and emotions that followed a climbing fiasco. He used the Half Dome story to secure a photo shoot for *Saturday Night* magazine a few months after the climb, and he let his partners share the limelight. In the staged photos, Royal stands awkwardly in slings and struggles to make what he's doing look difficult, or even interesting. Harding, in real life a laconic and reserved lead climber, hams it up and grasps at the air in fake panic.

"These danger-loving climbers seldom conquer lofty mountains," wrote Hal Burton in the article, "just 'impossible' cliffs in their own back-yard," adding that climbers are not "teenage daredevils with no means of support, Robbins was a banker . . . " The article, which Royal found distasteful, made him question Harding's motives for climbing. Royal had been annoyed when he didn't receive the attention he deserved in RCS newsletters, but he was inherently suspicious of the press in general. The embarrassment he felt about the shoot never diminished. When he used a photo from it in his memoir *Fail Falling,* he captioned it "Checking in with the Park Service, registering for Half Dome."

· · · · ·

The Half Dome attempt left Royal in an unsettled and introspective mood. In September 1955, looking for answers to the mysteries of life, he enrolled as a student-at-large in literature at Los Angeles Junior College.

His favorite course was English, where he could indulge his voracious reading habit. He admired Thomas Hardy's villagers shaped by the half-wild landscape of Wessex. He sympathized with Captain Ahab and his obsessive quest to destroy the white whale, an apt symbol of the big wall. The conflict between the self and society attracted him to Fyodor Dostoevsky's *The Brothers Karamazov.* A taste for ancient traditions, warrior codes, and sagas revealed itself in his love of J.R.R. Tolkien's *Lord of the Rings* and Homer's *Odyssey.*

He loved Walt Whitman's *Song of Myself,* and quoted it in his memoir: "I celebrate myself, and sing myself. . . . I wear my hat as I please indoors or out." The college reading list, however, contained within it the seeds of Royal's egress from academia. Ralph Waldo Emerson's musings on the transcendence of nature and the limitations of human philosophies and learning made college seem superfluous, and so in the fall of 1955, Royal quit. A few weeks later he was promoted at the bank.

On the romantic front, Royal appeared as eligible as any 5'11", handsome, up-and-coming fellow in a department-store suit, but he had climbed away the years when many experiment with relationships and intimacy. Now, he fretted over how to get the women in his office to pay attention to him. Climbing seemed useless in this regard. He enrolled at the Arthur Murray Dance Studio, but quit when George Harr told him that climbers don't dance.

After the failure on Half Dome, Royal withdrew from climbing almost completely for a year and a half. He had climbed seven new routes at Tahquitz from 1952 to 1954. From 1954 to 1956, he established only one. If he was seriously thinking about giving up on climbing, however, it didn't take much to draw him back in. In fall of 1956 when Powell asked Royal to join him on the first ascent of Liberty Cap, a 1,000-foot-high white granite dome overlooking the Mist Trail to Half Dome, he responded *yes* immediately and enthusiastically. Here was his chance to complete his first new big route in Yosemite.

Royal proposed Fitschen, despite his inexperience, as the third climber. Fitschen was delighted. "Of course!" he said. "Finally a chance to play with the big boys!" Fitschen remembered sparks flying from Royal's hammer as he led a hard pitch in the dark. The trio spent a night on sloping ledges. It was an adventure, but the route lacked character and sated Royal's appetite for new Yosemite routes as quickly as it had galvanized him to action.

After Liberty Cap, Powell left Camp 4 to join Wilson and Gallwas for the conquest of Cleopatra's Needle in the Navajolands of New Mexico. Royal returned to the bank and the romantic challenge of a coworker, Graciela (Grace) Elba Balderamma.

Grace, said Royal, was "of Hispanic heritage, fiery and natural, while I had Irish ancestry and was rather bookish." Royal knew that Latinos were poorly treated in the city, but he also held some unexamined ethnic stereotypes. When Royal's sister, Penny, drove to Las Vegas with her boyfriend, Arturo, without Beulah's permission, Royal called Arturo her "Latin lover." Likewise, his comments about Grace's sexuality echoed the white press's fascination with the sexuality of *pachucas*, the heavily made-up Latinx women said to be irresistible to white men. When they broke up, he was self-conscious about the impression he had made in the office by dating Grace in particular.

In 1956, Royal made a final attempt to reconnect with his father. "The address of any veteran is confidential," wrote a Veterans Administration caseworker. "If you wish to contact your father, you should enclose a letter to him in an unsealed, stamped envelope. The envelope must not show a return address. The Detroit Regional Office will then address your letter to the last known address of your father." Royal sent a letter, but never received a response.

Early the following spring, Royal learned that Harding would return early from a job in Alaska at the end of the summer to attempt Half Dome with Powell. Both men would be free to launch numerous attempts, if necessary. Harding and Powell may have accepted Royal as the third climber, with the implied condition that Harding was the leader, but Royal made his own plans. And, as usual, his transition from apparent inactivity to action was abrupt.

He hoped to try the wall that June, as soon as the weather was warm. He reckoned it would take five days. He had only a week's vacation, so his schedule was tight. For Royal, there would be no second attempt that year.

On June 13 at the Koffee Kup in the town of Idyllwild—below Tahquitz—Royal asked Gallwas to join him. Gallwas would start his summer job at Mammoth Lakes on July 1, and he was eager to make an attempt as soon as possible. As if to seal their agreement with a display of prowess, they made the first ascent of *The Step*, a difficult free line with a few points of aid.

Wayne Merry, Gallwas's friend from the San Diego Chapter RCS, was a candidate for third climber, but he couldn't get time off from his job as a Yosemite ranger. Hemming had dropped out of the Air Force Academy, but he wasn't asked. "Gary claimed he was disappointed that Royal didn't consider him," said Gallwas. "My impression was that Royal considered Gary too erratic." Royal invited his mentor, Chuck Wilts, who turned down the invitation because the wall was still considered a dangerous proposition and he had a family.

Fitschen, who was now a strong climber, couldn't get away from his new job repossessing cars, but Fitschen's friend Mike Sherrick agreed to come along instead. In 1955, Sherrick had taken some of the hardest snow and ice leads on the first ascent of the *Wishbone Arête* on Mount Robson in the Canadian Rockies, and he had also ticked off several Yosemite testpieces, including the *Steck-Salathé*. In September of 1954, after the pair made the first ascent of *The Reach* at Tahquitz, Royal had called Sherrick the most talented climber he had yet met.

For gear, they mostly made do with what they already owned or could easily buy. An army surplus store supplied cheap plastic bladders that doubled as water bottles, and flight suits for bivouacs. In addition to Gallwas's collection of hand-forged pitons, they brought twenty-five ⅜-inch Dryvin bolts and handheld star drills. Bolts were essential between crack systems and on cracks wider than a few inches since pitons were at most a couple inches wide.

A few days before he headed for Half Dome, Royal noticed Grace "sauntering down the aisle between the adding machines, fixing her beautiful, irresistible eyes on me." That evening, in the back seat of his black 1939 Ford Coupe, they made love.

. . . . .

A few days later, on Sunday, June 23, 1957, Merry, Royal, Sherrick, and Gallwas carried their gear, food, and water up the trail to Half Dome. Merry left his load at the base, wished his friends good luck, and hiked up the cables to the summit, where he posted a sign warning tourists not to throw rocks because there were climbers below.

On the first day, Royal and his friends climbed fifty feet beyond their 1955 high point and rappelled to a bivouac ledge. They zipped up their flight suits and waited for the Firefall at Glacier Point, the signal to flick their flashlight on and off twice so that Merry, at Mirror Lake, could see that all was well.

The next day, Gallwas spent five hours drilling a ladder of bolts across a blank wall that separated them from a 500-foot-long crack system. When Gallwas was exhausted, Royal took a turn and got a few pitons in a crack above the bolts, but there was still thirty feet of blank rock between him and the crucial crack. He lowered forty feet and, on his second try, made a wild pendulum to a ledge, where he placed an anchor and rappelled. In the morning, their third on the wall, they left a rope across the traverse, anchored to a flake that would not support a climber's weight. It was a safeguard for retreat, not an expedient for the next party.

Difficult free climbing led up the long crack system to a bivouac behind a seventy-five-foot-tall sheet of rock leaning against the main wall. The next day, pebbles dribbled down the wall as Royal squirmed up behind the flexing wafer of granite. At sunset, they reached the flat ten-by-five-foot ledge that would later become known as Big Sandy. Five hundred feet above them loomed the tiered Visor overhang that they had to find a way around in the morning.

Shortly after dawn, the temperature reached the 90s. They were at least two days from the top, with only two quarts of water left. Gallwas mimed drinking from a water bladder to preserve water. The others copied him. That day, three pitches of vertical aid climbing led to a tiny alcove, where, too exhausted to find more suitable lodgings, they crammed into the crack for an uncomfortable bivouac.

The closer they climbed to the crackless overhangs of the Visor, the farther it seemed to jut out from the wall. Gallwas spotted a horizontal ledge a foot wide and fifty feet long, leading to a crack left of the over-hang—"a Thank God ledge," as Sherrick described what would become one of the most famous rock climbing pitches in the world. It took them straight to a crack system that led to the final slab.

After five days on the wall, they stumbled onto the flat granite summit like sailors stepping onto land after a long sea voyage. Harding had come to Yosemite to try Half Dome with Powell only to be surprised to find Royal's party high on the route. Harding hiked up with ham sandwiches and a gallon of water for his rivals.

"Hey, congratulations," he said, "you rotten lucky bastards."

Royal instantly felt like Harding's next climb, whatever it was, would be motivated by competition and jealousy, feelings to which Royal was himself vulnerable. In fact, Harding was upset by the Half Dome climb, but did not know what to do next.

"Warren was complaining about Royal Robbins finishing the *Regular Northwest Face* of Half Dome without him," recalled Valley climber Bea Vogel in an interview. "He was pouting and moaning because he had been left out. Well, I told him, 'Oh, hell! There are lots of other walls. Why don't you do El Capitan?' and standing in El Cap Meadow and pointing at a line, I said, 'You can climb right up the South Buttress.' And he looked at it and said, 'Well, OK, maybe we can.'"

But El Capitan was still a big maybe and Half Dome was a real, new, American type of climb: vertical, committing, huge, a big wall in the most literal sense—a pure, technical rock climbing tour de force. Gallwas and Royal didn't even own crampons. Severe weather was all but impossible. It had been climbed from the bottom up in a continuous push, without any of the fixed ropes so essential to the first ascents of the 8,000-meter peaks then seen as the apex of world climbing. There were no flags at the top. The four Los Angeles climbers in their early twenties reinvented climbing as a deeply personal, aesthetic act. Any rewards were purely symbolic.

"Half done [sic] first ascent 5 days," Gallwas telegrammed his mother, "but late to work Love Jerry." The National Park Service's press release was almost as brief. The rangers called the climb "the first ascent of the east shoulder of Half-Dome." The same description was used in newspaper articles. Some used the even less impressive "east slope." The attention of the average reader of the *Bakersfield Californian* was more likely to be drawn to the adjacent story, "Grandma Holds Suspect for Police." California climbers, however, were agog. In the July *Mugelnoos*, published two weeks after the ascent, Wilts asked if "Half Dome was the hardest north face yet?" and described the climb as "fantastic and formidable" with "staggering statistics."

Royal gave the route the name that stuck. His full report, "The Northwest Face of Half Dome," appeared in the *Mugelnoos*, almost eight weeks after the climb. He called the climb "arduous," "perpendicular," "enervating," and "seldom-remitting." His tone suggests that the privations of heat, thirst, and fatigue were routine for his party. The use of the third person gives the impression of a youngster straining to be taken seriously.

In December, a longer piece by Royal was published in the more polished *Sierra Club Bulletin*, "Half Dome—The Hard Way." The photograph of Half Dome by Ansel Adams with the route and the bivouacs scrawled over it foreshadowed a clash between those who, like Royal, saw themselves as legitimate figures on the Yosemite landscape and the high-wilderness aesthetic in which the only evidence of humans was the artist's gaze.

Half Dome's *Regular Northwest Face* was, as expected, crowned the first grade VI. Now, Royal's presence in the campground at Idyllwild excited a kind of low-intensity celebrity gossip. His friends began to comment on his masculine appearance, his shyness was now sometimes interpreted as arrogance, and his voice struck some listeners as terse and manly.

· · · · ·

Outside of climbing, Royal's life was less glamorous. After Half Dome, Grace Balderamma told him that she was pregnant, "probably," as Royal put it, "by him." He met the situation with what he called "honor" and proposed marriage. They eloped to Las Vegas, where, according to the Clark County marriage registry, they were married on July 14, 1957. Royal was twenty-two; Grace was nineteen.

Back in their small apartment in Los Angeles, they quarrelled most nights. The victor of Half Dome bivouacked on the floor of his own apartment. Royal thought that he bored Grace, which was a fair observation. Instead of getting to know Grace's friends and family, he spent almost every weekend at Tahquitz. He avoided her in the evenings. Compared to fighting with Grace, climbing seemed more attractive than ever.

At Tahquitz in late August, Royal and Fitschen heard a scream and looked up to see a lead climber falling from the *Fingertip Traverse*. They were unimpressed by whoever had just fallen from a 5.4, but they admired the skill of Dave Rearick, the belayer. Rearick was an unknown at Tahquitz. A graduate student at Caltech, he had learned to climb at the Shawangunks, a 280-foot-high escarpment 70 miles north of New York City, known to climbers as the Gunks.

Later that day, Royal and Fitschen met Rearick at Lunch Rock. Royal and Rearick climbed *Open Book* and *The Innominate*, two of the hardest routes at Tahquitz. Harry Daley and TM Herbert, twenty-one-year-olds from Los Angeles, were so impressed after watching them climb that they decided to do everything they could to emulate them on the rock. They became regulars at Stoney Point and part of Royal's growing cadre.

Rearick was more circumspect about his new friend. "We were at a belay stance and [Royal] told me he was an existentialist," said Rearick, according to Fitschen in his book, *Going Up*. "I was impressed by Royal, so I later checked out the books. They didn't make me a better climber but they might have made Royal better." At the end of the weekend, Royal invited Rearick to come with him, Fitschen, and Sherrick to Yosemite on Labor Day. Rearick, however, would have to find a climbing partner: Royal and his friends had plans of their own, namely the *Lost Arrow Chimney*, a route known for difficult free climbing and cracks too wide for pitons. Royal had been "dizzy with fear" looking up at the 1,000-foot gash below the Lost Arrow Spire, but Harding had climbed it and so would he.

Sherrick was ill and rappelled after the first pitch. Royal refused to follow Fitschen up the Harding Hole, the last pitch to the notch, and toproped a difficult crack instead. "It was the only pitch I ever led," said Fitschen, "that Royal didn't want to follow." Royal and Fitschen finished the *Lost Arrow Chimney* in two days, setting a new speed record. Royal, who had always climbed efficiently, began to promote speed as a way to improve on previous ascents.

After the *Lost Arrow Chimney*, Royal joined Harding and Janie Dean, a climber and the Yosemite Valley Lodge coffee shop manager, at a camp-fire. Royal noted her presence and her long red hair in his diary, but in the midst of his unhappy marriage, climbing was an escape from women, not a way to meet them.

Royal's fear that excluding Harding from the Half Dome climb would force Harding to attempt an even bigger climb had become a reality. If Harding had made the first ascent of Half Dome, Royal would probably have sought to repeat it faster or in better style, then done his own route, but Harding, as some of his contemporaries observed, seldom repeated routes.

El Capitan's 3,000-foot-high, glacier-carved wall of granite was only steps from the Valley's main traffic arteries. It had been much surveyed and discussed, and before the Northwest Face of Half Dome had been climbed, dismissed as impossible. When Harding, Powell, Merry, and Bill Feurer debated the merits of various lines up discontinuous cracks and across blank walls, some climbers thought they were joking. Harding settled on a route up the 3,000-foot South Buttress, aka the *Nose*. His proposed climb was bigger and steeper and had fewer ledges than any other climb ever attempted, anywhere, but it looked like the easiest line up El Capitan.

It was generally agreed that a wall of this magnitude could be climbed only by fixing ropes up the face, rappelling down, and prusiking back up with supplies. By these methods, they reached the 1,200-foot mark in August 1957, but attracted so many onlookers in El Capitan Meadow that the rangers shut down the climb until after Labor Day.

Royal believed that Harding's methods were the only way to climb the *Nose*, but he wasn't willing to use them. He had climbed Half Dome in a continuous effort partly because the bank gave him a short vacation, and he hadn't trumpeted his ascent as a victory of good climbing style. As he watched Harding crawl up and down El Capitan, it occurred to him not that Harding was a poor climber, but that there was something unseemly about his relentless use of ropes and supply camps—that it was how you rode the trail that counted most. To hold back and not throw himself body and principled soul into the climbing arena while Harding sieged El Capitan proved intolerable.

Royal quit the bank's bowling club. He had told himself that by climbing only weekends, and being a good employee, one day, he would be cured of climbing and anything else society found so wayward in him. Such a cure was now tantamount to death. "Climbing," he wrote, "was life." After two unhappy months of marriage, the most dramatic manifestation of his quest to become a regular middle-class American, he left Grace and moved back to Beulah's house on Berkeley Avenue. Royal's only new route in that autumn of life changes was *Hoodenett* at Tahquitz, named after a piton of unknown provenance found partway up the climb. Around this time, however, a more serious mystery presented itself. Grace gossiped to her coworkers that she was unsure of her child's paternity.

Bad luck was in season. On September 20, Powell fell on the Arrowhead Spire and shattered his left ankle. As soon as he was out of his cast, in the spring of 1958, he rejoined Harding's team on the *Nose*. They made it to the 2,000-foot mark, but Powell quit the team. When Harding asked Royal to join him, Royal turned him down. "I didn't feel too competitive about it," said Royal. "I was happy with Half Dome and I knew that if they did El Cap, it would be with different methods, so our position would not be threatened directly."

Together, Harding and Royal would have made the most formidable big wall team in America and finished the *Nose* in faster time. But by 1960— two years after the climb's first ascent—Royal would come to see himself as Harding's competitor on the rock, the champion of a different vision of climbing. He had swerved between commitment and waywardness, honor and crime, passion and reason. The Boy Scouts, the courts, and marrying Grace had not quite set him on his true course. The rebel Harding's challenging deeds had finally nudged Royal into the moral positions that would define and shape his life and American climbing.

4
The Big Daddy

ROYAL CONTINUED AT THE BANK through the winter of 1958, but without his former ambitions. In the evenings, he played chess, drank beer, and listened to classical music with Fitschen, who had quit college and was unemployed. Fitschen's mother, unlike the ever-indulgent Beulah, threatened to make him leave home and look after himself. On weekends, Royal burned off some of his frustration in ski races, but he no longer aspired to compete at a high level.

One night, Fitschen surprised Royal with the news that he was depressed and had enlisted in the army. He had volunteered instead of waiting to be drafted so he could play his trumpet in an army band rather than serving in whatever post the army chose for him.

"Do you know what the army *is*?" Royal sputtered. "You just gave away two precious years of your life. No more freedom, no more climbing, just saying *yessir* all the time."

The last person close to Royal who had volunteered for the army had been his father, Shannon. He claimed that he had enlisted to defend Royal and Beulah from the Japanese, although he had refused to support his family in any more ordinary way. After service, his alcoholism and depression had worsened. In January 1958, Royal's own draft papers arrived. He reported to the Induction Center in Los Angeles at 8 a.m. on March

23, 1958. Fitschen reported on March 24, the same day Elvis Presley was inducted at Fort Chaffee, Arkansas.

If Royal had still been with Grace, he could have applied for a deferment, but men who were separated and divorced had to serve. In February, Grace gave birth to a son she said was Royal's. When Royal arrived at their former apartment, however, he was apprehensive. "The child," he wrote, "a boy, though he may have been mine, was foreign to me; I didn't feel any connection to him." Despite Royal's doubts, the Selective Service bureau docked more than half his monthly pay to support Grace and the child. Grace eventually admitted that she did not know whether he was the father, and said she would pay him back. He filed for a divorce.

At Fort Ord, near San Francisco, Royal was assigned to basic training Company B, where, by coincidence, he served alongside G.I. Joseph Fitschen. Royal hated the sadistic discipline and weapons drills. "Oh God, to live and love and to love and live live and love to love and live," he wrote in a tiny wire-bound journal that August. "Live grenades are being thrown—maybe—killers are being made amidst all this overflowing of life." Discussions about the use of nuclear artillery made him even more cynical. "More murder," he wrote, "how to kill with radiological agents—goody-goody."

Photos of the Fort Ord training facility—unlike photos of Camp 4 or the RCS—show a mix of white and Black young men. Sergeant Steen, Royal's platoon leader, was a Black veteran of World War II and the Korean War. Royal's habit of climbing the barracks buildings for practice amused Steen, who made Royal a squad leader. Royal accepted the promotion without enthusiasm. "I can't really believe in the principles and ideals of the army," he wrote Beulah, "and would suffer if I were put in a position where I had to make it appear that I did believe in them."

Royal and Fitschen spent their first weekend leave in San Francisco. The extensive classical music collection on display behind the bar at Opus One was an obvious attraction (although they seem not to have noticed that it was also a famous gay bar), as was the beatnik Coexistence Bagel Shop, whose walls were decked out with notices of jazz sessions and poetry readings. They also spent hours in Lawrence Ferlinghetti's

City Lights Bookstore, a multistory rabbit warren stocked with the latest literature.

Royal read Kerouac, Ginsberg, Snyder, and Ferlinghetti. It seemed to many climbers of their generation that Kerouac's *On the Road*, with its valorization of wandering, dropping out of society, and the pursuit of risky thrills, was written for them. Kerouac's language seeped into Royal's discourse, and he began to refer to his circle of friends as the "scene" and El Capitan as "the Big Daddy." Royal also related to Kerouac's preoccupation with women and sex, writing in his journal of Eleanor, a nineteen-year-old from Berkeley he dated while he was at Fort Ord, that she was "Beautiful, vivacious, and full of love."

After Basic Training, Royal was sent to Fort Bliss, near El Paso, Texas, and became an officer's clerk. Before he and Fitschen parted, they agreed to save up leave so that they could take a month together to climb in Yosemite in the fall of 1959. Royal was bored and passed the time with army courses on regulations, the Geneva Convention, and anything else that didn't involve actual combat. Eventually, his divorce was finalized. Grace remarried and the army ended Royal's support deductions.

While he was at Fort Bliss, Royal teamed up with Pete Rogowski from the Southwest Mountaineers club. They frequented the 300-plus-foot-high domes of Hueco Tanks, east of El Paso, and the Organ Mountains in southern New Mexico. They even found a two-day route in the Organs, the *Direct South Face* of the Wedge. Royal's interest in climbing in New Mexico and Texas, however, evaporated when he discovered a form that entitled its bearer to free military flights anywhere in America. The flight time to most Southern California locations was about four hours, less than a quarter of the time it usually took to hitchhike to Los Angeles.

Royal received a pass for home leave in early November of 1958. To get home faster, he forged signatures on the air travel permission forms and two flights later, he was in San Diego. He hitchhiked to Los Angeles and surprised Beulah at home on a Thursday morning, attended a ski club party at San Onofre Beach on Saturday (where he ruined a rear tire on Beulah's car), hitched back to Fort Bliss, and arrived just in time to avoid a charge of absent without leave.

. . . . .

The upcoming 1960 Olympics inspired Royal to even more imaginative mis-
uses of army resources. That year, America would host their Communist
athletic adversaries at the Winter Olympics in Squaw Valley, California.
The American military encouraged eligible servicemen and servicewomen
to train and compete in the Games, including the first Olympic biathlon.
The army was especially keen to show that its ranks included expert skiers
and marksmen, and so sent personnel to compete at the national-team
trials from February 21–23 in Steamboat Springs, Colorado.

Royal's score in marksmanship was poor and he wasn't a Nordic
skier, but he convinced the army to send him to the trials anyway. When
he returned, he told his superiors that he had made a mistake and had
intended to go to the alpine ski trials at Mammoth in California a few
weeks later. The army gave Royal two more weeks of leave and three hundred dollars for his expenses. Before Royal got to Mammoth, however, he
gambled away his expense money in a Nevada casino. He phoned Fitschen
at Fort Mason, who bailed him out with a one-hundred-dollar loan. In
Mammoth, Royal took a part-time job on the ski hill and earned enough
money to pay Fitschen back before he returned to his base.

Royal's knowledge of army flights and connections grew. He surprised
his friends at Tahquitz, Stoney Point, or Pacifico Mountain. New faces had
shown up at the rocks while he was away, including twenty-seven-year-old
Yvon Chouinard and his friend twenty-five-year-old Tom Frost.

Frost, a decorated sailboat racer, had advanced quickly in his two years
of climbing. He had converted from Roman Catholicism to the Church of
Jesus Christ of Latter-Day Saints, and his quiet, self-possessed demeanor
struck some as spiritual. He was also a recent engineering graduate from
Stanford, and, like Wilts, applied his technical knowledge to hardware
design. Royal found Frost competent, good-humored, and reassuring.

Climbers found Chouinard intense, likeable, and astute, but he and
Royal were not fast friends. Royal learned that Chouinard had done one of
his boulder problems at Stoney Point with one hand. "I remember thinking," said Royal, "he had done it on purpose. It didn't really bother me, but
I just felt that I would do better."

Chouinard, for his part, took stock of Royal's abilities at an early stage in their relationship. "Royal Robbins did some very hard climbs," Chouinard later said in an interview, "but [was a] totally unnatural climber; he was a mental climber, he had to think before he made a move."

Also at issue was Chouinard's preference for alpinism. At fifteen, he had impressed Don Prentice, an older climber from the RCS, on alpine terrain in the Wind River Range in Wyoming. The next year, he had ignored Yosemite and gone to the Tetons, climbing alpine routes in work boots— perhaps favoring the alpine crucible of the Tetons over the Valley, mused Royal, because " . . . at first he thought, 'That's just rock climbing.'"

In the summer of 1959, Royal traveled from Fort Bliss to Tahquitz some ten weekends in a row. He might have gone to Yosemite as well, but it was farther from military airports. The army either didn't notice or didn't mind Royal's activities and offered him a place in officer school, which he promptly turned down.

TM Herbert and Royal climbed together and bonded over shared ambitions and Herbert's relentless, occasionally sardonic sense of humor. "On our way to Tahquitz Rock, TM would have us doubled over with laughter in our chairs before our malts and hamburgers," journaled Royal, whose own sense of humor had its main expression in corny puns. "I don't know why Herbert was so very, very funny. Perhaps because most of us climbers were a bit on the serious side."

·····

Royal negotiated with the army to be released in December 1959. That fall, when he arrived in Yosemite to spend his saved-up leave, Herbert was in Camp 4 on his last climbing trip before military service. Frost and Chouinard were there, too. Royal climbed with Berkeley's Chuck Pratt, who, at twenty, had already made the second ascent of *The Worst Error*, the hardest crack climb in the Valley, and the first ascent of the 2,000-foot North Face of Middle Cathedral with Chuck Wilts and Steve Roper.

Royal found Pratt "affable, strongly built and a pleasure to be around." That September, they climbed *Crack of Dawn* on the Royal Arches, the first new climb by a team made up of both Southern and Northern Californians.

A new identity, "Yosemite Climber," was born, and nobody would represent and define it as fully as Royal.

In 1959, the biggest subject in Camp 4 was the *Nose*. The year before, after forty-seven days of effort spread over thirteen months, Harding, Merry, and Los Angeles climber George Whitmore had finally made it to the rim. Harding drilled the final bolted section through the night to complete the final seven-day push. They had used fixed ropes and ferried supplies up the wall, assistance that Royal eschewed on Half Dome, but he nonetheless called the *Nose* "a monumental achievement—world class" and admitted that it "permanently put Yosemite on the climbing map." San Francisco's papers ran what Steve Roper called "war-sized" headlines for the story; the *Los Angeles Times* also ran the El Capitan story on the front page.

Harding wrote up his climb in the *Sierra Club Bulletin* and sent it to local RCS newsletters; to *Summit*, a monthly climbing magazine; and to the *American Alpine Journal* (*AAJ*). He also sold articles to *Argosy*, a men's pulp magazine, and *Life*. A sidebar in *Argosy* read: "Challenging the deadly granite façade of El Capitan, 2,900 feet above Yosemite's Valley. A handful of human flies faced almost certain death to make mountain-climbing history in the greatest adventure of the year."

Royal's first written response to Harding's climb is a letter to Yosemite's chief ranger. "I am writing to request permission to attempt a second ascent of the face of El Capitan," Royal wrote. "Mark Powell, Joe Fitschen, and myself are the interested parties."

Royal contrasted the first-ascent party's hunger for publicity with the more personal motivations of he and his friends. "Few people," he wrote, "are less interested in money and the awe of the masses and more sincerely interested in the mountains and in climbing." He proposed to make the climb over ten days in the spring of 1960—in a single push without fixed ropes.

Climbers in the muddy, perpetually bear-pillaged Camp 4 in the fall of 1959, however, spent more time on their day-to-day survival than big walls. Royal and Fitschen stored some food in army surplus footlockers, but bears broke the lids off and clawed into the cans. Royal's tent leaked in the rainstorms that pummelled the Valley. He snuck into the car of a visiting climber, but a bear drove him out by jumping on the trunk. Chouinard boasted that he didn't own a tent, so he slept in his car when it rained, at least until the same bear that had already broken in and destroyed his equipment once before returned to smash the car window in the middle of the night.

Royal and Fitschen spent hours drying out in the Yosemite Valley Lodge coffee shop. Janie Dean, the climber who managed the shop in the peak season, had left, so they talked to the girls working the concessions. A couple of them came to Camp 4, but they left after some casual conversation. Camp 4 was awash in unrequited love and sexual longing. Even Hemming breezed through Yosemite that fall in anguished pursuit of a woman he had met in the Shawangunks. Meanwhile, the inauspicious weather made for indifferent climbs. Royal and Fitschen ended the season with the only important climb of their trip, the second ascent of the North Face of Middle Cathedral Rock.

On the route, Royal added a bolt to one of Pratt's hard leads, the first of three that he would add to established routes over his career. The rule that a climber must take the same risks as the first ascensionists or retreat was understood, but unwritten. That day, Royal broke it. In the October 1959 edition of the *Mugelnoos*, Royal described the pitch as "certainly one of the most remarkable leads in the history of American mountain climbing," which both praised Pratt and declared, perhaps a year or two prematurely, Yosemite's primacy in American climbing.

Bad weather allowed time for other dreams. Chouinard tried to start the invitation-only Yosemite Climbing Club. The club's goals were to prepare a guidebook to Yosemite, since the 1954 guide by the Sierra Club included only half of the 150 routes that had been climbed by 1959, and to "assemble together devoted climbers interested in raising the standards," wrote Steve Roper in his book *Camp 4*. Chouinard invited Royal and the rest of the Camp 4 inner circle: Harry Daley, Bill Feurer, Joe Fitschen, Warren Harding, TM Herbert, Bob Kamps, Mark Powell, Chuck Pratt, Charlie Raymond, Dave Rearick, Steve Roper, Herb Swedlund, and Chuck Wilts. Fitschen says Tetons climber Dave Dornan was also on the list. Notably excluded were members of the old guard, like Roy Gorin, George Harr, Allen Steck, and Bob Swift.

Royal was jaded with the rules and restrictions of army life, and his history with clubs made him wary. Along with Pratt and Fitschen, he ignored the invitation. In the end, the club never met.

· · · · ·

After the North Face of Middle Cathedral, Royal returned to Fort Ord. December 1 would be his last day in uniform. Around midnight on the Saturday after Thanksgiving, he surprised his friends at the campground in Idyllwild. Wilson, whose marriage and academic studies protected him from the draft, was there. That weekend would be the last time he and Royal climbed together.

A group from the Caltech Hiking Club at Berkeley had joined the RCS campfire party. Seventeen-year-old college freshwomen Janie Taylor and her friend Judy McFarlane were among them. Royal had met Taylor bouldering at Indian Rock in Berkeley a year before. They stayed up talking after the others retired; Royal asked her if he could write to her, and she gave him her address.

Royal described Taylor that night as "sweet," "a sharp observer," and "good with words." She knew about books and music. She played the violin in the Berkeley university orchestra. And best of all, she climbed.

Instead of taking the job at a ski resort for which he had secured early release from the army, Royal moved back in with Beulah and returned, without enthusiasm, to the Union Bank. Over the winter, he and Taylor wrote each other long letters. They discussed E. E. Cummings, D. H. Lawrence, Thomas Hardy, Herman Melville, Robinson Jeffers, and Allen Ginsberg. Jeffers became one of Royal's favorites. "When the cities lie at the monster's feet," wrote Jeffers in "Shine, Perishing Republic," his most well-known poem, "there are left the mountains."

In January 1960, Royal traveled to San Francisco for his first date with Taylor. Fitschen thought Taylor was "successful at breaking some of Royal's reserve," Royal would later write. Taylor, however, didn't find Royal reserved at all, but "witty, serious, completely supportive and enthusiastic about my growing abilities as a climber."

In mid-February, Royal moved to Berkeley to be closer to Taylor and Yosemite. He took a room at Krehe Ritter's pad, an outbuilding off Spruce

Street in north Berkeley, a few blocks from the climbing at Cragmont Park and Indian Rock. Ritter, a climber, mathematics graduate student, folk dancer, and French horn player, lived on the main floor and sublet the upstairs bedrooms. Royal's roommates were Lito Tejada-Flores, whom Royal described as "a young and very intelligent one-time Bolivian," who had actually grown up in Pasadena and started rock climbing at Tahquitz at thirteen, and Charlie Raymond, whom Royal described as "a not very exceptional person but a good climber."

Ritter's pad was equipped with a stereo system and a collection of reel-to-reel tapes of classical music, which played constantly. Nonetheless, Royal's taste for music was so voracious that he asked Beulah to send him his own record player and a list of some eighteen records, mostly Beethoven pressings, with a smattering of Bach and Haydn. Elvis Presley, Fats Domino, and Roy Orbison all had chart-topping hits that year, but Royal seemed oblivious to rock and roll. In addition to the music, the monthly rent of fifty dollars included groceries, which were rumored to include horsemeat.

In 1962, a revolution in the California wine trade changed the drinking habits of the state's climbers, Royal included. Gallo released their Mountain Red, the first wine sold in a gallon jug with a finger ring, for two dollars. The intellectual scene in Berkeley was soon awash in Mountain Red, which Ritter supplied as part of room and board. Although this hunger for inebriation eventually had its victims in the climbing scene, Royal was always ready to climb the next morning, no matter how late the party had gone on.

"We all spent a lot of time at Krehe Ritter's pad," said Taylor, "talking about everything: literature, music, climbing. Royal and I discussed Hardy, Lawrence, the poetry of Whitman and E. E. Cummings, and the tragic flaws of mankind!" Conversations were held over chess games, while climbers did pull-ups on the doorjambs.

Tejada-Flores remembered bouldering sessions at nearby Indian Rock. "We would be doing these long, traversing bouldering problems that were only a foot off the ground. You could step down . . . any time you liked, and so I would give up if it got too hard, but Royal was so fierce trying them, he would put so much effort into it, as if his life depended on it." Tejada-Flores said that Royal's strength came from his prodigious mental focus—"from what he could make himself do more than what he could do easily."

With the climbing season a few months away, Royal, out of financial necessity, took a job as a teller at the American Trust company in downtown Berkeley. By the time the park granted permission for the *Nose* attempt—not for the spring, but the post–Labor Day season—Powell's injured ankle had become worse and he dropped out. Pratt and Frost joined the team. "As to style," said Fitschen, "it was just a matter of doing it in one continuous push. It was mainly a logistics problem."

· · · · ·

In early May, Royal quit what was to be his final bank job, grew a beard and long hair, and scootered to Tahquitz to begin preparing for the awesome challenge of El Capitan. He dropped in on his mother on the way. Back on his home cliff, Royal did his first new climb with Frost. Frost was calm, courteous, and unaffected by Royal's personality, which some saw as reserved but others found arrogant. He quickly became one of Royal's favorite partners.

In that era, most male climbers did not climb with their girlfriends or wives, but Royal's first Yosemite climbs that season were with Taylor. They even set a new speed record on the difficult *Arrowhead Arête*. He was genuinely proud of her abilities and even told Colorado ace Layton Kor, "If you can climb as well as my girl, Janie Taylor, I will buy you a beer."

Royal remained, however, unnecessarily protective of Taylor in a way he was not with his male partners. "Ever the chevalier," wrote Fitschen, "if Royal was leading a difficult pitch and he thought a fall was a possibility, he would tie his climbing rope to a belt loop [instead of around his waist], assuming that Janie wouldn't be able to hold a long fall and she might be hurt trying." If Royal fell, he would certainly have been killed, but at least Taylor would not have suffered rope burn.

In mid-June, Fitschen, Pratt, and Frost made the second ascent of the *Regular Northwest Face* of Half Dome. They raced past two of the first-ascent party's bivouac sites, and Fitschen reported that they were "surprised to find that six of the twenty-five pitches were fourth class" and that "only four of the pitches required extensive nailing." It seemed like Royal's biggest climb was not such a big deal after all.

Royal monitored their progress with binoculars from Mirror Lake. He was astounded to see them already at the top of the Zig-Zags, a series of cracks on the last third of the wall, on their second day. They cut his time on the wall in half, finishing half a day later.

"He was happy to see his friends Fitschen, Pratt, and Frost climbing this route he loved," Royal wrote in the third person, "but aghast to witness the speed and ease with which they were doing it. How dare they make a mockery of his great route! . . . He hated them, for a while, with an intensity of hatred he had never felt before or since." However, Royal quickly responded with a program of new climbs, speed records, and first free ascents that would make 1960 a year like no other.

First, with Rearick, he made the first free ascent of the East Chimney of Rixon's Pinnacle, Yosemite's first 5.10. "Rixon's was the only time I ever saw Robbins take a lead fall," said Rearick, "but he made it on his second attempt." Then they teamed up to set a new speed record—one and a half days—on Half Dome. He told Rearick, "I don't think anyone will climb it faster than that."

Royal's first new big wall that spring was the North Face of Lower Cathedral Rock with Fitschen and Pratt. The most memorable pitches climbed the Gong Flake, a thin, 300-foot-high, 40-foot-wide piece of rock perched on fractured rubble. Royal wrote in the *Sierra Club Bulletin* that he and his companions "considered this the most unpleasant, yet one of the most challenging climbs we have ever done."

Royal and Fitschen's next project, on the 1,400-foot Royal Arches behind the Ahwahnee Hotel, turned out to be even harder. On June 24, they liebacked and aided 750 feet of slabby climbing to the final, vertical band of rock. A wet overhang sprouting clumps of grass jutted out above them.

Fitschen tried the roof, pulled out a piton, and fell. He gave the lead to Royal, who choked on the dirt as he dug for piton placements. After his first solid piton, he decided to free climb. Twenty-five feet higher, he tried to place a Knifeblade piton behind a flake, lost his balance, and fell.

"I heard a small ping and saw Royal's silhouette splayed against the sky," wrote Fitschen. "The rope momentarily looking like a pile of spaghetti." The next morning, after an uncomfortable bivouac in slings, Royal tried again, fell again, but got back on and kept climbing. When he finally finished the pitch, it had taken a total of ten hours. They reached the top after one more bivouac, a day later than planned.

Royal admitted that he would not want to repeat *Arches Direct*. When Layton Kor made the second ascent in 1965, he concurred. In early April, the first climb to be graded A5—the most difficult aid-climbing rating—had been completed on the Southwest Face of the 200-foot Kat Pinnacle by Yvon Chouinard and Tom Frost, but Royal and Fitschen were the first to climb the grade on a big wall.

Arches Direct was so dirty and dangerous that it was left out of several subsequent guidebooks. Half Dome, Lower Cathedral Rock, and *Arches Direct*, Royal's three greatest contributions to date, had long, loose, or unaesthetic sections. He ended the 1960 spring season with an attempt on another dangerous project, the vertical, 1,000-foot-high North Face of Cathedral Spire, also with Fitschen. So far, Royal's routes showcased his nerve, but they weren't enjoyable. Climbers mostly avoided them.

Royal had permission to try the *Nose*, but only after Labor Day. The Valley would soon be too hot for hard climbing, so Royal and Fitschen took their first trip ever to the cooler altitudes of the Tetons in Wyoming.

The Tetons' legends and prestige situated the range firmly at the center of American climbing. Every summer, its glaciers and ridges drew more climbers than the sheer walls of Yosemite, and by the time Royal and Fitschen arrived, the climbers' camp at Jenny Lake was full. Late arrivals were sent to an old Civilian Conservation Corps site without bathrooms or water, to camp in a disused concrete incinerator. A week later, Chouinard and his partner Ken Weeks, who was AWOL from the army, took up residence in the unoccupied chamber next door.

In the evenings, there were guitars, folk songs, and Teton Tea, a hot mixture of lemonade and port wine. One rainy day, the Gunks climbers held a push-up contest, but Royal supposedly demurred. Some said they later saw him practice push-ups in the woods before he proposed another contest.

Layton Kor hobbled around the campground using a stick. An injury he'd suffered on the North Face of the Grand Teton made him a limping warning for rock climbers to take high alpine peaks seriously. On the advice of local climber and guide Dave Dornan, one of the only Tetons climbers familiar with Yosemite, Royal and Fitschen made their first climbs on the rock formations of Baxter's Pinnacle and the South Buttress of Mount Moran.

In late August, Hemming set up camp on top of the incinerator. He had found Judith, the woman he had been searching for when Royal had met him in Yosemite, but there had been no rapprochement. Royal noticed a new seriousness in Hemming. The easygoing kid from San Diego had become a gaunt, bearded wanderer, obsessed with literature and uninterested in joining Royal and Fitschen on hard routes. His sudden departure to the University of Grenoble on a scholarship surprised everyone.

On July 30, Royal and Fitschen climbed the North Face of Middle Teton, their single new alpine route of the season. Royal's report on the climb was also his first submission to the *AAJ*.

Their most substantial alpine effort was the second ascent of the Northwest Chimney of the Grand Teton. Weeks had been arrested by the military police in Jenny Lake, leaving Chouinard free to climb with the two alpine neophytes. Crucially, Chouinard brought an ice axe, a piece of kit neither Fitschen nor Royal owned. Chouinard led most of the route, and Fitschen and Royal followed as well as they could, their rock climbing shoes slipping on the ice and their numb fingers clawing at the snow.

On the trail back to Jenny Lake, they met Irene Ortenburger, who had driven Royal and Fitschen from Berkeley. She was hiking up Garnet Canyon on a sad mission to retrieve the camping gear of her friend Tim Bond, a young guide who had died on Nez Perce a couple of days before. They were all tired, but Royal, who was more familiar with grief than some young climbers, volunteered to help her.

Up in Garnet Canyon, above the Platforms camping area, Robbins and Fitschen tackled a 300-foot wall using the postage-stamp-sized Realized Ultimate Reality Pitons (RURPs) for the first time in the Tetons. "Probably no one who has camped at the Platforms in Garnet Canyon," wrote the editors of the 1961 *AAJ*, "has given any thought to climbing the overhanging cliff directly above [the Platforms] that is until Royal Robbins and Joe Fitschen climbed it on August 12." Fitschen was more straightforward when he wrote the climb went unrepeated "because of our hubris and a lack of a sense of place, our inability to sense the characteristics of a truly great climb in the Tetons."

Royal did not make a name for himself in the Tetons in 1960 and left his visit out of his memoir. He had, however, probed the alpine world, with its poor rock, dangerous weather, and omnipresent dangers, and he and Fitschen had brought Yosemite techniques to the range. A new, American synthesis of climbing began to take shape, not because Teton climbers came to Yosemite, but because Royal and Fitschen had come to the Tetons.

· · · · ·

Back in Yosemite, as Labor Day approached, final preparations were made for El Capitan. Royal, in an iconic photograph by Frost, sits bare-chested at a picnic table with pitons and carabiners lined up in front of him like chess pieces. His hair is shorn, but his beard is fuller than ever. In another photo, Fitschen, with a goatee and mutton-chop sideburns, looks on. Pratt has a white patch over an eye grazed by a shard of piton steel.

Chouinard loaned them more RURPs. Frost had made some steel bong-bong pitons that could span cracks as wide as three inches for the Stoveleg Cracks, where Harding had used scrap-iron pitons. Royal convinced the others to live on slim rations. As a concession to the number of nights they would spend on the cliff, however, they packed sleeping bags instead of the usual down jackets. Their four haulbags weighed about fifty pounds each.

Despite Royal's assurance to the rangers that he was uninterested in publicity, *The Fresno Bee* sent a reporter to Camp 4. Fitschen (whom the newspaper called "Fitschem") and Frost gave interviews to the *Los Angeles Times*. "They plan to climb 500 feet today to Sickly Ledge," declared the *Times*.

They drank their last beers before the climb in the Mountain Room bar and discussed their plans a final time. At five o'clock the next morning, Fitschen and Royal lay in their sleeping bags and listened as the car rolled away from the campsite with Pratt and Frost, who had drawn the straw for the first climbing shift. They would leave a few ropes behind them for Royal and Fitschen to prusik with the bags later that same day.

On the third day, Boot Flake expanded while Royal hammered in a piton. Terrified, he placed a bolt in the main wall as a back-up. He felt ashamed of this concession to fear as soon as he clipped his rope, but it was too late to do anything about the transgression.

"Air Mail thanks again for your support," Royal wrote on a message in a tuna can jettisoned from the wall. "Everything is going well, but we are feeling tired and thirsty. We get more shade in the evenings but the afternoon sun is fierce! However, the situation is not at all serious and we are mostly enjoying ourselves . . . " He closed with "à bientôt," although he neither spoke nor read French.

Newspapers called the climb "the first sustained effort" and "continuous climb," and contrasted it with Harding's "series of weekend climbs." Frost captured the climb in black-and-white photographs with a borrowed Leica. Pratt coils a rope over a boulder, Fitschen a few inches away, and less than a foot behind stands Royal, still in his underpants. The mental stress of the wall shows on their faces.

After seven days and only a couple mishaps, they were on top—three days ahead of schedule. Friends met them on the summit with fruit, milk, juice, and a bottle of champagne. A second celebration in the LeConte Memorial Lodge in the Valley went on until dawn.

The continuous ascent of the *Nose* was a more significant historical breakthrough than Half Dome. Harding was a good climber, but there was something inevitable about his success, given his methods. There was nothing inevitable about the success of a single team relying only on one another and what they had with them, even taking into account the benefit of Harding's routefinding and bolts. Royal was a driving force on both Half Dome and the continuous *Nose* ascent. He saw El Capitan not as an irreducible behemoth that could only be defeated by any means possible, including bending the unwritten rules of the game, but instead as a goal that could be achieved by the means available and within the boundaries accepted by most climbers. It was a kind of democratic moment, heralding the arrival on El Capitan of every climber. Royal, Pratt, and Fitschen were climbers, as others were climbers, repeating a climb, albeit a very big one, as others climbed. Harding, who rarely repeated anyone else's climbs, aided by a special supply of bolts, ropes, and hardware unknown outside his endeavors, remained a brilliant force unto himself, his only followers the revolving door of partners he allowed to share in his obsessions.

The top of El Capitan's only route was, for now, the vanishing point in American climbing. Royal and Fitschen set their eyes on the Alps, the ancient seat of alpinism, where no one had yet heard of Royal Robbins, Chuck Pratt, Joe Fitschen, or the *Nose.*

5

Poste Restante, Chamonix

IN DECEMBER 1961, ROYAL TOOK a job at Sugar Bowl Resort, ostensibly to make money for Fitschen's and his European trip. The cluster of ski lodges and chalets near Donner Pass was accessed by an aerial tramway, and the young people who lived and worked there in ski season were largely isolated from the world below.

At night, Royal tended the bar in the employees' lounge, and during the day he helped out the ski instructors. He had already shown some talent as an instructor by teaching his friends how to climb, and reported to Beulah that he was "moderately successful in improving my students [sic] ability to ski."

As Royal saved his wages, his daydreams about taking on even harder climbs in Yosemite grew into plans. He fretted that others would beat him to unclimbed walls that in reality, only he and his friends would consider. Without telling Fitschen, Royal made his decision. The Alps could wait another year; Yosemite could not. In the *Mugelnoos*, he described Fitschen as "currently a busboy in the Yosemite Lodge coffee shop, but hopes to work his way up to bellboy at the Ahwahnee Hotel. All this to pay for a trip to Europe." As far as Fitschen knew, Royal was saving money for the same purpose.

Janie Taylor visited with Royal at Sugar Bowl over Christmas, and when ski season ended and he moved back to Los Angeles, she transferred to UC Santa Barbara to see him more often and climb at Tahquitz. Her admiration for Royal continued to grow. "Some people have described him as cold," she said, "calculating, overly serious, etc. But what I remember is that . . . he was a kind, thoughtful, and generous person, open to new ideas, and learning about everything."

That May, Fitschen quit his job and moved into Camp 4. On the day Royal arrived, it rained, and they whiled away the afternoon at the coffee shop where Fitschen had worked all winter and where Janie Dean was the manager. Royal confessed that he would not be going to Europe because he wanted to climb in Yosemite that year. Fitschen had already booked his passage and made his plans. He felt betrayed.

When the coffee shop closed, Dean invited Royal, who knew her moderately well by now, and Fitschen, who was smitten by her, to her cabin. She had much to tell. That winter, she had sold her motorcycle to pay for a berth to Tahiti on actor Sterling Hayden's boat *Wanderer*. She had cut her hair, learned to sail, and acquired a sarong.

"When [Janie] went to take a shower," Fitschen wrote of the visit, "Royal said, 'I'm sorry, Joe, but she wants to be with me tonight.'" Fitschen politely took his leave, and when Royal left Yosemite shortly thereafter Fitschen and Dean "had a few more ardent evenings together" though, wrote Fitschen, "Many years later when I asked her about that night, she responded that she had never said that to Royal, which made me contemplate the limits of friendship and the accuracy of memory and the muddle that desire makes."

Fitschen left for Europe and the rain stopped. Royal and Frost threw themselves at one of the hardest free climbs Royal had yet done in Yosemite. A smooth, 400-foot-high slab provided *The Diehardral*, a bad Robbins pun and another 5.10, but Royal had not foregone Europe for routes that were only a few pitches long. In May, he and Frost completed the 1,100-foot Northwest Face of Higher Cathedral Spire with no fixed ropes and only six bolts. In Roper's *Camp 4*, Royal was said to have described the crux—a leaning, shallow, unprotectable groove—as "psychologically devastating," but he climbed it anyway. "I was not alone," wrote Roper, who had attempted the climb, "in regarding Robbins as Yosemite's best climber."

That June, Royal and Frost stared at El Capitan for hours, looking for a route left of the *Nose*. Wayne Merry had already pointed out some crack systems; scoping from the ground, Royal, Frost, and Pratt linked them, naming the visible features. A thousand feet up, beneath a massive heart-shaped depression, was Heart Ledge. A pitch above it was Mammoth Terrace. High on the wall, El Capitan Spire stood proud of the face. The crux headwall bulged above it. The wall was known as the Southwest Face, even after Chouinard suggested calling it the *Salathé Wall*.

Royal and Frost concocted a climbing plan, at first half-seriously and then with intention. They would climb the 1,000-foot lower slab to Mammoth Terrace, rappel to Heart Ledge 150 feet below, and fix ropes to the ground from there. Since El Capitan's base rose acutely to the left of the proposed route, they would only need six ropes. The compromise would avoid gruelling bag hauling up the climb's slabby lower third. They would then prusik their fixed ropes, drop any they didn't need, and head for the top in a single push. They hoped to minimize their use of bolts, but "bolts, if necessary," wrote Royal, "would get us up the last five hundred feet."

The park service and the summer heat kept climbers off El Capitan until after Labor Day. They brought Pratt into their plan, but otherwise Royal kept it secret for the moment, even from Janie Taylor, with whom he spent the summer in the Tetons.

The previous summer, Royal had forgone an alpine apprenticeship for hard rock climbing. This season, he spent more time on the big peaks. In addition to ticking off classic itineraries like the North Face of the Grand Teton, he and Taylor climbed a difficult new route on Middle Teton. Royal named it the *Taylor Route* as a statement against the common practice of excluding second climbers and women from the climbing record.

In August, Taylor wrote her family from Jenny Lake. "It rained all day yesterday and only began to clear up in the late afternoon. I discovered something that will be joyful news to you all. There is a man here in camp

[Tom Cochrane] with a violin and a lot of Vivaldi, Handel, and Bach and so I spent the afternoon playing."

Royal listened to the concertos and the rain and dreamed of Yosemite. In September, they hitchhiked home, Taylor to Berkeley and Royal to Yosemite. Soon afterward, Royal revealed his plans to her in a letter:

> . . . . *Here in the valley something new has arisen, which will affect my activities for the next couple weeks.*
>
> *This "something new" is a new route on El Capitan. Yesterday Tom [Frost] and I were down casually binockulering [sic] the s w face when we suddenly realized that there is a route there! It's beautiful!*
>
> *The facts are that I'm afraid someone else might get it, I will be gone next summer, Tom is just starting a two weeks vacation. All these make an immediate start imperative. Chuck [Pratt] also will be with us.*
>
> *We plan to try to do it in two pushes. The first will involve (1) a long line of bolts, (2) a long traverse diagonally upward over and past the 'half dollar,' (3) a 200 or 300 ft rappel, and possibly, a swing traverse hanging 300 feet below the suspension point.*
>
> *All this will bring us to the end of a long traverse. From the end of the traverse it is a straight line to the summit, 1,800 feet away. The second push will go from the end of the traverse. We plan to leave fixed ropes from the end of the traverse straight down. We will start the first push Tuesday. I hope to be down Thursday night but we might be held up until Friday night.*
>
> *I so much want to see you that I hate to put it off past Wednesday but as you can see, the circumstances <u>are</u> pressing. . . . The coyotes are howling in Yosemite again—weird, eerie and siren-like.*
>
> *So far [Teton climber Bill Briggs] hasn't arrived.*
>
> *Today Tom and i climbed Sentinel north wall in 3 ½ hours.*
>
> *Avec l'amour (je pense)*

Royal devotes only a couple phrases to his longing for Taylor after the details about his proposed route. His closing line, in French, translates as "With love," moderated by *"je pense"*—"I think"—in parentheses.

· · · · ·

Pratt, Frost, and Royal took three and a half days to reach Mammoth Terrace, a third of the way up the wall. They had used only thirteen bolts—mostly on a ladder on blank rock—fewer than were found on many Yosemite routes of the same length. The next day, they rappelled to Heart Ledge. Three days later, they prusiked back up and set off for the top. Continuous crack systems led to the top of El Capitan Spire, a triangular ledge with twelve-foot sides and one of the most exposed and comfortable bivouac sites in Yosemite.

In Frost's photographs, the climbers look more relaxed than they did on the *Nose*. Royal stands in slings as he climbs around a roof and goes through his rack of pitons casually, as if looking for his car keys. His clothes and grooming radiate more beatnik swagger than ascetic determination. His beard is a neat goatee, the chunky glasses replaced by Ray-Ban shades. Instead of the ballooning, protective knickers he wore on the *Nose*, he sports shorts. He looks lighter, more honed.

Royal, who could wax French even on El Capitan, named a ledge two pitches below the overhang marking the start of the overhanging headwall *Sous le Toit*—"Beneath the Roof." Hidden piton cracks gained them a thin crack system in the headwall. From the meadow below, they looked like tiny figures in a desert of rock, surrounded by limitless space.

"We felt like we were explorers up there on El Capitan," said Glen Denny, who was later active on El Capitan, "like the astronauts." On September 12, while Royal and his friends climbed the *Salathé Wall*, President John F. Kennedy asked, "Why, some say, the moon? Why choose this as our goal? And they may well ask why climb the highest mountain? . . . We choose to go to the moon in this decade and do the other things, not because they are easy, but because they are hard." There was something of this epochal appetite for difficult endeavors, even in the wayward, beatnik world of Camp 4.

After six and a half days, Royal, Frost, and Pratt stood atop El Capitan. There had been no water or food shortages; no long falls, routefinding errors, nor dropped pieces of crucial equipment. They had used 500 feet of fixed rope. The climb was made in two continuous efforts—one three days long and one six days long—for a total of nine days. Harding's team had spent a total of forty-seven days on the *Nose*, seven of which were on the final push up the last third. Royal, Frost, and Pratt used 13 bolts in total, mostly on a single pitch. Harding had used 125 bolts on the *Nose*. By any measure, the *Salathé Wall* was an improvement in style.

Janie Dean and Janie Taylor met them up top with champagne and wildflower chaplets. In a photograph, Frost beams beneath his flowers, Pratt looks tired and indifferent, and Royal looks annoyed. "We wore our conqueror's wreaths for the first part of the hike, but soon took them off," wrote Royal. "We felt more 'conquered' than 'conquering.'" Royal simply wasn't the kind of fellow who wore flowers.

The *Salathé Wall* was a new standard in difficulty, commitment, and style, but Royal told the papers, "[We] encountered no difficulties," and the climb "was much easier than our previous [El Capitan] climb." Climbers, naturally, wondered what he could have meant.

Royal's last notable climb of 1961, a solo of the *Steck-Salathé* using a self-belay on three pitches and free soloing the rest, was the first solo of a Yosemite big wall, but it was overshadowed by both the *Salathé* and Harding's latest project.

Three weeks after the *Salathé*, Harding, Merry, and Al MacDonald completed their year-long siege of the West Face of Leaning Tower. The 1,000-foot wall overhung almost continuously, and its first few hundred feet were smooth and crackless. The whole route was climbed with fixed ropes. The climbers placed 110 bolts—almost as many as on the *Nose*, which was three times longer. Harding convinced a television station to film his ascent from below.

Leaning Tower was the last of Harding's fixed-rope siege climbs. Royal complained about the fixed ropes, but he'd later write that he admired Harding's audacity, if not his love of publicity.

MacDonald's lavishly illustrated report appeared in the December 1962 *Sierra Club Bulletin*, alongside a single-page article about the *Salathé Wall*. Royal complained to David Brower, the club's executive director, explaining the difference between the two climbs, but Brower had already decided to be cautious in the future about reporting on dangerous big walls. Royal overcame his apprehensions about the East Coast editors of the *AAJ* and sent them a report on the *Salathé Wall*. Instead of his article, however, they ran a three-sentence report on his climb. Royal was livid, dismissing the AAC as hopelessly out of touch with California climbers. Perhaps his plans to meet Janie Taylor, Joe Fitschen, and Janie Dean in the Alps the next summer for the deferred alpine debut would give him a chance to prove California climbers' mettle in an arena the club would have to respect.

At night, Royal and Taylor joined the campfire gatherings of climbers and young Curry Company employees, drank Teton Tea and red wine, talked about climbing, sung folk songs, and discussed climbing plans. One night that fall, a newcomer to these soirees caught Royal's eye. It would turn out to be the most important chance meeting of his life.

· · · · ·

Florence Elizabeth Burkner, known to her family and friends as Liz, was born on June 22, 1938, to Carrie Burkner, née Hartley, and her husband, Earl. Carrie grew up working in her parents' railway-station hotel in Texas. As soon as she was old enough, she sought her own fortune in California. Earl was born in Kreischa, a hamlet in Saxony, Germany, and came to America as a child. His love of his new country was undiminished by his incarceration as an enemy alien during World War I, and afterward, he headed west to make his fortune. In Stockton, California, he met Carrie.

Earl and Carrie married and settled down in Modesto, a growing community surrounded by almond and fruit orchards, ninety-five miles east of San Francisco. After the tragic death of a prematurely born baby boy, ten years passed before they had Liz. "They lived with the memory of their first child's death," said Liz, "and I became pampered and overly important to them." Even as a child, she went to the symphony and wore fashionable clothes.

They opened the Valley Paint store in the 1930s, and over the next three decades, the town's population tripled and so did its demand for paint. The small family prospered, and purchased a rambling Spanish-American style bungalow on Magnolia Avenue with an iron driveway gate and a ninety-five-foot sequoia in the backyard.

Liz fulfilled her parents' high expectations with brilliant school years. Her mysterious smile in the Downey High School yearbooks, however, concealed her emotional attraction to the forces of nature and ambivalence about becoming an ornament to society. When the Burkners visited relatives in the Midwest, Liz fell in love with the nights full of fireflies and storms so violent that, on one occasion, a bolt of lightning flashed down the chimney. At twenty, on vacation in Switzerland and Austria, she got her first view of the mountains. Their beauty impressed her, but it didn't occur to her that she would ever climb them.

At the University of California, Berkeley, Liz lived in the Tri Delta sorority house. Football games and parties bored her, so she snuck away to the less structured environment of the international students' residence whenever she could. In the spring of 1961, after her fourth year in college, Liz took a summer job as a social hostess at the Ahwahnee Hotel dining room in Yosemite. She liked the idea of earning her own money and craved a reprieve from the university.

Male recollections of Liz's arrival in Yosemite tend to emphasize two things: First, that she could come across as either haughty or pleasingly self-assured. (Men either sought her approval or commented on why it didn't matter to them.) Second was her beauty, generally and, at times, acutely observed in public and private—in casual comments, letters, articles, doodled cartoons, plangent letters from ex-boyfriends, and photographs.

"Pretty quickly after I started work," said Liz, "the gentleman who was managing the place brought me over to work at the front desk." He also fell in love with her, causing a minor scandal, as he was married.

Her coworker Herb Swedlund and his friend, the Camp 4 troubadour Mort Hempel, were eager to take her climbing. Hempel's folk singing won him more romantic attention than any other climber in Camp 4, but he fell hard for Liz—who was less interested—and he never fully recovered. Liz liked climbing and her new friends, and took advantage of the offer to attend a campfire in the boulders behind Camp 4.

By the forgiving light of the fire, the climbers sprawled on the rocks world-weary and lean, rather than merely underfed and in need of showers.

Their passionate conversations about the esoterica of climbing seemed to Liz to reveal an appealing penchant for free thought. The climbers, who were mostly young men, immediately took notice of Liz. "I was like a bird," she said, "with unusual feathers they'd never seen before."

Swedlund pointed out Royal. "My impression was that he was bold and shameless," said Liz. "He stared at me, even though he was with his girl-friend. He thought nothing of it, or that he was doing something wrong. I didn't want anything to do with him." It was a sentiment that would not last long.

When Liz went to relieve herself in the woods she ran into Royal, who had left the gathering for the same purpose. "He stopped and looked right at me," Liz recalled, "and said, 'You are a beautiful woman.'" His words, said Liz, "sent shivers down my spine." Moments later, they were making love in the bushes.

There was something pampered and refined about Liz that unintentionally engendered longing in many lonely young climbers, but there was something exquisite about the degree to which Royal, himself, had been so quickly ensnared. The next day, in the employee parking lot, with one foot on the bumper of her father's Mercedes, Royal told Liz he wanted her. Although Royal always shied away from physical confrontations, he showed his devotion by confronting an ex-boyfriend who was stalking Liz.

For Royal, the sudden appearance of a person he felt was his destiny shook his faith in his relationship with Taylor. When the Yosemite scene dispersed at season's end, he was, however, still with her. Liz was bemused, rather than overcome, by Royal's attentions. Royal resumed his job as ski instructor and bartender at Sugar Bowl, and Taylor returned to babysitting the manager's children. In April, she left for Europe.

"When Janie left, I was in Berkeley and had three months to graduate," said Liz. "I got a letter from Royal, saying, 'Come up to Sugar Bowl and ski with me.' I never went back to school; I spent two weeks there. We lived together and skied together, and it was fabulous." When ski season ended, they went to Yosemite. Long-legged, brave, and light, Liz was a natural climber. When she climbed, Royal said he "saw her as creative and vivacious." Royal nicknamed her "the Lizard." She was charmed.

. . . . .

Liz happily hung out in the Valley while Royal and Frost added a new, direct route to the north face of Sentinel Rock. Royal described it as a casual, almost contemplative excursion. His report in *Summit* contained a sentence that was not quickly forgotten: "How easy it is to become anaesthetized to the simple and grand things of nature," he wrote, "which really are the best—better, even, than Mozart."

Yosemite had other classical music fans besides Royal. Chuck Pratt had once consoled himself after a romantic fiasco by listening to all of Gustav Mahler's symphonies in succession, but Camp 4 ridiculed Royal's Mozart name-drop. The young climber Eric Beck wrote up a farcical report on one of Royal's new routes on the Apron. "Better than Rimsky-Korsakoff [sic]," he japed, "but not as good as Tchaikovsky." Beck even dubbed Royal's new Sentinel route *The Mozart Wall*, but the name didn't stick. After the "Mozart Wall" episode, in Steve Roper's words, "a kind of polarity [concerning Royal] existed in Camp 4, subtle, but ever present."

"Royal," said Liz, "was unscathed and untouched by what other people did or said or thought. It didn't mean anything to him. He had no intuitive side to figure out what people really meant or wanted. He didn't see himself as others saw him."

Janie Taylor awaited him in Europe, but to join her he had, at least for now, to give up Liz, who saw him off to Europe to return to his girlfriend. For Liz, the fling was over.

Royal followed Kerouac's example and booked a berth on a Yugoslav passenger-freighter liner, via the shipping line Jugolinija, from New York to Tangier. He hitched a ride to Colorado with Jack Turner. They stopped on the way for a few hours to make the first ascent of the overhanging capstone of the Mexican Hat. Turner dropped Royal off at the bus station in Denver, and two days later, Royal was in New York City with a day to kill until his ship sailed. Deciding to save the $2.50 a hotel room would cost and sleep under a park hedge, Royal was awakened when a stranger crawled toward him to warn him that he could be arrested for sleeping in a park. Royal wrote that the man "might have had something else in mind," and found another park to sleep in.

In the morning, Royal found a Yugoslavian ship at the Brooklyn docks, but the gangplank was raised. The Jugolinija office told him that the next ship sailed in six days. He spent a week with Jerry Carrico, his friend from the Standard Bank who was studying at Princeton University. Whiling away the hours in the neo-Gothic splendor of the Firestone Library gave Royal his first experience of where rich kids read books. On the nine-day voyage to North Africa, Royal was seasick, disgusted by the food, and separated from his fellow passengers by language barriers. It was his first experience of being a foreigner.

Fitschen had been on the road since early that year. He had climbed in England, Austria, and the Italian Dolomites; he'd toured Germany and Italy, split up with a girlfriend, bought a van, and been seduced by an innkeeper's wife. He picked up Janie Dean in Alicante, where they briefly became lovers, before moving to Ibiza, where Dean met a musician addicted to heroin. Most recently, Fitschen had joined a jazz band, learned to play flamenco guitar, and moved in with Lois, an American woman with children and a novelist husband back in California.

Fitschen and the two Janies missed Royal in Tangiers, and left him a note to meet them in Madrid. Janie Taylor waited for Royal on the platform for five or six days in a row. When Royal finally stepped off the train, she was unaware that his affections were now divided. "It was good to see her," Royal wrote, "as fresh and effervescent as ever."

Fitschen sat behind his shades on a restaurant patio, waiting to tell Royal the bad news. "Lois's warm bed seemed more appealing than the cold granite ledges of the Aiguilles in Chamonix," Fitschen wrote. "Love was a good reason for doing almost anything, I thought. Besides, Royal had left me in the lurch the summer before when he decided not to come with me to Europe. He couldn't take it too hard when I decided not to go climbing."

But Royal did take it hard, and cursed his erstwhile climbing partner while the women looked on awkwardly. Without Fitschen's van, Royal and Taylor would have to hitchhike and take the train. Taylor was a good climber, but for the hardest routes Royal would have roped up with Fitschen. The only other climber in France Royal knew was the skilled but erratic Gary Hemming, who was living in Grenoble. In a postcard to Beulah from Paris, Royal reported on Impressionist paintings and Notre

Dame, and requested the last hundred dollars he had left with her. His travel expenses were mounting.

Before he left Paris for Chamonix—the true end point of his European peregrination—Royal wrote to Liz and asked her to respond to him at Poste Restante, or general delivery, in Chamonix. "I had no idea he would write to me," said Liz. "I didn't know if I would ever see him again, but he was good at writing love letters." Her response awaited him in the post office on Place Balmat before he and Janie even arrived in the damp Biolet campground on the edge of town. There, with alpine pilgrims from all over Europe, in a state of some romantic turmoil, Royal prepared to drink from the fountainhead of the pursuit that defined his life.

Royal knew all about the granite aiguilles of the Mont Blanc massif. He considered Italian Walter Bonatti's solo first ascent on the Petit Dru in 1955 to be one of the best climbs ever made. He owned a copy of Chamonix guide Gaston Rébuffat's *Starlight and Storm: The Conquest of the Great North Faces of the Alps*, in which Rébuffat effused about Chamonix's perfect rock pillars. The aiguilles played a central role in Royal's favorite climbing novel, *First on the Rope*. Top British rock climbers Joe Brown and Don Whillans had transitioned from cragging to alpinism in the aiguilles with legendary success. Most importantly, the long granite crack systems resembled Yosemite climbs.

Their first big route was the 1,500-foot Charmoz–Grepon traverse. Steve Miller, one of the few American climbers in Chamonix that summer, joined them. They sprinted up the rock climbing on the traverse itself, but the crevasses on the Nantillons Glacier approach terrified Royal. Taylor fell on an icy patch.

When it came to pure rock climbing, however, Royal measured up well against the best in the world. The *Fissure Brown* on the West Face of the Aiguille de Blaitière, first climbed by British cragsman Joe Brown in 1953, was the hardest free pitch in Chamonix. Royal made the second ascent. "There is one wooden wedge in place which cannot be avoided," he wrote in *Mugelnoos*, "but which was not in place when Joe Brown made the first ascent," and conceded that he would not want to lead the crack as Brown had, without it. After *Fissure Brown*, Royal started wearing a flat hat like Brown himself, a symbol of working-class British cragsmen.

Gary Hemming visited Royal in the Biolet. In Grenoble, a couple hours' drive from Chamonix, Hemming studied sporadically and shared a house with a young Frenchwoman. After a single season, he had convinced himself that "there is no comparison between mountain climbing or rock climbing in the States and true unadulterated alpine climbing. . . . It's ten times more dangerous, 20 times more exhausting." So far, however, Hemming's lack of big wall experience and quarrelsomeness had stood in the way of his dreams of alpine greatness, but with Royal, he saw a new chance. He proposed a first-ascent attempt on the west face of the Petit Dru, a vertical 3,000-foot wedge of stone across the Mer de Glace from the Montenvers railway station.

They decamped to the seaside limestone cliffs of the Calanques to climb with John Harlin II and wait out a predicted week of bad weather. Royal knew that Harlin was a married family man, a Stanford-educated reserve fighter pilot who had tried a couple of Europe's hardest climbs, but he had never met him. On first meeting, Royal felt that Harlin lived up to his credentials.

Harlin, Hemming, and Royal made the first ascent of the giant aid roof of *La Machine á Laver* (*Washing Machine*) at En Vau, and above it, *Machine á Sécher* (*Clothes Dryer*), later known as *Le Pilier des Américains*, two of the hardest pitches in the Calanques. Harlin, who wanted to make his mark in European climbing, took note of his new friend's rock skills.

After a brief, unsuccessful visit to the Dolomites, they were back in Chamonix, where the weather was improving but still unstable. Royal and Hemming were driven off the west face of the Dru by a violent afternoon lightning storm. They left a fixed rope and rappelled. On July 24, they tried again. Two and a half days of hard free and aid climbing gained the 90-Meter Dihedral; a combination of established routes brought them to the summit. The first American ascent of a new route in the Alps had been completed by two California bohemians. There were no flags.

"I waited alone in a little camp on the moraine above the Mer de Glace," said Taylor, "sitting high above the glacier, trying to see Royal and Gary as they climbed on the Dru and reading *Moby Dick* while swatting horseflies." After a few days there she left to get food and supplies to celebrate their climb back at the Biolet, but Taylor's happiness that Royal had completed his climb was overshadowed by her growing realization that she wasn't the only woman in his life.

"That month in Chamonix was a very special and wonderful time but marred by my gradual awareness that Royal had found another woman," said Taylor. "Royal would occasionally put a letter from Liz in his shirt pocket that I couldn't miss seeing." (For his part, Royal knew that she'd seen the envelopes and that "something was up.") Taylor said she felt "incredible pain and sadness," but also relished her final stint with Royal in the sublime French Alps.

Royal had successfully dodged confrontation on the wall with the volatile Hemming, but back at the campsite, Hemming exploded. Royal wanted to carry the camping garbage out, but Hemming was fixated on burying it. Royal let Hemming have his way. Hemming, wrote Royal in *The Vertical World of Yosemite*, had "turbulent emotions and wanted to control them. He wanted an answer, a way of dampening the suffering he was going through. . . . He thought—obviously we all do—that if he did a certain climb, things were going to be better." Royal admitted that he and Hemming shared a certain amount of personal anguish and insecurity, but unlike Hemming, he strove to contain it.

Domenico Rudatis, one of Europe's premier alpine commentators, wrote in the book *Sesto Grado* that the *West Face Direct* proved Yosemite climbs "are at a par with if not above, the most sensational achievements by Europeans," although like many European climbers, he referred to the route as the direct start to the *Magnone-Bernardini* route, not as its own entity, the *West Face Direct*. Royal, however, was understated. "The line on the Dru," which he acknowledged as Hemming's idea, "was just right for the time," if not, in his opinion, especially difficult.

While the Dru won Royal only a modicum of fame in Europe, it was a watershed for American alpinism. In August, Harlin and German climber Konrad Kirch succeeded, on Harlin's fifth attempt, on the north wall of the Eiger. The same month, Hemming and fellow Californian Henry Kendall climbed the *Walker Spur* on the north face of the Grandes Jorasses, the hardest great north face of the Alps. Europeans now recognized Yosemite as the seedbed of American alpinism. Hemming, who hadn't climbed much in Yosemite, began a French treatise on the "Yosemite School."

The 1963 issue of the *AAJ* heralded the arrival of American alpinism on the world stage. Royal's report on the Dru used French terms, such as *bloc coincé* and *voie normale*, and almost Victorian understatement; "lightning," he wrote, "counseled descent." Harlin's thirteen-page account of his ascent of the Eiger described the use of a RURP and a Knifeblade piton, items in the Yosemite kit likely still unfamiliar to most AAC members. Kendall wrote up the *Walker Spur* and sent in one of the first European-style topo maps of the route. All of these climbers had been trained in Yosemite.

· · · · ·

Royal and Taylor left Europe on separate planes due to a mix-up with their passports, and met up again in New York. As they drove back to California, they discussed the end of their relationship. "[Royal] was seven years older than I was and in a different place," said Taylor. "I was trying to please him, but it wasn't completely healthy. . . . Except for Liz, [Royal] was very honest with me and never said anything he didn't mean." She asked Royal to climb the 1,000-foot East Buttress of El Capitan with her before they broke up.

However, on the route, Taylor twisted her ankle; by the time they got to the top, she couldn't hike out. "Royal walked out to get some food for me and I stayed on top alone," she said. "Sometime after 1 a.m., Royal arrived with food, wine, and a group of friends." The crew partied on the summit almost until dawn, and then made their way back to the Valley floor, with Taylor using a stick.

"We continued to write to each other after he was with Liz," Taylor said. "In one letter he expressed some doubt about their relationship, which gave me some false hope, but in the end, it worked out very well for both of them. . . . I had already experienced so much of life and I thought, 'If I die right now, it would be enough.'"

"Janie is fabulous, a wonderful person," said Liz, "a better person than me."

That autumn, Royal and Frost made the second ascent of the overhanging East Face of Washington Column and chiselled the heads off twenty-five of Harding's twenty-seven bolts. Royal had tried to improve on Harding's performance in the past. This was the first time he tried to materially remake a Harding climb to match his own vision. Many of the bolts had anchored fixed ropes in place or protected cracks too wide for pitons during the first ascent in 1959 (wider bong pitons were available by 1962), so the incident generated little controversy, but Harding noticed. Like a chess player forcing a move on an opponent, Royal had nudged Harding into a defensive position.

In 1962, Washington climber Ed Cooper, Canadian Jim Baldwin, and Californian Glen Denny made the first ascent of the *Direct Southwest Face* of El Capitan. The *Dihedral Wall*, as the climb became known, was a popular topic of conversation in Camp 4 because Cooper had fixed ropes on his months-long siege and was rumored to have used bolts where piton cracks were available. "We took great offence to this," said Royal, "especially me."

Royal held that the new standard on El Capitan was the *Salathé Wall*, where five fixed ropes and thirteen bolts had sufficed. Herbert, Frost, Pratt, Roper, and others held the same opinion, often with even more conviction than Royal.

Royal confessed that he found Cooper "like Harding, but darker and more somber, without Harding's liveliness." At first, he only shared this opinion with a handful of friends, perhaps because, as Denny said, "Royal really wanted to do [the first ascent of] the *Dihedral Wall*." Inevitably, however, word of Royal's displeasure spread, and if anything, encouraged Cooper to bolt more—to get the climb done before someone else did. "Cooper had fixed ropes on it," said Denny. "He wasn't about to rappel off when he got to the blank section. Competition drove him into bolting."

When Cooper took a break from the climb to appear in a tobacco commercial in New York City, Royal's enmity grew. He hated smoking.

Royal called Cooper an outsider who "carefully avoided" doing an established big wall in Yosemite before he set out to "get himself a route on El Capitan." To some, the outsider insult left Royal open to criticism. That summer, Royal had added a route to the Dru before he'd climbed any other European big walls. The crucial difference, as Royal saw it, was that he and Hemming climbed within the boundaries of good style. They used neither fixed ropes nor bolts, and finished their new climb in a single push.

On the climb, Cooper annoyed Denny when he asked him to switch to a red jacket so that he would show up better in the photographs. Denny was even more disheartened when reporters met them on the summit. Newspapers from coast to coast praised the *Dihedral Wall* as "the most difficult rock climb to date in the U.S." For Royal, however, the way it had been done decreased its value, and much to his chagrin, the route also inspired others to contemplate even more protracted sieges. Al MacDonald, who had been with Harding on Leaning Tower, proposed to take years to complete a route on El Capitan he had already dubbed *Odyssey.* But after a bitter exchange of letters with Royal, MacDonald gave up on the idea before he even started.

According to Royal, anyone who hoped to do a new big wall should pay the same dues as him. They had to move to Yosemite, give up regular work, join the Camp 4 scene, complete an apprenticeship on a variety of Yosemite climbs, and earn a reputation before adding anything new.

The logic of Royal's own beliefs, however, left him vulnerable to criticism for having used fixed ropes on the *Salathé Wall.* Before he got a chance to live up to his own ideals on his greatest route, Chouinard and Roper attempted a continuous ascent. Royal predicted they would fail. "Yvon's too short," he said, "and Steve's too chickenshit." "Fuck you, Robbins!" Roper shouted after he climbed the crux on the lower wall, but a worn-out haulbag forced them to retreat from Heart Ledge.

"Tomorrow, we have decided to climb the *Salathé Wall,*" Royal declared at a campfire the night before his first attempt on a continuous ascent. The climbers applauded, but they could hardly have been surprised. Royal had begun to attract what he called "camp followers," young men with varied abilities who looked to him for advice and sometimes climbed with him. A few became highly skilled climbers in their own right. In Camp 4, a world mostly without adults, a twenty-five-year-old with a great climbing record could become a paternal figure.

Royal took jokes about himself gracefully, but he was deeply wounded by the attacks on his camp followers. "[I] have cringed when I have seen

[Harding] crush the spirit of someone he has chosen to attack," Royal wrote to Roper in 2000, "most often a camp follower on our side who can't defend himself."

On the biggest climbs, however, Royal relied on his most tested partnerships. Frost and TM Herbert joined him on the *Salathé Wall* that September 1962. They were turned back at Heart Ledge by rain and a stomach ailment that afflicted Herbert and Royal. Royal and Frost returned in mid-October, failed, and then succeeded later in the month. The four-and-a-half-day climb was the first two-person ascent of El Capitan.

On the other side of the country, Carlton Fuller, the new president of the AAC, took note. Most of the club's members lived in the east, but to broaden the membership, Fuller sponsored projects designed to unify the national scene and raise the profile of climbing, like the successful American Everest expedition of 1963. Hubert (H.) Adams Carter, the editor of the *AAJ*, and Fuller invited the Yosemite climbers to contribute. When the Californians ignored him, Fuller flew west to meet them in person and convinced them to write.

In "The Salathé Wall," in the 1963 *AAJ*, Royal acknowledged Harding's ascent as the beginning of the El Capitan climbing era, but he also criticized Harding's use of thousands of feet of fixed rope, 125 bolts, and numerous attempts. "We wished to avoid such methods if possible so as to keep the element of adventure high," wrote Royal, who also noted that on the descent, he and Frost felt "very spiritually rich indeed."

In his own article in that same *AAJ*, Cooper declines to name Royal and calls the *Regular Northwest Face* of Half Dome "barely even a VI." The first ascent of the *Nose*, Cooper says, "remains perhaps the greatest achievement of its type in the history of climbing." The continuous ascent of the *Nose* goes unmentioned. The *Salathé*, Cooper says, was merely "repeated this year." Cooper complained that "someone had intended to complete [the *Dihedral Wall*], perhaps the spirit of competition which exists in the Valley brings out weaknesses in some."

The best and longest of the pieces about Yosemite in the 1963 *AAJ* was by Chouinard, who was now in the army and had time to write. "Modern Yosemite Climbing" touched on Yosemite achievements, techniques, and definitions of free climbing, and the differences between Yosemite and

French climbing. He made the case for the emergence of a new American school of climbing that was in a position to take over the climbing world. But Chouinard had complaints as well: "An outsider is not welcomed and accepted until he proves that he is equal to the better climbs and climbers," he wrote. "He is constantly on trial to prove himself." Competition, said Chouinard, "was initially spread by a few."

Fixed ropes, Chouinard wrote, were "popular in other parts of North America, especially in the Northwest," where Cooper came from, and "manifest American love for security, and show that the climber should not be there in the first place." According to this logic, the patriotic, employed squares who dug America were the real chickens, not Camp 4's collection of beatniks and dropouts, led unofficially by Royal.

Climbers came to Yosemite not in spite of but because of its reputation for fearsome walls, elitism, competition, and partying. In the preface to the first guidebook to Yosemite, Steve Roper lamented that there was an influx of new climbers who climbed "only when they 'feel' like it, which if they're feeling good is once a week." "One cannot help wonder," he lamented, "what reasons compel these people to remain in Camp 4."

But the reasons were clear enough. Camp 4 hopefuls were eager to improve their climbing skills and gain some of the swaggering self-confidence and sense of belonging they associated with the place. Before there was the Haight-Ashbury in San Francisco, a kind of climber's Camelot came into being in Camp 4. Royal had become its leader the day he walked into Camp 4 at age seventeen and asked Allen Steck if there was anything worthwhile to climb there. And, for the time being, no one had the ability nor the climbing record to steal the crown from Royal.

By the mid-1960s, the Tahquitz Decimal System, now known as the Yosemite Decimal System (YDS), was America's grading system, infusing even the most modest climbs with a hint of Yosemite's mystique. Teton climber Leigh Ortenburger, however, objected and wrote letters asking climbers to adopt his National Climbing Classification System (NCSS) instead. Royal vacillated and wrote a letter to *Summit*, enjoining the use of the NCSS with more generosity than conviction. In 1964, however, Art Gran's new Shawangunks guidebook and Roper's new Yosemite guidebook both used the YDS, effectively blocking the NCSS from being applied to two of America's most popular areas.

When the preponderance of American climbers talked about difficulty, their common language came not from the Tetons but from Yosemite, the new capital of American climbing.

6
We've Got Nothing Else But Climbing

IN THE WINTER OF 1962 AND 1963, Royal resumed his position as assistant ski instructor and staff bartender at Sugar Bowl. Liz worked at the front desk and stayed in the basement of manager Ed Siegal's house. Royal's official residence was, once again, the staff barroom. He had begun the process of ski instructor certification and would study the manual at the bar until the lights went out at the manager's house and then sneak over to spend the night with Liz.

Budding photographer Paul Ryan worked at Sugar Bowl that year, and he knew about Royal's status as a climber. "It seemed like the demands of his position distanced him from casual conversation," Ryan wrote. "Everything had a formality about it. An intellectual loftiness. 'Don't you think it's redundant to speak of the High Sierras? Sierra is already plural and does not need an *S*.'"

Ryan was smitten by Liz, who rewarded his attention with her own. Royal reacted mysteriously by inviting Ryan to Yosemite to climb. In April, Liz and Royal picked up their camping and climbing gear at Krehe Ritter's and headed for Yosemite. On the way, they detoured to Modesto, where Liz debuted Royal with her parents.

Royal liked the Burkners, but they were tentative. "Royal didn't spend a lot of time around Mom and Dad at first," said Liz, "but he respected my dad so much. My dad was very optimistic and believed Royal was going to be the right person for me. My mother was more nervous about him. She didn't know anything about him except that he was a climber."

Camp 4 climbers tended to be inexperienced in relationships. There were temporary romantic pairings, but the few married climbers rarely brought their spouses to Yosemite. By contrast, Ryan wrote that "Liz and Royal were there and, like First Lady and President, much deference was given." Ryan had followed Liz and Royal from Sugar Bowl, on Royal's invitation. The thought of another climber crawling up a rock wall before Royal got a chance triggered emotions about "owning" rock formations, but in relationships, he displayed an unusual lack of jealousy.

Royal invited Ryan to climb *Via Aqua*, high on the wall left of Yosemite Falls. It was an easy route, Ryan's first. Ryan worried that Royal might be testing him, or had chosen a frightening climb to take revenge for his relationship with Liz, but the climb went without incident.

Royal told Liz that Ryan had done pretty well "for a beginner." There's a photograph of Royal defeating Ryan at chess in Camp 4. Royal looks relaxed. He has taken a bishop, a knight, and two pawns, and holds Ryan in check with a bishop and his queen. Tejada-Flores lounges in the background, toying with a shoot of grass. "The next day," Ryan wrote, "I drove out of the Valley in my 1955 Chevy. Back to San Francisco. I had achieved something and concluded something. But in the end, I was leaving Yosemite alone."

At Liz's suggestion, after ten years of visiting Yosemite, she took Royal out for breakfast in the dining room of the Ahwahnee Hotel for the first time. Liz then used the Blue Chip Stamps Beulah collected to buy a gas lantern, stove, cooler, and water container—basic camping items Royal had never owned in a decade of spartan living at Camp 4.

Royal asked Liz, and only Liz, for advice on soloing the West Face of Leaning Tower. Their partnership gave him a new, intimate creative environment, unaffected by advice, onlookers, expectations, and gossip. It would be a second-ascent, single-push solo of a Harding siege route, as

well as the first solo of a Yosemite grade VI. It was also the most overhanging route in Yosemite. Retreat would be difficult. Liz, however, gave Royal
the answer he wanted when she agreed it was a grand idea. Two days later,
when he set out behind a cover of clouds and rain, only she knew.

The climb was strenuous and exacting. Royal's prusik self-belay system
was hard to use and not as reliable as an actual belayer. Royal had to lead
each pitch, rappel back to the belay, and prusik back up, carrying the pack
of water and food while he hammered out the pitons.

He maintained an internal dialogue with Harding as he climbed.

"I complained about your fixed ropes," wrote Royal. "And you just put
up more of them. It reached a point where I began to imagine you a pranc-
ing figure in a black cape with horns and a pointed tail. . . . I don't like your
methods, but I love your attitude. You don't care what anyone thinks. And
you don't give up. . . . I admit my stunt on the Tower is meant to be a blow
for our side. . . . It's another move on the Yosemite chessboard."

Royal took breaks from his imaginary dispute to daydream about Liz.
He pictured her as "radiantly alive," making "everything around her dance
to the rhythm of her buoyant spirit." At night, ever picturing Liz, he rested
his head on a pillow of slings and carabiners, dropping immediately into
an exhausted sleep.

Out of sight behind the storm, Royal climbed the dry, overhanging
wall. After a couple of days, Liz worried about how he was faring and asked
Jack Turner and Layton Kor to check on him. "That fucking Robbins," said
Kor, at least according to legend, "no matter what you do, he's always one
step ahead." Royal theorized that solo climbs were mirrors that privately
revealed a climber's strengths and weaknesses. They were also, however,
public displays of skill and determination. Most Yosemite climbers hailed
his Leaning Tower climb as the best ascent of 1963.

The solo also emphasized the increasing gap in skill and vision between
Royal and other climbers. When Royal practiced a boulder problem by
lantern-light, some climbers admired his solitary drive; others gossiped
that Royal couldn't allow himself to be bested, even on the smallest rocks.
Any exceptions between the ideas Royal espoused and the way he climbed
were subjected to scrutiny. A month later, on the third ascent of the *Nose*,

Roper shunned the bolt Royal had placed next to Boot Flake and encouraged Kor to remove it while seconding. At the bivouac, Roper brandished the bolt, a rare piece of proof that even Royal sometimes gave in to fear.

After the *Dihedral Wall*, Cooper, accompanied by twenty-three-year-old Galen Rowell, set to work on a route a few hundred feet right of the *Regular Northwest Face* of Half Dome. They retreated after a few pitches and left fixed ropes.

Royal had decided that despite having himself used a fixed rope on Sentinel Rock to claim a route the year before, fixed lines no longer reserved the route for their owners. He decided to try Cooper's route, despite the ropes. He went with Dick McCracken, a quiet but experienced Berkeley climber who had impressed Royal on the first ascent of *Far West* on Rixon's Pinnacle.

The three-and-a-half-day ascent of the *Direct Northwest Face* was made miserable by rain and high winds, but McCracken was unfazed. After the *Direct Northwest Face*, he became Royal's most trusted new big wall partner outside his inner circle of Pratt, Frost, Herbert, and Chouinard.

Circumstances soon gave Royal a chance at a second Cooper project. "One evening in late May, 1963, as several of us climbers sat in the lounge of Yosemite Lodge," wrote Royal, "a Curry Company employee walked up with some startling news. He told us of a radio report describing an attempt which was to take place next day on the right side of the Upper Fall. This attempt, the report said, would probably take five days and involve several nights spent in slings. The participants were to be Ed Cooper, from Washington, Glen Denny, of California, and Jim Baldwin, a Canadian." However, the latter two climbers, upon learning of the mystery leak to the media, promptly dropped out.

McCracken joined Royal on the first ascent of the *Misty Wall*, a 2,000-foot grade VI. Although they had done the climb partly because they'd been tipped off via the rumor mill, Royal waxed poetical in his report in the *AAJ*. *Misty Wall*, he wrote, "awakened in our minds and spirits a lust for life and a keener awareness of beauty."

After *Misty Wall*, Cooper gave up on Yosemite walls and became one of the twentieth century's leading mountain photographers.

· · · · ·

In the winter of 1963, the council of the AAC asked East Coast climber Jim McCarthy to "pick an objective that you feel will contribute something to the development of American climbing, gather the strongest group of technical climbers available to do the job and the AAC will back the venture." The club earmarked six thousand dollars to pay for the expedition, and McCarthy proposed an attempt on the 2,000-foot southeast face of Mount Proboscis in the Cirque of the Unclimbables, a remote area recently discovered by climbers in the Logan Mountains, in Canada's Northwest Territories.

McCarthy, who would become a close friend and associate of Royal's, was a thirty-year-old New York City lawyer. He dated ballerinas, lived in a Manhattan apartment, and was the best climber in the Shawangunks. The Gunks, however, were seen by Californians as an inferior sibling to Yosemite, partly because of how poorly climbers from the Shawangunks performed in Yosemite.

But McCarthy had a style and sangfroid that appealed to Yosemite climbers right away. On Chouinard's first day in the Gunks, McCarthy had shown off by leading *Never Never Land*, one of the hardest routes at Near Trapps cliff. When the belay ledge at the top of the pitch crumbled, McCarthy plummeted eighty feet. Hanging upside-down, a few feet from the ground, he looked Chouinard in the eye and said, "Welcome to the Gunks."

McCarthy wrote that he knew Royal, his first choice of teammates, "by reputation. For those less well informed on the latest goings-on in technical climbing I shall simply say that Royal is now and has been for some years one of the finest American technical climbers." Royal accepted and invited Fitschen, on condition that he train in Yosemite first. But Fitschen was in New York and could only manage a few trips to the Gunks, so McCracken came instead.

McCarthy also invited Layton Kor, whom he called "one of the most astonishing climbers anywhere," noting his tremendous reach (Kor stood 6'3") and energy, his incredible speed and technical proficiency, and his voracious appetite for difficult climbs. Kor accepted immediately.

The team agreed to meet in late June. After a few training climbs in the Tetons, they would drive to the Northwest Territories together. Royal and Liz planned to spend the first three weeks of June climbing in Colorado. Liz, however, almost missed out on the trip when she fell off a boulder problem at Indian Rock near Berkeley and broke her wrist.

Nonetheless, she joined Royal hitchhiking on the shoulder of Highway 99, sticking her thumb out of her plaster cast as best she could. Just east of Sacramento, they squeezed into a two-door 1950 Dodge with a man determined to drive to Chicago without sleeping. Liz called him "insane and terrifying." They got out and hitched another ride. A few days later, they met Kor in Rocky Mountain National Park.

In 1960, Californians Dave Rearick and Bob Kamps had climbed the vertical wall of the Diamond on Longs Peak. Although only 1,000 feet high, it ended at 14,000 feet, making it the highest big wall climb in North America. On June 11, 1963, Kor and Robbins climbed it in a day. After a rest day, they made the first ascent of *Jack of Diamonds*, a steeper and harder route on the same wall.

On the descent, Royal lagged behind, fretting about the impression he had made on Kor. "I suppose Layton might not have found me that simpatico a partner," he wrote in the unpublished story "Strolls with Kor," "a bit too serious perhaps. One of the things I loved about climbing was I could be myself, and if I climbed well enough I had to be accepted for what I was. Still, it must have been tough, at times, to be my partner. It's hard to get on with a chunk of ice. Inside I churned with heat waves of passion and desire, but I didn't let it show. You had to be in control."

Kor returned to Boulder, while Royal brought Kor's sixteen-year-old friend Pat Ament on the first ascent of the *Gangplank* on the nearby Ship's Prow. Older climbers sometimes found Royal socially awkward or aloof. Ament, however, was starstruck. In his biography of Royal, *Spirit of the Age,* Ament wrote that he felt like Royal looked "almost darkly into your soul as though truth, adventure, and perfection were for him an inward necessity and, to get along with him, the same were going to be required of you." Ament continued, "As I stood there in the door of that dark shelter-cabin, I could feel his aloneness—that mood. It settled over Longs Peak."

Ament also shared Royal's interest in chess and books, and ended up closer to Royal than most of his young friends. "I was immediately drawn to [Ament]," wrote Royal in an unpublished story titled "The Diamond." "He had quick, intelligent eyes, excelled at gymnastics, and loved climbing. . . . And he impressed me as an excellent climbing partner—cautious, reliable, talented."

Royal had viewed Mendenhall and Kamps as helpful, avuncular figures, if not quite heroes. Royal's Yosemite "camp followers," and now Ament, saw him as a star. Royal paid back their affection with a sincere concern for their well-being and interest in their lives.

· · · · ·

Back in Modesto after her and Royal's jaunt to Colorado, Liz came down with mononucleosis and checked into the hospital for a few days. "It had been the trip from hell," Liz said, "but it was just me doing what I wanted to do. I was reacting to my overprotected upbringing. I didn't let on about how sick I was to Royal when he came back. I was ready to do it again." Meanwhile, after a few warm-up climbs in the Tetons, McCarthy rolled his overloaded Volkswagen Beetle out of Jenny Lake Campground, bound for the Yukon, with Royal, Kor, and McCracken on board.

A floatplane and a day of carrying fifty-pound packs through groves of fallen trees, over boulders, and up shifting talus slopes brought the climbers to the Cirque of the Unclimbables. Three days of rain and snow gave them time for conversation. Kor and Royal argued about the comparative merits of classical versus rock music. "I shut it down and they went back to their tents," said McCarthy. "That night, Layton told me, 'Don't worry about me and Royal. We're both the same; all we have is climbing.'"

After a false start up Proboscis in a short-lived spell of good weather, they set out a second time. They spent the first night in a sleepless bivouac in slings. At the end of the second day, they discovered that ledges they had seen in photos were too small for a bivouac and spent another bad night hanging from pitons.

Kor, famously unafraid of leader falls, ripped out an aid piton and fell forty feet. McCarthy caught the fall but injured his hand in a carabiner. Higher up, one of McCarthy's jumar ascenders popped off a diagonal rope, a mishap that could have had serious consequences. Royal and McCracken took over the lead, but Royal was so exhausted that he fell asleep while he belayed. Progress was slow, with most of the pitons in thin cracks and tied off with slings, but the team had cracked big granite walls by slow increments before. Late on the third day, they made the summit.

McCarthy summarized the climb in the *AAJ*. "We feel that this is one of the most difficult technical rock climbs ever done under remote alpine conditions, as well as one of the most elegantly direct routes that one can hope to climb." Despite their success, the team never revisited the Cirque of the Unclimbables together.

Proboscis gained Royal the attention of mountaineers, but instead of moving on to another alpine objective, he returned to Yosemite. In September 1963, Royal nurtured a new obsession: the smooth, overhanging 2,000-foot southeast face of El Capitan, which was emblazoned with an intrusion of black diorite shaped like North America.

What would become the *North America Wall* appeared impossible to most climbers, but Royal had traced a series of faint weaknesses up its lower flanks. The upper half, despite some huge, mysterious overhangs, had more cracks. In the *AAJ*, he described the wall as "treacherous," "ogrish," and "lacking in elegance and majesty." "We didn't expect to get up this wall in particular," he wrote. "We didn't know where the route went or even if there was a route."

In the fall of 1963, Royal had confessed to Glen Denny that his motivation for big wall climbing was fading. The *North America Wall* would demand a tour de force of climbing skills and stand as a masterpiece of his principles of bold, ground-up climbing, hopefully with a minimum of bolts. The *Salathé Wall* had been graced with cracks where none were expected and comfortable bivouac ledges. The *North America Wall*, if Royal could do it, would be a work of his own imagination, with few natural weaknesses or ledges.

Royal "wanted to create climbs no one else could do," said Denny, "or, if they could, they'd have to do them with more protection than he had used, more aid, more bolts."

In September of 1963, a month before his first reconnaissance on the *North America Wall*, Royal and Chouinard costarred in *Sentinel: The West*

Face, produced and directed by ski filmmaker Roger Brown. Tom Frost, who had made the first ascent with Chouinard, prusiked beside the climbers with a handheld camera while Brown tracked them from the ground using a telephoto lens on a movie camera. On film, Royal climbs without superfluous movement, flourishes, or hesitation. He has momentum, but he lamented that the film made him look "stony and cold," while Chouinard seemed "warm and human." The glimpse of himself as the great climber had left him wanting.

The film begins with Chouinard climbing a graffiti-covered boulder at Stoney Point. He falls, and, in scriptwriter Barry Corbet's words, "A man climbs on the graffiti of his society. He falls, not from a mountain, but into a city." The lonely bivouac on Sentinel is contrasted with shots of busy city streets. "Relate to me please," says the narrator, but at no other stage in Royal's life did the thoughts of the average urban commuter matter less to him than when he was preparing for the *North America Wall.*

In October, Royal, with Denny, finally made his first reconnaissance. As Royal led the difficult third pitch, "his emotions were fighting against the grip of his logical mind," Denny said. He told Denny to watch him, to let some rope run out if he fell to soften the impact. A wild fall that ripped out several of Royal's tied-off aid pins ended just above the belay.

"Nice catch," Royal said.

"I had to drop the camera and grab the rope with my hands," said Denny, "which got terribly burned."

Royal was now reporting to *Summit, Off Belay,* and the *AAJ,* and was conscious of how his activities would be captured on film. Denny assured him he had taken some good photographs of his lead.

"That's real A5 up there," said Royal, referring to the highest aid-climbing grade. He unclipped the pulled pitons hanging from his belay rope. "What a challenge," he said. "I'm not going to put in a bolt until I get to that blank section."

"His blood was up," said Denny. "He *had* to conquer that pitch."

After five pitches, they rappelled. In addition to climbing some of the most difficult-looking rock on the wall, they had successfully experimented with a bag-hauling technique that used jumar ascenders. The new method would reduce the strain of hauling on the leader and free the second climber to concentrate on cleaning pitons. The Yosemite hauling method, invented by Royal, drastically reduced the labor of one of the most hated big wall tasks.

. . . . .

That winter, Royal was scheduled to return to Sugar Bowl to work. The manager, a religious man, told Royal he could only bring Liz back to Sugar Bowl if he married her first. Royal and Liz thought it was a fine notion, and on November 17, 1963, they were married.

Royal's first wedding had been at the justice of the peace in Las Vegas; this time, it was at the Swedenborgian Church in San Francisco's Pacific Heights. The Arts and Crafts building had been completed in 1895. The first minister had been Joseph Worcester—a camping partner of John Muir, the second president of the AAC and legendary savior of Yosemite. Liz and Royal exchanged their vows below roof timbers fashioned from Pacific madrone trunks that evoked the forests where they had first met. The tiny wedding party included Liz's friends and family, Beulah, and Royal's sister, Penny. The climbers were represented by Mort Hempel, whose continuing devotion to Liz must have made the event excruciating for him, and Janie Dean.

Royal didn't buy a ring, but Liz's mother supplied one. "I wore it all the time," said Liz. "There were a few sizes of cracks where the ring came in handy for finger jams." Janie Dean loaned them her houseboat in Sausalito for their honeymoon.

They were still on their honeymoon on November 22, when President John F. Kennedy was assassinated. The previous August, Kennedy had made a highly publicized visit to Yosemite, an event mostly ignored by climbers. Royal seldom mentioned politics or world affairs, but like most Americans, he and Liz were deeply upset by the assassination. The 1960s of history had begun.

Five days after the wedding, Roper was sent for basic training in Georgia. Royal mailed him a copy of H. L. Mencken's "The Sahara of the Bozart," a critique of Southern culture. Roper joined the Civil Rights Movement and marched with Martin Luther King Jr., and Ralph Bunche.

Royal's generation of soldiers had spent their service outside combat zones. Roper was deployed to Vietnam, the conflict that would become a symbol of how America had lost its way.

Folk music became the voice of American dissent. Royal had been introduced to the genre by campfire troubadours like Bill Briggs (whom Royal considered the best campfire musician of the era) in the Tetons and Mort Hempel in Yosemite. He had listened to it in coffeehouses in San Francisco. Bob Dylan, the muse of the civil rights and anti-war movements, became the first popular musician Royal listened to with interest and quoted in his writing.

Life for the Robbinses, as for most Americans, went on with little external change. The newlyweds moved into a duplex on a working-class street in western Modesto. Although Royal had lived in tougher neighborhoods, Liz had not.

In the fall of 1963, Royal took a job at Valley Paint, the Burkner family business. Earl taught him to mix and sell paint. "Royal loved my father," said Liz, and Earl, whose only child was Liz, loved Royal. If Earl hoped that Royal was ready to settle down to learn the family business full-time, however, he was soon disappointed.

Royal had seen what middle-class life could provide. Other climbers had intellectually rewarding careers. Frost was an engineer. Most of the men he had known at the RCS were white-collar professionals. Royal, who lacked the education to catch up with them, began to wonder how his skills could improve his way of life.

In 1962, Royal had climbed *Royal Arches* with French alpinist Lionel Terray, who explained how he made an income from giving presentations. San Francisco travel agent Leo Le Bon, who had brought Terray to California, had come along with them and told Royal about an increasing demand for adventure- and experience-based vacations. Unlike Royal, however, Terray had actively publicized his climbs.

Royal overcame his misgivings about self-promotion and put together some slide presentations. He reevaluated his ambivalence about fame and publicity. "I started thinking in terms of doing climbs mainly for fame," said Royal, "rather than of doing them just for the fun of it."

After another winter at Sugar Bowl, where the newlyweds were entitled to their own chalet, they returned to Yosemite. Royal went from one big wall to the next, cramming as much climbing as he could into the spring season before his summer road trip and his first paid presentations. A fall attempt on the *North America Wall* loomed.

He began with the second ascent of the *Dihedral Wall*, with Frost and without fixed ropes. At the post-climb summit celebration, Royal overcame his aversion to smoking to try "grass." "When I first started having the occasional joint behind a boulder in Camp 4, Royal was slightly disapproving," said Fitschen, "but later he came around. I remember going up to meet him on top of El Cap after he and Tom finished the *Dihedral Wall*. Tom went down but Royal and Liz and Linnea (my wife) and I stayed on top for the night and laughed and giggled a lot."

In his journals throughout the 1960s, Royal referred to "grass trips," which could be either "good" or "good but strange." Smoking remained a nighttime recreation, associated with conversation, meals, and sex. He scorned people who smoked weed during the day.

Camp 4 artist Sheridan Anderson often sketched Royal as a muscular homunculus with his signature hat, glasses, and beard, even though at 5'11", he was taller than most of his counterparts. Anderson also drew Royal on the cover of *The Royal and Liz Coloring Book*, dressed as Superman and smoking a long joint. Marvel comic books graded their publications with letters to warn readers of any potentially morally questionable content. Anderson invented the "M" grade for Royal's coloring book, presumably for marijuana.

Royal was curious, if not game, when it came to hallucinogens. "Drugs? You ask if I've taken any?" replied Roper to a letter from Royal. "Nothing powerful—I shall wait until your return." But Roper was only joking. LSD, said Fitschen, was "too far out" for Royal.

After the post–*Dihedral Wall* weed wore off, Royal offered a decidedly un-giddy assessment of Cooper's route. He complained that Cooper had removed the hangers and nuts from more than thirty-five bolts, making it difficult to repeat. He and Frost removed eighteen bolts from the wall. Royal suggested that Cooper had deliberately underestimated the number of bolts on the route in his *AAJ* report. Later, he said that the climb had no aesthetic qualities, besides its difficulty.

A few days after the *Dihedral Wall*, Royal and Pratt climbed Kor and Roper's West Buttress of El Capitan in three and a half days. The route had no long bolt ladders and had been climbed in a style Royal approved of. Then, on June 19, during a nighttime retreat from the East Face of Washington Column, Canadian climber Jim Baldwin, a friend of Cooper's, slipped off the end of a rappel rope and fell to his death. Baldwin was the first person close to Royal's circle to die climbing. Royal speculated that Baldwin had been rendered incautious by an unsuccessful love affair.

In late June, Frost joined Royal and Denny on a second reconnaissance of the *North America Wall*. They climbed 1,200 feet to a long ledge they named Big Sur. The remaining 800 feet looked loose and strenuous. They made plans to return after Labor Day. In the interim, Royal and Liz packed their gear into their wedding present from the Burkners, a beloved green Mercedes Earl had bought in Germany, and headed out on their first extensive American climbing road trip. This also marked Royal's first engagements as a professional presenter and his first shot at making his name known outside Yosemite and the Tetons.

On the granite spires and sweeping buttresses of Wyoming's Wind River Range, Royal, McCracken, and Charlie Raymond made the first full traverse of the Cirque of the Towers and the first ascent of the South Buttress of the Watchtower. On the Watchtower, a stone dislodged by the haulbag barely missed Royal but jammed the rope in a crack. On the seventh pitch, they were caught in an afternoon storm.

"Although this is perhaps the most difficult route in the Cirque of the Towers," wrote Royal in the *AAJ*, "with perhaps the finest 'line,' the actual climbing did not meet the expectations engendered by the beauty of the buttress. The rock is often poor and the belay spots not well situated."

The vertical 1,800-foot North Face of Mount Hooker was next. For three cold days, Royal, Raymond, and McCracken switched leads and hauled bags. The wind was so strong that Royal struggled to maintain his balance in his etriers as he nested pitons and used hooks on small nubbins. The wall ran with cold water. They spent a night in hammocks Liz had made on her Singer sewing machine. It was a fine adventure, but Royal was unimpressed by the copious loose rock on the climb.

At a picnic table in Custer State Park in the Black Hills of South Dakota, the next stop on the road trip, Royal penned a letter to Roper, fretting about the *North America Wall*. "I know that Galen Rowell, stung by [Royal and McCracken's] Half Dome coup [of climbing past Rowell and Cooper's fixed ropes], is seriously trying to cut us out on [the *North America Wall*]." He also repeated a rumor that Ed Cooper was going to attempt to solo it. Roper, who was now in Vietnam, had other things to worry about; moreover, both he and Royal knew that the park service only allowed El Capitan climbs after Labor Day.

The Needles of the Black Hills were, in some ways, the opposite of Yosemite. Face climbing predominated. Piton cracks were rare. The climbs were rarely more than 150 feet long, but they demanded superb technique and nerve.

The area's reputation as a seedbed of futuristic free climbing and bouldering was greatly enhanced by John Gill, a mathematics professor based in Colorado. Gill had searched the outcrops and boulders of North America for hard boulder problems, applying his prodigious skill, strength, and self-directed passion. His ascents were rarely discussed in *Summit* or the *AAJ*, but he achieved an attractive sort of fame untarnished by controversy or competition. Royal's main reason for visiting the Needles was to try Gill's unrepeated 1961 climb on a thirty-foot-high, mitten-shaped pillar known as the Thimble, rumored to be the hardest boulder problem in America.

Climbing with locals Dick Laptad and Sue Prince in the Tenpins area at the Needles, Royal and Liz made the first ascent of the Tricouni Nail pillar. Royal renamed the pillar Cerberus, following the tradition that entitled the first ascensionist to rename a climb, but the old name stuck. All three followed Royal up the bald and dangerous Queenpin, another 5.9. The leaning pillar of Sandberg Peak and the steep-sided cone of the Tent Peg rounded out Royal's first ascents in the Needles.

Royal failed on Gill's route on the Thimble, his real reason for visiting the Needles, and left a short message in the summit register: "Hats off to John Gill." "I consider my greatest failure to be my effort on the

Thimble," Royal wrote. "I could see that even if I worked on it forever, it was very unlikely that I'd ever climb it. I really came face to face with my own limitations."

·　·　·　·　·

At Wyoming's Devils Tower, a 500-foot plug of phonolite porphyry, Royal made the first ascent of *The Window* with Colorado climber Pete Davidson, establishing an aid route that passed through the tower's biggest over-hangs. He also made the first ascent of *Danse Macabre*, at 5.10 the tower's hardest climb.

There, Colorado teenager Michael Covington had his first encounter with Royal. "I mentioned we were on our way to the Needles in South Dakota," said Covington, "and he said he was just there. He recommended the *Needle's Eye*. . . . I recall thinking that this guy is really good. I never would have attempted that run out without knowing that it had been done before."

Royal moved on to Colorado, where he teamed up with Ament, whose skill, drive, and admiration for Royal had all increased exponentially. Some referred to Ament as Royal's teenage sidekick, but the age difference wasn't quite so apparent at the time. "Pat was so young and in a way, we were too," said Liz. "He was an eager kid who wanted to excel in things. He worshipped Royal, took to Royal. Royal was always so open to people; if someone wanted to be his friend, he let them."

Together, they made the first free ascent of the *Yellow Spur* in Eldorado Canyon at 5.9+. In Boulder Canyon, they climbed *Final Exam*, a 5.10 crack. They also climbed *Athlete's Feat*, a five-pitch 5.10 (today rated 5.11a) with a difficult mantelshelf that favored Royal's well-honed granite-bouldering skills. A toprope ascent of the hard, thin face on the first pitch of *Country Club Crack*, now graded 5.11, and an ascent of the second pitch's overhang-ing crack with only a couple of points of aid (this pitch is also rated 5.11 today) marked the next step in free climbing.

After a visit to Estes Park, where Royal made the first free ascent of *Turnkorner* at 5.10, Royal, Liz, and Ament headed southwest to climb the desert spires of Castleton Tower in Utah and Shiprock in New Mexico.

A two-day event in Salt Lake City for the Alpenbock Climbing Club began Royal's career as an awkward, if committed, lecturer. "I would typically hide at the back of the room," he wrote in the unpublished essay "Life on the Lecture Circuit," "lurking out of sight behind the slide projector, while I lectured the group about the pictures they were viewing. I didn't fancy myself a public speaker. I was too shy, too solitary, too sullen, and I took myself with way too much deadly seriousness." He was more relaxed in the outdoor sessions at Big Cottonwood Canyon, where he demonstrated Yosemite climbing techniques.

Before he left Utah, Royal and Salt Lake City local Ted Wilson made the first ascents of a direct route on the south face of the Thumb and the *Robbins Crack*, an unprotectable 5.10 offwidth on the summit block. It was the last new route on his road trip that summer. Climbers in less famous areas enjoyed the whiff of celebrity Robbins's routes added to their cliffs so much that by the end of the decade there were rumors he had accomplished first ascents in some areas he hadn't even visited.

In Yosemite a few days later, Royal and Herbert climbed with Spaniard Josip-Manuel Anglada. Anglada had climbed the Eiger Nordwand, dressed well—even when he climbed—joked about bad American food, and charmed Royal, who was not easily charmed by Europeans. They became lifelong correspondents and friends. In August, Glen Denny contracted dysentery on the first ascent of Jirishanca Norte in Peru and told Royal he wouldn't be able to join the *North America Wall* climb that fall. Royal decided not to postpone until the spring.

"By this time," said Royal, "things had gone so far that I was getting greedy. I was anxious to get [the *North America Wall*] before anyone else did. . . . I dislike certain elements in my personality."

Pratt and Frost were already committed to the team. The loss of Denny meant that the plan to have two parties share the work on the wall was in jeopardy. Royal invited Chouinard, and told Ament he could come if Chouinard didn't make it. As Chouinard, fresh out of the army in 1964, wrote, it was to be his first big wall—"I mean it was a miracle that I was asked to come along really, but Royal, Royal was the captain on that one," he noted. Royal, however, secretly dreaded repeating even the parts of the climb he had already done and was likely relieved when Chouinard led the third-pitch crux.

In the Black Dihedral above Big Sur Ledge, the leader had to clear loose rock and clumps of grass as he climbed. On October 17, their seventh day on the wall, they bivouacked under the Black Overhang. "It looks like a tenement house on a work day," said Chouinard, "hammocks every which way, blue parkas, hauling ropes splayed out, shoes all hanging in a haphaz-ard fashion from anchors." A helicopter filmed them at the bivouac, and Chouinard's parents saw him climbing on television for the first time. The next day, a storm moved in; the rain trapped them beneath their overhang and soon soaked them to the skin.

Mort Hempel sung folk songs over their radio at night, reminding them of the pleasures of Camp 4. Royal hadn't been away from Liz this long since the Cirque of the Unclimbables. On Leaning Tower, thoughts of Liz inspired him. On the *North America Wall*, he wrote, "I didn't give her much thought at the time, on a climb we don't think about girls much." Robbins wrote in the *AAJ* that "jocose badinage" at the bivouac sometimes took a darker turn. "You remember your nightmares," said Pratt to Chouinard, "and I'll remember mine, and each morning we'll trade. OK?"

When they set out again, wet, overhanging rock led to the Igloo cave. A half foot of snow awaited them on the summit the next day. There were no reporters and no champagne toasts. In the summit photo, the climbers look drawn and dirty, their smiles wan. They had just watched a passing driver steal the haulbag full of gear they threw off the rim.

During the climb, a reporter for the *Modesto Bee* called Glen Denny. "I was surprised when they told me that Royal had called them ahead of time," said Denny, who knew Royal's views on publicity. "Apparently, he had changed his attitude."

The newspaper stories about the *North America Wall*, however, came and went in a few days, leaving Royal with little lasting fame or satisfac-tion. Climbers who sought publicity and the error-prone reporters who provided it remained favorite subjects of disapproval.

Royal's report in the *AAJ* was his most creative piece yet. "But what was Yvon doing on a nightmare-inducing wall like this?" he asked. "If there was ever anyone who has an eye for elegant routes on esthetic walls it is he. A poetic soul, Chouinard really rather disdains the analytical mind, for he hates to see beautiful things ripped and torn. . . .

"Pratt, on the other hand, had already climbed three great routes on El Capitan, though never one like this. Chuck's fantastic native talents and unassuming demeanor make him the finest of climbing companions; while his infinite patience and sense of humor make him an excellent teacher and guide. He enjoys severe climbs and easy ones, and will repeat a route many times if he likes it. Like Jack London and Thomas Wolfe, Pratt is an incorrigible romantic and suffers from the anguish which is a corollary of that *Weltanschauung*. Perhaps Chuck loves climbing partly because rock walls, unlike humans, are without malice."

Only Royal, with his extensive and idiosyncratic reading habits could have put the authors of *The Call of the Wild* and *Look Homeward, Angel* in the same camp.

He concluded with philosophical musings heavy with the language of closure. "The earth in turn would be a mere dot on the sun, and there are suns many thousands of times larger than that fiery orb giving us life. Mankind is truly insignificant. Man's fate, indeed, is to have to swallow these truths and still live on. If one could only find meaning to make these hard truths of insignificance and omnipresent death acceptable. Where to find this meaning? Again the search . . . and we climb on."

Camp 4's literary experts called the article overblown, but it resonated with many aspiring climbing writers. "The NA [*North America Wall* piece] changed, and inspired my whole life," wrote British climber and writer Edwin Drummond to Royal, "with its awesome vision of belonging, arising out of the spirit of the climb." Ken Wilson, another British writer, praised the climb in *Mountain Craft* magazine, setting the foundations of British interest in Yosemite and its greatest climber.

The *North America Wall* showed that fixed ropes were unnecessary and that bolts could be minimized by daring aid climbing. A small, skilled team, cut off from the ground, could climb a new route on El Capitan. Yosemite climbing was now without parallel. There were climbs in the Italian Dolomites that were about as hard and long, but none had been climbed in better style. The torch of climbing tradition had been passed from the Old World to the New.

· · · · ·

In 1964, the year Royal climbed the *North America Wall,* a generation for whom spending a week aid climbing was admirable but not tempting took over the Yosemite free-climbing scene, showing just how forward-looking Royal's free-climbing summer road trip had been.

Twenty-four-year-old Frank Sacherer, who simply would not do a climb if he had to aid it, had the best free-climbing season on record. Sacherer kept a list of climbs he wanted to free. He charged up cracks with scant protection, and terrified his seconds by keeping the rope slack so that they had to free climb just like him.

At Tahquitz, where Royal had recently been the undisputed master, Tom Higgins put up *Jonah,* a six-pitch 5.10+. "It was very hard," wrote Royal, "and I was determined to get up it, because Higgins had done so. I got up it, but I remember it as the hardest climb I had done up to that point."

At twenty-nine, Royal knew he was no longer the best climber in California. He would make a few more great climbs, but nothing to rival what he had already done. He would no longer reside for months in Camp 4. He now came when he had a specific climbing agenda, and left when he was done.

Royal ended the volume of his memoir entitled *The Golden Age* with the 1964 season. A new stage of his life was about to begin. He concluded his account of the *North America Wall* with a quote from American alpinist John Harlin II: "such beauty . . . turns satisfaction to pure joy."

Royal did not quote his contemporaries in passing. Harlin's ascent of the Eiger Nordwand made him the leading American alpinist, poised for preeminence in the global arena. Marriage and the need to maintain some kind of household on his modest wages from the paint store and fees from articles in mountaineering publications made it hard for Royal to return to the Alps. In 1965, however, Harlin himself would reach out across oceans and continents like God in the Michelangelo painting to offer Royal his second chance in the Alps.

Royal Robbins taking notes while belaying Chuck Pratt on the first ascent of the *Salathé Wall* in 1961. *(Photo by Tom Frost)*

Top left: Royal saluting in his Boy Scouts uniform at age 10. *(Courtesy of Robbins Collection)* **Top right:** Beulah holding her son at age four *(Courtesy of Robbins Collection)* **Bottom:** Hanging out at local crag Stoney Point, circa 1956, after dropping out of high school *(Courtesy of Robbins Collection)*

Top: Conducting a climbing lesson for Leysin American School students on the Miroir d'Argentine in Switzerland in 1966. *(Courtesy of Robbins Collection)* **Bottom:** Playing chess at Camp 4 in 1964; from left to right: Royal Robbins, Lito Tejada-Flores, Paul Ryan, and an unidentified climber. *(Courtesy of Paul Ryan)*

Top left: Belaying on reconnaissance for the first ascent of the North American Wall in Yosemite in 1964 *(Photo by Glen Denny)* **Top right:** Joe Fitschen and Royal Robbins (behind Joe) on the first continuous ascent of the *Nose* of El Capitan in 1960 *(Photo by Tom Frost)* **Bottom:** The team after the first ascent of the North American Wall: from left to right are Tom Frost, Royal Robbins, Chuck Pratt, and Yvon Chouinard. *(Photo by Tom Frost)*

Top: Liz Robbins and Royal enjoy each other's company atop the Muir Wall in 1968. *(Photo by Glen Denny)* **Bottom:** Liz Robbins in Yosemite, circa 1967 *(Courtesy of Robbins Collection)*

Top: Tom Frost and Royal bivouacking on the 1964 North American Wall ascent *(Photo by Glen Denny)*
Bottom: Celebrating on the Kichatna Spires, Alaska, in 1969 *(Courtesy of Robbins Collection)*

Top left: Setting up the booth for a trade show *(Courtesy of Robbins Collection)* **Top right:** Five-year-old Tamara on her father's shoulders on a family vacation in England in 1975 *(Photo by John Cleare)* **Bottom:** The Robbins family (left to right: Liz, Damon, Tamara, and Royal) enjoying a day outside *(Courtesy of Robbins Collection)*

Robbins enjoying a quiet, reflective moment on a weeklong annual company retreat, a rafting trip along the Middle Fork of the Salmon River in Idaho *(Courtesy of Robbins Collection)*

7
When the Saints Come Marching In

ROYAL GAVE AN AFTERNOON PRESENTATION at the 1965 annual meeting of the AAC in Philadelphia. Harlin, presenting under his full name, John Elvis Harlin II, was the keynote speaker at the evening black-tie dinner, which Royal attended—without a tie. Carlton Fuller introduced a confident and relaxed Harlin as a Californian and a "mountaineer extraordinary." Royal, who was nervous at presentations, was impressed not only by Harlin's alpine prowess, but also by his "subtlety and the strength of his personality."

Harlin's subject was the world-famous Eiger, whose history of ascent reached back through decades of lore and tragedy. Royal's best climbs, by comparison, were only famous after he did them and still not much understood outside his circle. The Eiger also required an array of skills in which Royal had only dabbled, with limited success, in the Tetons. "There was an atmosphere of euphoria at that meeting," recalled Robbins. "The successes on the Eiger, in Yosemite and on Everest [in 1963, five Americans made it to the summit of Everest by two different routes] gave one the feeling that one was witnessing a renaissance in American climbing."

Harlin was the director of sports at the Leysin American School (LAS), where his wife, Marilyn, was a mathematics teacher. With investment from British climber Bev Clark, Harlin had started the International School of Modern Mountaineering (ISMM) "to enable the individual to introspect into his character," as he put it, "and then build upon it through analysis and adventure. . . . To strive, through the study of perfection in the sport of mountaineering, to understand and express our lives in the environment of our choice."

Royal accepted a position at the ISMM in the summer of 1965, partly because it included an apartment within a few hours' drive of Chamonix and a paycheck that would allow him and Liz to live comfortably. There would be no more waiting out rainstorms in a damp tent in the Biolet. That summer, Harlin quit as director of sports at LAS to train for a new direct route on the Eiger Nordwand, and convinced LAS to hire Royal for the fall and winter terms. It seemed an ideal arrangement.

Liz and Royal packed up their green Mercedes and drove to New York, only to learn from Jim McCarthy that nobody in Manhattan had a spare place to leave a car for a year. Royal left the vehicle with a dealer who promised to sell it for him.

The Robbinses were captivated by Leysin, a hillside town in the French-speaking canton of Vaud. The ski slopes of Les Masses and the 500-foot-high limestone rock walls of the Tour d'Aï, Mayen, and Famelon overlooked the town. A *laiterie* selling milk, cheese, and butter, a butcher and a baker, some bars, modest hotels, and a newsagent composed the local businesses. Their apartment had no refrigerator, and so they adopted the local practice of shopping each day. In the shops, Royal interpreted what had been said to Liz, who read the responses from her phrase book.

On August 7, Royal wrote Beulah on ISMM's stationery with its blue-and-white cubist mountain logo and "John Harlin, Director" in the upper left-hand corner. Royal complained that there were so few students that after a month in Switzerland, he and Liz were short of money. The Mercedes hadn't sold, and the dealer wanted to reduce the price. Royal asked Beulah for a loan of $100, which she sent him. "I am afraid," Royal wrote, "that John Harlin, the director, although he is a great climber and a strong person, is a very poor organizer, so things have not gone as well as they might have. There will have to be some changes if I am to be associated with the school next summer."

At the end of June, Jan Herbert, wife of TM, wrote the Robbinses about her husband and Chouinard's first ascent of the *Muir Wall* on El Capitan. The *Muir*, a direct line between the *Salathé* and the *Nose*, was the first new El Capitan route climbed by a party of two, done without reconnaissance or fixed ropes.

"[John] Muir used to roam the Sierra for weeks," wrote Chouinard in his report in the *AAJ*, "eating only bread and whatever he could pick off the land, sleeping under boulders," sounding a lot like Chouinard during climbing season. Chouinard promised climbers in pursuit of the most demanding style "profound mystical experiences," "unity with our joyous surroundings, this ultra-penetrating perception [that] gave us a feeling of contentment."

It sounded like a lot to miss out on, and as Jan Herbert wrote to Liz, "a year-and-a-half sure is a long time to be away from Yosemite." Royal had been away less than eight weeks when he wrote Steve Roper to tell him how much he missed Yosemite, without conveying much enthusiasm for his European activities.

After the *Muir Wall*, Chouinard went to Canada, and then Europe. He and the Robbinses reunited in the Dolomites, the birthplace of big wall climbing. Royal and Chouinard warmed up on the North Face of the Cima Grande. The first ascent, in 1930 by Emilio Comici and Angelo and Giuseppe Dimai, had been a technical tour de force. Californian Allen Steck had used the experience gained climbing it in 1950 on the first ascent of the North Face of the Sentinel. There were harder routes on the Cima Grande now, and the two Californians made short work of the former testpiece, noting the excessive fixed pitons.

Liz and Royal followed up with the *Spigolo Giallo* on the Cima Piccola. The 1,000-foot vertical ship's prow was graded VI+, or 5.10-. "It was my best route ever," said Liz. "Royal belayed me as I did the traverse pitch. He said it was the only time climbing with me when he was scared, and he looked it."

Chouinard and Royal also climbed the *Cassin Route* on the north face of the Cima Ovest, one of the most overhanging walls in the Alps. From there, they saw the bolts on the much-attempted but incomplete roof between the *Scoiattoli Arête* and the *Swiss-Scoiattoli Route*. Royal had been dismayed by the scores of fixed pitons on European climbs, but the bolts on the Cima Ovest were too much to countenance.

Recent super-direct climbs in the Dolomites had used fixed ropes and hundreds of bolts. Concerns about sacrificing style to technology had been voiced, but did little to check the proliferation of *superdirettissime*. Chouinard and Royal, however, decided to try the bolted route they had seen using Yosemite techniques, in a single push, removing the bolts as they climbed.

British climbers Eric Jones and David Harwood met the Americans at the Auronzo hut, near Cima Ovest. "Royal was quiet and reflective while Yvon was entertaining us with stories and humour," said Harwood. "We saw them hauling massive packs up the face the next day."

Chouinard said that whoever had tried the route before had "used a lot of bolts, and we had more modern hardware and were able to not use the bolts.... We started to chop the bolts, but then there were so many of them we stopped."

"I wanted to go on," recalled Royal in the *AAJ*, "but Chouinard demurred. There was something wrong with the climb and he felt it. Perhaps we were climbing for the wrong reason: going too gung-ho for glory in mountains new to us, when we should have been enjoying ourselves." The climb was completed three years later by Gerhard Bauer and Erich and Walter Rudolph, who also relied on bolts, although in smaller numbers than the first party. The Cima Ovest would mark the first and last time Royal tried to convert Europeans—or at least one of their climbs—to Yosemite norms.

· · · · ·

Back in Leysin, there were still few clients for ISMM. Royal climbed the *Bonatti-Ghigo* on the east face of the Grand Capucin with Bev Clark and young American Larry Ware. "[Royal] was unspectacular to watch, no balletic grace," said Clark, as he watched Royal give each piton a single hammer tap each to test its reliability. "He had a workmanlike approach to climbing, with huge powers of concentration. He was hard to stop." Yet Royal remained unsure of himself on the snow: on the descent, recalled Clark, "he climbed down difficult rock rather than walking down lower-angled snow."

Harlin convinced Royal to join his second attempt on the steepest section of the West Face of the Dru. Tejada-Flores and French climbers Pierre Mazeaud and Roberto Sorgato had already tried it with Harlin, and afterward the Frenchmen questioned Harlin's climbing judgment. Whether or not Royal had heard the gossip, he had his own reservations. "A nice line," he said, "but we have many routes like that in the States. I didn't really see the point in coming all the way to Europe for that."

Nonetheless, Royal began to gather the equipment, using a list Harlin had written in French on a sheet of foolscap. Royal, whose French comprised a few shopping phrases, snippets of Camus, and what he'd gleaned from Tintin and Asterix comics, would have had to use his phrase book to translate some of it. "I recall being struck by the meticulous way [Royal] sorted through the hardware from the climb," wrote LAS teacher Sid Eder in an unpublished manuscript. "Through his horn-rim glasses he carefully inspected every piece of equipment, reminding me of an accountant poring over figures in a ledger."

Rain and snow foiled their first two attempts, but gave Harlin a chance to show Royal a side of Chamonix that foreigners rarely saw. Harlin eschewed the Bar Nationale, where drunken, mostly British climbers relieved themselves outdoors because there was no restroom, for the comfort of Le Choucas, the watering hole of guides and locals. With his masculine features and blond hair, Harlin looked the part of the best American climber in the Alps—which he was. The French liked him so much that Le Phoque had even named their top-of-the-line mountaineering boot after him.

On August 9, 1965, they made their first real attempt. They climbed well together at first, taking turns leading the hard pitches. Things only became tense when a helicopter with a photographer tipped off by Harlin photographed them on the climb. Royal deliberately made the photographer's job more difficult by snapping photos of the aircraft with Liz's camera.

"Harlin," Royal wrote in a book review in the *AAJ*, "strikes a heroic pose, just as he has chosen the clothes which will show him off to best

effect, perhaps subconsciously. Not that Harlin was being false in project-
ing a heroic image of himself. He certainly had the makings of a hero."

On their second day, a rock smashed into Harlin's thigh. The pain was
so severe he thought his leg was broken. Royal navigated 1,000 feet of
overhanging and unstable rock to the summit, while an injured Harlin
struggled to second him. Near the summit, they radioed Liz, who had
camped out at the base, and asked her to send a team up the normal route
to help Harlin down. Liz contacted Marilyn Harlin in Leysin.

Clark, who was in Leysin with Lito Tejada-Flores, said he heard
about the accident from Marilyn Harlin; the two drove to Chamonix and
ascended to the top of the Dru to meet the climbers. Tejada-Flores's training as a combat medic might have come in useful, but by the time the parties met on the rappel route off the summit, Harlin's leg felt better. "Royal
was very unsure of himself on snow," said Clark. "He couldn't do much to
help John, and actually, it seemed like Harlin was helping him. We lived
through the worst storm I've ever experienced. Lightning and thunder,
sitting on our heels."

"We were bivouacked at the bottom of this big dihedral, and there
was a kind of overhang above us," said Tejada-Flores. "There were ava-
lanches; snow plastered the wall. I was just watching these sheets of ice
and snow coming down thirty or forty feet out in front of us." Said Clark,
"An atmospheric aberration set our radio playing loud and clear: 'When
the Saints Come Marching In.'" In the morning, the skies cleared and they
descended to Montenvers. On the glacier, Royal realized that he had left
Liz's camera at the bivouac site.

Liz told American alpinist Steve Miller to wait until Royal got to speak
to the reporters before greeting him. Royal struggled with his French until
Harlin stepped in and gave them the quotes they craved for the next day's
copy.

American newspapers occasionally reported on big climbs, but the
European press treated climbing as part of the mainstream sports scene.
The *Direttissima*, as the reporters referred to the climb, was a major front-
page story. The next day, back in Leysin, Royal read about how Harlin,
"the leader" and "a top American mountaineer," climbed the Dru "with

his companion, Royal Robbins, a ski instructor"—though, of course, Royal had led almost the entire climb, as he would write to Beulah.

Harlin's account in the *AAJ* differs in some details and themes from Royal's. "Tense, dangerous climbing," Harlin wrote. "Perhaps one of the most dangerous rope-lengths of my career—Delicate work." He called Royal "eminently qualified for this kind of [rock] climbing," but somehow Royal, in Harlin's mind, seems to have taken a supporting role.

Royal felt used by Harlin for his big wall skills, and said that when it came to other, stronger climbers, "my impression was that [Harlin] used them, so that he could get as good as they were. If he ever did, they were dismissed."

In the tiny Anglophone community of Leysin, Royal's views quickly reached Harlin. Sid Eder, an American living in Leysin, was, he wrote, chopping wood in his yard when he saw "John Harlin, ice axe in hand, walk over from his chalet. His face was flushed. He was hyperventilating. He was obviously upset." Harlin told Eder he was en route to the Robbinses apartment, furious over something that had happened recently. "He had an 'axe to grind' (a prescient expression in light of what happened several minutes later). And, if he couldn't resolve things to his satisfaction, then he just might bury his ice axe in their 'sanctimonious skulls,'" recalled Eder. Perhaps fortuitously, as they talked, a distracted Eder accidently brought his axe head down hard on a large log; when the axe skidded, it cut deeply into his left leg, the blood gushing like a geyser. Continued Eder, "[Harlin] half-carried me up to the road, put me in our van, and drove to Dr. Bonzon. More than fifteen stitches were required to close the large gash that nearly reached the bone. By the time John drove me home, the emotional storm that had gripped him had passed."

Royal said that Harlin "let a lot of misleading things develop. . . . The idea that he cut his teeth on El Capitan—or that he was a Yosemite climber at all—is all nonsense. . . . When we brought Yosemite techniques to the Alps, or, in particular, when Gary Hemming did, Harlin took all the credit for it."

Despite these tensions, Liz and Royal's marriage flourished. "Lizard really is a fantastically good girl," Royal wrote Beulah. "She's got everything and my love for her is growing. Sometimes I feel it so strongly it scares me. But she really is a princesse [sic]. She takes good care of me and I take good care of her." Liz wrote Beulah that her husband was "really a kind, understanding, wonderful human being—the most admirable I have ever known."

The Robbinses' relationship appeared especially solid in expat Leysin, where the center of climbing and skiing social life was Club Vagabond. The Vag (with a hard "g") was famous—and in some circles, infamous—for its parties, casual relationships, and bohemian morality. When a Swiss television station sent a reporter to ask the townspeople of Leysin what was happening in the old hotel on the hill, bemused locals commented that the club's guests kept to themselves, but held wild parties and practiced free love. At a folk music singsong in the Vag's basement bar, the camera lingered suggestively on handholding young people, and especially on two bearded young men, both with an arm around the same girl.

Registration for ISMM courses was taken at Club Vagabond's reception desk. Parties and girls at the Vag were additional lures for the British climbers Harlin had invited to Leysin on the promise of work at his school. A few of these Brits achieved fame, but even those who didn't partied with principled intensity.

Royal was impressed by the British climbers' extraordinary fitness, despite the alcohol and wild nights. "The startling sinews in his neck when his head is craned," wrote Royal to Roper of Dougal Haston, who was fresh out of Scottish prison for accidently running over a pedestrian while inebriated, "the austere lines in his face. The quick, directed, intense movements." Royal also noted, with admiration, that Haston had made the only complete ascent of a bouldering traverse across Club Vagabond's dining room ceiling.

Royal reserved judgment even when British climbers were less amusing, often under the influence of alcohol. Don Whillans smashed a beer glass into a man's face in the bar. Royal claimed that Davie Agnew knew how to break an opponent's fingers in a fight. Glaswegian climber Stewart Fulton, who had made the first ascent of the difficult South Face of the Fou in 1963 with Hemming and Frost, mistook one of the LAS teachers in the street for a mugger and took a swing at him, said Ware. They all remained among Royal's friends.

British climbing was becoming something of a melting pot for the class system, and Royal also got along well with the generally less volatile middle-class climbers. Twenty-two-year-old Mick Burke was skilled, determined, and easy to get along with. Royal asked Harlin to hire him. Even-keeled Rhodesian climber Rusty Baillie had made the second "British" ascent of the Eiger Nordwand with Haston in 1963, and stayed in Leysin that summer. Royal also became fast friends with Bev Clark, an investor in ISMM and an Oxbridge graduate.

Even educated and polite British climbers revered the pugnacity and adopted some of the mannerisms and dress of the working-class hardmen. And Royal himself—like many of the best British climbers and few Camp 4 climbers—had survived a tough, working-class upbringing. He was no brawler, but he shared the British hardmen's notion that a hard life was the best preparation for hard climbing. "I think that the more you can approximate the rigors of climbing to the rigors of life," Royal wrote, "the more complete a game it is."

Camp 4 had prepared Royal for Club Vagabond in other ways: evening entertainment, as in Yosemite, was the mixture of folk music and conversation British climbers knew from pubs back home. Climbers "revered Bob Dylan and the Stones, read *The Lord of the Rings* and enjoyed intoning Irish rebel songs," wrote Ware. "Discussions ranged from literature to philosophy, politics and travel. Mountains were rarely discussed unless a current foray into the high Alps was imminent." Most of the climbers were autodidacts like Royal.

"Royal loved the conversation and the atmosphere in pubs," said Liz, "where he could be himself." In Camp 4, Royal was sometimes read as arrogant and pompous. British climbers in Leysin, however, were amused. "He was reserved," said Scottish skier Davie Agnew, "he had a dry sense of humour. He loaned me a pair of skis, which I broke and returned to him, and he wasn't angry, he didn't even bat an eyelid."

Whillans, described by Jim McCarthy as "perhaps the champion bad house guest of all time," stayed in the Robbinses' small apartment. "The bravest thing I ever did," said Royal, "was to ask Don to mind his smoking habits [in his apartment]. Actually, he was surprisingly gracious about not grinding his cigarette butts into our floor." Climbers are natural gossips and raconteurs, and Royal's reputation reached the crags and pubs of Britain before he did.

In September, Royal and Liz began work, respectively, as the Sports Director and Assistant Sports Director at LAS, where they hoped for more stable working conditions and regular paychecks. The LAS occupied the Belle Époque edifice of the former Savoy Sanitarium. "The students were mostly the kids of people who worked in business or the military in Europe," said Kathy Gaylord, who attended from 1965 to 1967.

Despite the appearance and expectation of quality education, Harlin had left the sports program in an inspired shambles. Students skilled enough to accompany him on difficult trips like the Haute Route ski traverse in Chamonix loved it, but imparting basic skills interested him less. There was no set program, and Royal had to put something together on the spot.

"I think, initially, Royal and Liz were twenty-five or thirty," says Gaylord. "I imagine they thought 'Oh, my God, what do we do with these kids?' But as students, we didn't see them that way—they were role models. In the mid-60s, there was a very different, more formal student-teacher bond."

Royal taught the kids hiking, rock climbing, and skiing, the sports he knew best. It didn't occur to him to train kids only on topropes or bunny hills. The culture of outdoor sport emphasized mental control over movement, and so did Royal. With realism however, came risks. One girl quit the climbing classes after being dropped by a classmate who was an inexperienced belayer.

"Royal was a remarkable person," said alumnus Kathleen Galvin. "He required us to do things well and do them right. 'You could do anything on a rock wall you want to do,' he said, and this translated to the rest of my life. He believed that women could climb just as well as men, and Liz was a great example of what he meant."

Students were introduced to climbing basics in the disused quarry behind Harlin's house. Longer climbs on the local limestone towers were the next step, followed by the 450-meter slab of the Miroir d'Argentine for advanced students. Assistant instructors were hired, as necessary, from the roster of ISM (the school dropped "modern" from its title that fall). Students, forbidden from going to Club Vagabond on pain of expulsion, sometimes visited the Robbinses', where, Gaylord remembered, "Liz would sit there on the floor, peeling an orange" while Royal told climbing stories. By the time she left Leysin, said Gaylord, "I felt like a climber."

Royal was no less of an icon and role model for the students as a skier. Even in the ski-crazed European Alps, Royal's style on the slopes drew attention. He and Agnew were both hired to appear in *Ski Verbier*, a short film that won a prize at the Cortina Film Festival. As a teacher, taking LAS students up on the slopes of Les Mosses, Royal brought full-length skis and taught a completely parallel system—one that turned many of the kids into excellent skiers, recalled Agnew.

Lito Tejada-Flores had spent the climbing season in Chamonix. In the autumn, he followed Kor and Chouinard to Leysin. Tejada-Flores, who had never skied, asked Royal to rate his potential as a skier. Royal remembered Tejada-Flores dancing in Berkeley and told him that skiing was all about body movement. "If you want to learn to ski you can work for me," Royal said. "You'll pick it up." Royal loaned Tejada-Flores a couple of instructional books and arranged for Gaylord to teach him, Kor, and Chouinard snowplow turns.

Gaylord's brother, himself a climber, was starstruck when he heard his sister had taught some of his heroes how to ski. "But I had no idea who they were," said Gaylord. "Layton was big and not particularly coordinated. Yvon was small and quite coordinated. Lito ended up as one of the best skiers I ever skied with. That was Royal's way. He would say, 'I know you can do anything you set your mind to.'"

. . . . .

Royal saw outdoor education as an important part of the school syllabus and an indicator of broader academic talent. He wrote LAS student and keen climber John Feasler's father, a mining engineer, to convince him that it was worth Feasler missing family Christmas holidays for skiing in the Vallée Blanche and climbing in the Calanques. Feasler applied to the prestigious Colorado School of Mines, but the principal of LAS warned him LAS was almost unknown in America, so he was unlikely to be admitted. Royal, however, reached out to the school on Feasler's behalf. "In a demanding academic institution such as yours," wrote Royal, "success depends as much on a young man's character as upon his intellectual gifts. John has shown again and again his ability to meet difficult and challenging situations." The school accepted Feasler's application.

"On his own initiative," wrote Sid Eder, "[Royal] started a chess club . . . It met once a week after dinner. Royal would play simultaneous games with all five of us. At a certain point, he would stop the games, leaving the pieces in place. Then, the next week, he would return with the boards, having plotted out for each game the subsequent moves required for checkmate. I remember being awed by the time, concentration, and patience that it must have taken him to do that."

By contrast, Royal found the school administration "rather corrupt." "There is continuous graft," he wrote Beulah. "They do their best to cheat the teachers and the students." He accused them of keeping the 10 percent discount on ski sales offered to students in shops in town. He protested a decision to charge students for linens. "The headmaster from last year," he wrote, "is in jail for embezzlement. It is a rather sordid situation for us idealists to be involved in. . . . The more we get to know it, the more creepy it gets."

In spring, Royal and the students were back on the rock. Student Larry Ware recalled a trip up the Miroir d'Argentine on which instructors, including Mick Burke, Stewart Fulton, John Harlin, Chris Bonington, and the Robbinses, outnumbered the students.

Royal's abilities on the rock were as strong as ever. His free ascent of the Sphinx on the Tour d'Aï above Leysin with Utah climber George Lowe was likely the hardest free pitch in Western Europe. And yet, something about the way Royal moved on the rock intrigued and even perplexed knowledgeable observers.

"In bullfighting, you have matadors," Ware said, "who connect with the crowd, who give you a sense that this is something that is natural. . . . Then you have amazing technicians, who do everything very precisely and well, but you don't feel the same thing; it doesn't connect. Royal fit into the latter category. He was a machine, extremely precise. He could have made watches. He was not a natural climber, not beautiful to watch, he was brutish. But he was effective."

"I was kind of surprised by how methodical Royal was," said Rusty Baillie. "He climbed quite slowly and seemed to agonize over every move, being careful and thorough and double-checking his protection." Oddly, however, Royal seemed to climb at the same deliberate speed no matter how difficult the terrain was—he lacked, said Baillie, the natural flair of other period stars like Whillans, Joe Brown, and Martin Boysen. "Royal was like death and taxes: inevitable and unstoppable. Of course, he loved climbing, and was a compulsive analyzer of technique; he just seemed more like an orangutan than a treetops monkey," said Baillie.

Harlin, too, was impressed. Even after the arguments about the Dru, he invited Royal to join his Eiger Direct team. Royal turned down the invitation. "I'm not an expedition man," he later said, "and I didn't want to be involved with getting someone else to the top of a mountain." But these comments could only have been made after the climb: Harlin, intending to climb the route alpine style, only switched to expedition style during the climb itself. Kor joined the team. He had less alpine experience than Royal, but he was willing to learn on the job, and he liked Harlin.

Royal and Liz spent the Christmas break of 1966 in Spain. Josip-Manuel Anglada, who had climbed with Royal in Yosemite, met them in Madrid and invited Royal to return in the summer for a lecture tour. Back in Leysin, Harlin's proposed Eiger Direct route was going into production. The climbing team now also included Haston and Harlin. Chris Bonington, Mick Burke, and others had supporting roles.

In February, Royal taught snowplowing and chess moves and Harlin began the Eiger Direct, a route that many believed was going to be the hardest climb in the Alps. Eight climbers from Stuttgart, led by Jörg Lehne and Peter Haag, laid siege to the same route with fixed ropes and camps stocked with supplies. Harlin, however, intended to complete the route in a single push, or at least without fixed ropes

Bad weather, steep rock, and congestion slowed down and frustrated both teams, and the climb dragged into late March. Harlin finally used fixed ropes, and the project devolved into an expedition. Bonington was promoted to climber, and eventually the two teams joined forces. On March 22, 1966, Haston jumared up a fixed seven-millimeter line high on the wall. One of the Germans followed him up the rope. Harlin came next, but before he reached the anchor, the rope broke and he fell to his death. He was only thirty, and had left behind a wife and two children.

News of Harlin's death appeared on the cover of *Paris Match*, next to an image of the Rolling Stones sitting in beach chairs. The villagers of Leysin had liked Harlin. Many were grief-stricken at the news. The funeral was held in Leysin on a snowy day in late March. The mourners included climbers, school staff, students, and villagers. Kor was a pallbearer. Some reported that a beautiful young girl whom no one recognized wept in the crowd.

Speculation about how the accident might have been avoided was inevitable.

"I mentioned that I had overheard someone venture that such an accident wouldn't have happened to Royal Robbins," Sid Eder wrote that he told Kor and Burke, "because he would have made sure that all the ropes were in good condition. 'I bet he bloody well would have,' snorted Mick derisively. 'Being the kind of bloke he is.' I was taken aback at the negative tone of his remark. 'I would have thought that you admired Royal,' I said. 'Admire him?' Mick said. 'Let me tell you, Sid, I'll take twenty Royal bloody Robbins to one John Harlin. John had feelings. He had heart. Sure, he had faults. Sure, he had a temper. Sure, he lost it at times. But he had feelings. He was a sensitive human being, if you understand what I mean. No, give me a John anytime.'

"'I'll say amen to that,' said Layton."

Hemming, who had argued with Harlin more than anyone else, showed up in Leysin for the funeral. "John is one of my dearest friends," he wrote, "his death I refuse to accept and so far as I am concerned, he is still very much alive." He also propositioned Marilyn Harlin not long after the funeral.

"I wasn't involved in any way with the Eiger climb," Royal wrote Beulah, "except that I had loaned John Harlin, the fellow who fell, my pack."

. . . . .

Royal soon found himself back in the media limelight. The British Broadcasting Company's plans for an April 1966 live broadcast of an ascent of the 400-foot Red Wall at the Gogarth seacliff in Anglesey were threatened when one of the climbers, Chris Bonington, was injured.

"I was very aware that live television with climbing was acting," said the program's technical director, John Cleare. "I felt that live television climbing needed actors' repartee, and so the climbers had to be selected for that, not just because they were good climbers. We had Joe Brown, Ian McNaught-Davis, and Scottish climber and doctor Tom Patey, who had it."

Rusty Baillie had introduced Cleare to Royal in a Chamonix bar the year before, "and one was rather in awe of the chap. Who were we to climb with him? But I thought, 'Why not bring in Royal, who was calm, cool, and collected?' It might also mean the broadcast could be sold in America." As an extra incentive, a lecture tour by Royal about American climbing was planned.

In Patey's words, Royal suppressed "some of his Sphinx-like inscrutability" to make friends on the set. "It was brilliant working with Royal," said Cleare. "He was always ready with a wry joke; he went down very well in the UK." In an oft-repeated on-screen joke, Royal said that he could always tell a good aid climber by the lack of scars on their hands. Patey's hands were covered in cuts and scrapes from struggling with techniques as unfamiliar to him as they were to most British climbers.

Royal received a check for fifty pounds and an introduction to every climber with access to a television in Britain. He also found a community where he felt less restrained than he had in Yosemite. At the Anglesey after-party, he surprised the British climbers by standing on a table and singing.

Bev Clark introduced Royal to London climber and surgeon Max Gammon. Marianne Faithfull, Mick Jagger, and climbing stars Mick Burke and Dougal Haston were regulars at Gammon's parties in swinging London, and Gammon put Royal on the guest list.

At the parties, said Gammon, "Royal hung back, but I immediately knew that I had found someone special. Of course, I knew about his accomplishments, but there was something else as well. When I was a child, I always tried to catch a Camberwell beauty butterfly, but I never really knew what one looked like until I saw one. Royal was one of those people who you knew, right when you met him, was something special like that."

The first stop on Royal's lecture tour was the humbler environment of Cookridge, a suburb of Leeds, where they stayed at Anglesey rigger Dennis Gray's parents' house. Gray, who introduced Royal to the British climbing scene and its traditions, was, he said, pleased to find his student a man of "professorial demeanor, tall, spry, quiet, and contemplative."

British climbing intrigued Royal. On the gritstone crags of northern England, he adopted the British method of using slung pebbles, machine nuts, or manufactured nuts instead of crack-scarring pitons for protection. At Almscliff Crag, Gray impressed Royal by explaining how each route fit into the history of British climbing. Royal declared them "miniature masterpieces," higher praise than he had ever given the walls of the Alps. He studied British climber Geoffrey Winthrop Young's authoritative 1920 book, *Mountain Craft*, and underlined favorite passages about fair play, and the threat of "vulgarisation" to climbing's "glorious tradition."

Even as Royal imbibed these doughty traditions, he imparted an electrifying new vision of ethical—and importantly, sunny—California big wall climbing to his British audiences. "All of us in the room were stunned," said a young Chris Jones, who later wrote a history of North American climbing. "I was so impressed by these Americans that I changed my half-formed plan to live near the Alps, and instead headed for California."

Local climbers respectfully enjoined Royal to attempt their hardest climbs, as if for review and approval, an expectation Royal greeted with enthusiasm. After a night at the pub following a lecture in Sheffield, student climber Jerry Lovatt showed Royal the local climbing. "I took our honoured guest out to Curbar," recalled Lovatt, "to see how he would get on with some of its celebrated cracks. I started on *Peapod* and was standing on the halfway ledge when a head popped out of the top of the pod—it was Royal soloing the first section."

The tight-knit British climbing scene reveled in gossip about the American visitor. "One day we were at Stanage Edge," wrote American climber Chris Vandiver. "It's a Saturday morning, Royal is leading the climb, and . . . a huge crowd (at least a hundred) [has] gathered to watch. Right at the crux, Royal lost his balance and tipped over backwards. His fall pulled me off the boulder I was belaying from, and he and I met each other about ten feet from the ground!" The magazine editor Ken Wilson even caught news of the fall at another crag twenty miles away, a fact he conveyed to Royal in London that evening. Royal called Wilson "an authority on many things, delivering harsh, quick judgments, dogmatic, impulsive, abrasive, but often accurate," meaning to say that he liked him.

In Llanberis, the center of the Welsh climbing scene, Royal and Liz were hosted by Joe Brown. Royal failed on Brown's famous *Cenotaph Corner*, but he left Wales with his first set of crudely machined but purpose-built climbing nuts.

Royal was unsure of the effect of his lectures, particularly upon the more established set in British climbing. "I showed some slides and a movie, and said a few interpretative words," he wrote in the *Scottish Mountaineering Club Journal.* "Not really lecturing. I remember the reception at the Alpine Club: exceedingly polite, exceedingly unenthusiastic. One can't blame them. It was mostly the old guard, the conservatives who disdain pitons. And what I offered was mostly American ironmongery, and some monkey tricks on big rock walls, hardly *grande alpinisme.* They must have felt like spectators at a zoo."

Most audiences, and for that matter, venues, were not so stuffy. Rusty Baillie heard Royal speak in Glasgow, at eccentric veterinary professor Mary Taylor's house, where folk musicians, great expeditionary climbers, and goats lounged on the couch. "The subject was 'Yosemite Big Wall Climbing,'" Baillie recalled. "It was a long, interminable lecture with many, many, blow-by-blow pictures, but we were captivated and enthralled. I was impressed by his quiet self-confidence and his intense commitment to the details and implications of his climbing—single-push, self-contained big wall techniques."

The next year, Baillie and John Amatt applied Royal's ideas to the 2,000-foot overhanging wall of Sondre Trolltind in Norway's Romsdal area. Amatt was the first British climber to use Yosemite rather than the Alps as a benchmark of comparison in his report in the *Alpine Journal,* even though he hadn't visited the Valley yet.

The Robbinses' British itinerary concluded with a trip to Scotland. Back on the continent, they learned that the Mercedes dealer in New York had disappeared with the vehicle, so they borrowed money from Liz's parents to buy a Volkswagen van. "Royal lost things," said Liz, "and he lost the green Mercedes."

· · · · ·

The Richard-Pontvert company made the famous Galibier climbing boots. Company director Julien Richard had his eye on the American market, and asked Royal to design a boot specifically for California-style rock climbing. In exchange for Royal's ideas, and the use of his name, he offered a royalty on every pair sold in the United States. Royal and Liz, with Tejada-Flores as interpreter, dropped by the company headquarters in Izeaux, France, to discuss prototypes.

Royal had started climbing in basketball shoes and moved on to *kletterschuhe*, light boots with thin, lugged rubber soles. He had tried the smooth-soled Pierre Allain (PA) and Edmond Bourdonneau (EB) models, but despite their increased friction and sensitivity, many climbers were slow to adopt footwear that offered no protection from foot-crushing webbing etriers and was too flimsy for approach hikes.

The Royal Robbins Yosemite boot, or the RR, had a rubber toe and heel rand for extra friction. A four-layer, glued and riveted sole with a steel foreshank gave a solid platform for face climbing and protected the midfoot from etriers. The raised heel made the shoes more comfortable on approaches and descents. The royal-blue suede uppers made them the most ostentatious climbing footwear on the market.

Royal's prototypes were stolen from his van in Spain, and the RRs went into production before he had a chance to test them. When he finally tried them, he suggested replacing the steel shank with a more flexible plastic one, but the change was never made and most climbers liked the RRs as they were. Jim McCarthy called the RR the best shoe he had ever used for the Gunks. In Yosemite, British climbers found RRs more effective on some slabs than their smooth-soled EBs or PAs. The RR's toe was less sensitive to the rock than the EB's, although it could be a moot point.

Climbers wore hiking socks, making any model less sensitive than modern climbing shoes, which are worn barefoot.

In Spain, Royal gave eighteen lectures and finished a new route on the limestone cliffs of Pedraforca with Anglada. Some Spanish climbers who had attempted the climb before were annoyed, and attributed Royal's success more to his American bong pitons than his skill. "The Spaniards are extremely friendly, in general," Royal wrote Beulah.

At a picnic near the Calanques, Ramases, one of the Robbinses cats, wandered away from the van. Few things upset Royal as much as the thought of harm coming to his pets, and Royal and Liz searched for hours with no success. Before they left, they asked a nearby farmer to watch out in case Ramases showed up looking for food. Before they departed for America, Liz and Royal spent a couple of weeks guiding Jim McCandless, a wealthy American they'd met at Sugar Bowl. McCandless's fear of heights stymied their attempt on the Matterhorn, but they stayed in expensive hotels on his bill, and on a practice trip to the Calanques, the farmer reunited them with Ramases.

In August, they began a trans-American itinerary of presentations, meetings, and climbing. In California, Royal pitched Jene Crenshaw and Helen Kilness, the editors of *Summit*, on stories about European climbing. Taken by his enthusiasm, they gave Royal the title of Rock Climbing Editor.

Jim McCarthy took Royal and Liz on their first trip to the Gunks. Royal proposed the nuts he had acquired in England as a possible antidote to the area's severe piton scarring, but at first, only McCarthy and top Gunks free climber John Stannard were willing to consider them.

Gunks climbers were more interested in Royal's free-climbing abilities than his strange ideas about climbing protection. A small crowd gathered to watch him climb *Retribution*, a 5.10 and one of the hardest routes in the east. No one told Royal where to find a crucial, hidden handhold, but there were sighs of approval when he climbed the crux without it. McCarthy, however, had to take over the lead from Royal on the first ascent of *Grim-Ace-Face*. The strenuous overhangs common to the Gunks were a rare weakness in Royal's rock skills.

After visits to Seneca Rocks in West Virginia and the White Mountains in New Hampshire, Liz and Royal returned to New York City to find Don Whillans installed in McCarthy's apartment. McCarthy described Whillans as one of the worst houseguests ever, but Royal liked and respected him, despite his weaknesses, and offered to take him out West.

A few days later, in Eldorado Canyon, Whillans climbed the second pitch of *Ruper* without any protection. Pat Ament commented that if he fell, he would pull Royal off, but Royal just said he'd take his chances. That same day, Royal belayed Ament on the first lead of *Supremacy Crack*. Ament rested on a piton, but the route became known as Colorado's first 5.11.

"Ament was a young upstart," wrote the authors of *Climb!*, the history of Colorado free climbing, "and Royal Robbins, godfather of the free climbing game, supervised and sanctioned the *Supremacy* ascent." "Royal, a stickler for style," said Ament, "didn't see it as much of a flaw. . . . The best climbers of the age were quick to validate this ascent as a real and important one, while other lesser climbers, it seemed, were inclined to dismiss it."

Some wondered whether Royal, who was so strict with himself, bent his rules for his young admirers. Certainly, he indulged his friends, even when their views differed from his own. This charitability, however, contrasted with the stories of his uneasy interactions with strangers that became part of American climbing lore. That summer, when a customer at a climbing store in Colorado asked Royal if he was an employee, he answered enigmatically, "I'm Royal Robbins." Sometimes, when strangers approached him, he walked away in silence.

A small retinue of British and French climbers awaited Royal in Camp 4. "Royal invited every climber he met [in the United Kingdom] to Yosemite," wrote Roper in *Camp 4*, "and that fall, a few showed up." Whillans, Dez Hadlum, and Terry Burnell, climbing with Californian Jim Bridwell, became the first Britons to climb the *Regular Northwest Face* of Half Dome. Royal was happy that Yosemite was finally getting some international attention, and his prediction that foreign climbers would make an ascent of El Capitan came true when two French guides climbed the *Nose* that fall.

Royal soloed the *Steck-Salathé*, a route that had been unrepeated when he first came to Yosemite, in a stunning three hours and forty-five minutes, using a rope on the hardest sections, but his new dream was to slow climbing down. With Liz and the British climbers Victor Cowley and Mike Dent, he established *Boulder Gorge*, the first new route in Yosemite protected only by painstakingly using nuts.

"We had started out not using pitons," Royal wrote in *Summit*, "because the runners were good and because it was more exciting and interesting risking falls on nuts and runners. . . . You think you know the nuts are good and so you finish anyhow, trembling but with a slight smirk in your soul."

Even after *Boulder Gorge*, however, few Yosemite climbers even knew what nuts were, and those who did were skeptical. Pratt rejected them outright. Chouinard and Frost now owned the foundry Great Pacific Ironworks and produced carabiners as well as pitons. Chouinard said Royal's selection of the latest British nuts were "things that fell off the railway and vehicles"—he was appalled, even though Royal was "pretty big on it." On a more positive note, Chouinard agreed to become the North American distributor of RR boots.

After another lecture in Chicago and Royal's second annual dinner presentation to the AAC in New York City, he and Liz flew back to Europe, a place he was becoming less and less enamored of. Hemming, Harlin, and Chouinard had all fallen in love with the Alps, but Royal had not—and his French had remained rudimentary. He had neither Swiss nor French friends, except for his business contacts at Richard-Pontvert, and the only continental climber he had ever climbed with in Europe was Anglada. Europe no longer beckoned to Royal with the promise of fame, but instead confirmed his preference for the American mountains.

Many of Royal's complaints about life in Europe originated with British and American expats and visitors, rather than Swiss and French locals. There had been problems with Harlin and the LAS administration. Royal complained to his mother that apartment-sitting climbing friends left their place "an absolute pig-mess." Ramases the cat was "in a terrible state," one of their kittens was missing, and another had died from neglect.

"Don't trust friends in your apartment," Royal wrote in his letter. "Don't trust people to care for your cat with any sort of warmth or understanding."

Royal went about his work as ski and sports instructor and chess-club convener. Hemming and Haston contended, with some rancor, for control over the remnants of ISM. Liz wrote Beulah that Leysin "seems a better and more relaxed place without John Harlin," although Harlin's absence was keenly felt through the climbing community.

Hemming inherited Harlin's role as the dashing American alpinist. In the summer of 1966, while Royal was showing off his no-hands bouldering at Almscliff in Yorkshire, Hemming, Burke, and top French climber René Desmaison had rescued German climbers from the west face of the Dru. Chamonix guides called the rescue irresponsible, but *Paris Match* ran Hemming's account as a cover story. The French media paid the rent on his Paris apartments. He played the tragic English King Harold in a French television series. Women stopped him on the street for autographs, but he remained unhappy.

Haston and Burke were planning an expedition to Cerro Torre in Patagonia. The wind-battered granite pillar with walls higher than El Capitan had seen only one, generally disputed ascent; it remained one of the world's most coveted summits. Royal wanted to climb Cerro Torre, and his skills could have improved the chances of success, but he was not invited.

That winter, Royal's ski-racing program began to show signs of success. He organized a race with teams from different schools. The LAS boys' team won and the girls' team came second, although most of the kids had only started skiing a year before.

For Christmas 1967, Beulah sent Liz a tiger-print nightdress and Royal a tailored shirt perfect for the image of Monsieur Robbins. But Royal did not renew his contract with LAS after the 1967 spring semester. Before he left, he recommended Whillans as his replacement. Mick Burke, a more obvious choice, was understandably upset. Whillans didn't last in the role, but Royal was loyal to his friends, even after others lost patience with them.

In April 1967, Royal and Liz left Leysin for California. Royal never returned to the Alps to climb with any seriousness again.

They arrived back in California just as the Summer of Love began.

8

To Engrave
My Initials on
the Face Forever

IN THE SUMMER OF 1967, a hundred thousand or so kids flocked to San Francisco and turned California's fringe subculture into a groundswell of sexual freedom, self-actualization, revolution, free speech, nuclear disarmament, feminism, civil rights, and environmentalism. Behind the counter at Valley Paint, Royal plotted a revolution of his own, tinged with ideas about environmentalism and personal growth that were no less idealistic for being limited in scope to American climbing.

Royal knew that climbers, more than ever, were trying to show their respect for the rock. Yet they failed because pitons, the tool they had been given by history, destroyed cracks with repeated insertion and removal. With Royal's encouragement, they started to change their ways. He correctly sensed that small gestures like the National Park Service (NPS) closing small Yosemite crags because of unsightly piton scarring were only the beginning of a new, more environmentally aware park doctrine.

In "Nuts to You!" in *Summit*'s May 1967 issue, Royal suggested that for all of these reasons, nuts were not simply a possible alternative to pitons, but should replace them when possible. The "gadgets," as he called them, could—and should—transform American climbing.

"I find it convenient to wear the nut-slings around my neck, British style," wrote Royal, evoking the gameness of the *Boy Scout Manual*. A set of seventeen nuts was available from Joe Brown's store for ten dollars, including shipping, he wrote, with an urgency that suggested readers should order before supplies ran out. "Clean climbing," as Royal dubbed climbing with nuts, also had moral and spiritual dimensions. He suggested a new, tactile relationship with the rock, climbing without the ring of hammers, a true low-impact wilderness experience.

Although the old crowd was slow to adopt the new hardware, many young climbers, steeped in the environmentalist ideals of the counterculture, were quicker to adopt Royal's ideals—and also, on occasion, to judge him by them.

"Robbins's position in Yosemite in 1967 was not easy," said Chris Jones, "and likely uncomfortable. It was widely agreed among those of us then climbing in the Valley that Robbins was simply the best. Even though his time in the Valley diminished, he remained ahead of us all. The young guns [e.g., Kim Schmitz, Jim Bridwell, and Galen Rowell] were working to take his place; he surely wanted to remain as the top dog."

By 1967, however, the inner circle that had comprised Royal's most successful climbing teams had mostly moved on. Pratt worked construction in Washington, and on his occasional trips to Yosemite focused on short free routes. Frost took up expedition and alpine climbing. Chouinard only visited Yosemite on occasion.

Royal's single new big wall that summer was the 2,000-foot West Face of El Capitan, with TM Herbert. Lower angled than the other faces and lacking continuous crack systems, it was, said Royal, "the plain Jane sister of the *Salathé Wall*." For the first time in Yosemite history, Royal and Herbert used more nuts than pitons on a new big wall. Royal knew, however, that clean climbing needed a more accessible proof-of-concept climb. He chose the low-angled, 700-foot face of Ranger Rock, later known as Manure Pile Buttress, for his first ascent of *Nutcracker*, a multipitch clean route.

In his *AAJ* report on *Nutcracker*, Royal sold clean climbing hard. "A nut in a corner," he wrote, "a traverse out right and a runner on a flake and I was nose to nose with the hard part. So I fitted a so-so nut and draped a so-so runner on a so-so crystal (be brave, I thought, that's a good runner on the flake below) and moved up. . . . The next pitch is terrific: jams, laybacks, and face-climbing for 150 feet with 7 nuts and 2 runners along the way. You can fix the stance at the end with belays through holes in the rock." He continued, "A good slotted nut in a little overhang starts the next pitch; 15 feet higher I slipped in a couple of little wedges which would probably hold the sort of sliding, bouncing fall one would take here."

Pratt made his own statement by adding his own climb to the buttress, *C.S. Concerto*, protected entirely with pitons. Chouinard, however, overcame his skepticism about nuts and joined Royal to add a direct finish to the new, clean route.

As an inventor and builder, Chouinard saw that most British-manufactured nuts were too small to fit the most common Yosemite cracks, and began tinkering with lighter designs that fit a greater range of cracks. *Nutcracker*, despite its humble stature, turned out to be as influential, in its own way, as the first ascent of Half Dome in 1957, as it established clean climbing in America on an attractive and accessible route where American climbers could safely experiment with it.

Royal and Liz climbed the *Regular Northwest Face* of Half Dome on the tenth anniversary of the first ascent, making Liz the first woman to do a grade VI in Yosemite. Ten years earlier, Royal had been struggling with his direction in life. Now he was on the top of the climbing game, a position he had gained with Liz's input, support, and love. They both experienced the climb as an affirmation of what they'd achieved together. "The thrill of this exposure, the hammering of my heartbeat and the knowledge that I was sharing this experience with the man I trusted and loved brought a quiet mind and a soul-felt gratitude," Liz wrote in *Alpinist* magazine. "This is why I climb, I thought."

Liz did not lead on the route, but seconding, as Royal had pointed out when he named the *Taylor Route* in the Tetons, was an essential, if overlooked component of any team's success. On the *Nose*, their next wall, temperatures were higher than expected, and at Sickle Ledge, 500 feet up, they realized that they didn't have enough water and rappelled. Royal decided that a party of three would be more successful and asked Chris Jones to join.

"I felt I had an easy rapport with Royal," said Jones. "Although I [had] never had the good fortune to do a major climb with Royal, I accompanied he and Liz on a rather scruffy route that he had previously established: *Boulder Gorge.*" Royal then asked Jones to join him on the *Nose,* but when they met to talk logistics the next day, Royal surprised Jones by mentioning Liz would also be joining them. Said Jones, "However much I wanted to climb with Royal, and moreover on the *Nose,* I now felt like a dupe"— what would all his fellow Camp 4 denizens think of his willingly enabling a "first female ascent" that many would regard as illegitimate, since Liz was unlikely to do any of the leading?

"We spent a tense few minutes," remembered Jones, "and I declined his offer; I could see that he was upset. In my mind, he had hoped to take advantage of an admiring friend to further his ambitions. I felt let down." The pair's relationship was never the same again, though looking back now, Jones wonders how he might have responded had Royal been more forthright from the start about having Liz along. Said Jones, "I liked him tremendously, and maybe would have embraced the plan if I had had time to think it through. As it was, the event essentially destroyed our friendship."

That summer, Royal and Chouinard climbed Grand Sentinel, a 1,700-foot wall in Kings Canyon, with the intention of using as many nuts instead of pitons as possible. They were elevating the use of nuts to the same order of tenet as minimizing fixed ropes and excessive bolts. "Chouinard don't look back," Royal wrote in the *AAJ,* with a nod to Bob Dylan and his partner's new enthusiasm for clean climbing. "He's an artist of life. He delights even in the stray bits of wickedness which flit through his soul. He doesn't care much for intellectuals, or chess, or Mozart, for he's a humanist."

Royal broke a handhold and almost took a serious fall. "I thought how that wouldn't have happened to Chouinard," he wrote. "He's so cool, man, in climbing as in life." Coolness was a quality that Royal had occasionally envied but rarely evoked.

· · · · ·

In August 1967, Royal planned to make his first visit to the Canadian Rockies, where Chouinard had shown his cool on some of the hardest alpine routes in the range. Alberta's glaciated peaks had beckoned alpinists since the nineteenth century. The lack of a good showing in the Canadian Rockies—including, preferably, a significant first ascent—was a serious blank spot in any North American climbing legend's record. On the way, Royal visited Squamish, British Columbia, not principally to climb the 1,000-foot Stawamus Chief, but to teach the latest California techniques.

Royal had started guiding for Doug Tompkins's California Mountain Guide Service, the first commercial climbing guiding outfit in California. Tompkins, a displaced Easterner, charismatic natural athlete, climber, businessman, and trend-watcher, drove sports cars, socialized with celebrities, and dressed in the latest fashions. Although Chouinard, a friend of Tompkins, owned a hardware company, Tompkins was the first person Royal had met who expected to get rich from his passion for the outdoors. For Royal, the Squamish event was an experiment, perhaps not in getting rich but at least in making a living from climbing.

He hired Vancouver climber Jim Sinclair to help him. "At first," said Sinclair, "Royal and I got along really well, like Batman and Robin." Together, they made the second ascent of the 600-foot *Tantalus Wall.* "'I didn't sleep a wink the night before the climb," said Sinclair, "but I waited around until 10 a.m. for Royal to crawl out of his tent, wearing a little pair of white shorts and his famous white cap."

Sinclair told Royal they should get going because they planned to do the route in a day, although the first-ascent party had bivouacked. "'I thought it was only six pitches,' said Royal and he started cooking breakfast," remembered Sinclair. He disliked brisk morning starts. An hour later, Royal charged up the smooth-sided, vertical crack on the second pitch, pulling out wooden wedges alpinist Fred Beckey had used for aid on the first ascent and tossing them over his shoulder. Sinclair was impressed.

In the Rockies, Royal teamed up with John Hudson, a twenty-one-year-old Gunks climber. That season alone, Hudson had spent twenty-five days on an unsuccessful attempt on the east buttress of Mount Deborah in Alaska, climbed Mount Robson, and made the first ascent of the West Face of Mount Geikie with fellow Gunks climber Joe Kelsey. He was keen to complete a hard north face before the season ended and suggested Geikie's unclimbed, 4,000-foot quartzite north face. After the five-mile approach, Royal realized he'd forgotten his camera. Photographs were essential for his articles and presentations, and he left Hudson to set up camp while he went back for it.

Royal led the hardest pitches, and Hudson seconded with the bivouac gear. Hudson felt patronized by his comments, and complained that Royal climbed too slowly on an alpine route threatened by bad weather. In the *AAJ*, Hudson noted Royal's "exaggerated respect for snow slopes," which he had to be "nursed down" on the descent.

In his report, Hudson lampooned articles written by Royal and Harlin. "Here is where, if Royal were not so eminently qualified for this kind of climbing," Hudson wrote, paraphrasing Harlin's report on the Dru, "there would be but one decision—to go down . . . while those ballerinas, hope and confidence, dance in the shadow of a stone roof." He also revised a line from Royal's report on the *North America Wall* that had already amused Valley climbers: "We can . . . learn to face with a calm spirit the chilling specter of inevitable death."

Royal bought Hudson a beer in Banff after the climb, but they never climbed together again and did not remain friends. Hudson died in a climbing accident two years later. Their route was one of the hardest alpine walls in Canada, but the easygoing, almost playful mood that had attended Royal's climbs in California that summer had not followed him to Canada. "My writing has been a disappointment lately," Royal wrote in his journal. "Maybe I'll give up communicating with others. . . . Grave doubts lately about my future plans. The rock school etc. But one has to keep fighting."

He was drawn to the potentially deadly, 4,000-foot north face of Mount Edith Cavell that Chouinard, the Washington alpinist Fred Beckey, and Dan Doody had first climbed in 1961. In the *AAJ*, Chouinard had described the wall as "sheer and Eiger-like," threatened by falling seracs, and "a shooting gallery" for rockfall. Sections were "extreme," wet, and composed of "the loosest shale," and the last 400 feet comprised a steep snow slope and a sixty-degree ice wall. Royal's decision to solo it was one of the most enigmatic choices of his climbing career.

Royal's teenage solos in the San Gabriels had laid the foundation for a lifelong obsession with what he could do alone on the rock. He admired the climbs and writing of Italian solo climber Walter Bonatti. He had rope-soloed the Leaning Tower and the *Steck-Salathé* and done some free soloing in Yosemite.

Edith Cavell, however, was in a category of risk beyond that found in Yosemite. The near-constant rockfall could have knocked him off the wall or injured and stranded him. A broken hold could have sent him to his death. The snow and ice climbing below the summit ridge must have terrified a climber who was never at home on snow slopes. Royal joked darkly about having learned ice climbing on the route, but on the descent, he slipped on an icy slope and nearly fell to his death.

Some have said that Royal only soloed it because he could not find a partner, but he knew that was not reason enough to justify the risk. For once, his account of the climb revealed nothing about his mental state on the climb. Plaudits followed his ascent, but so did questions about his judgment.

"We were pretty pleased with ourselves for our efforts on Mt. Edith Cavell," said Chris Jones, after he and Californian Joe Faint had climbed the north face that season. "However, we soon got our comeuppance. In an unprecedented move, Royal soloed Chouinard's original Edith Cavell north face route. No Americans were soloing such climbs. This was unimaginable to me at that time, but of course that was the nature of what Royal had been doing all along. The bold stroke."

Beckey, the most experienced alpinist in North America, told Royal his ascent was "a pretty good stunt."

Royal's journals hint at a season of unrest and internal turmoil.

"Last night Liz and I had a rather wrenching discussion of what we were going to do with our lives," wrote Royal in his journal after Edith Cavell. "She doubts my ability to earn us a living in any but a drab way. She may be right of course, but I look upon it as climbing a mountain . . . I can't stand to be a non-entity. I must stand out. I must perform before the eyes of others. That's why I climb. Climbing Edith Cavell is like a little boy climbing up somewhere where people can see him. And I am going to engrave my initials on the face of Half Dome forever." Remarkably, he thought he hadn't yet achieved such a legacy with the *Regular Northwest Face*.

He stared at the smoothest expanse of the wall until he imagined features that would take pitons and hooks. He named it *Tis-sa-ack,* after the legend of a Paiute Ahwahnechee woman whose tears had made the wall's distinctive, plunging black water stains. The 1967 season, however, ended before there was time for Half Dome.

. . . . .

In the spring of 1968, with help from the Burkners, the Robbinses bought a ranch-style bungalow on Durant Street in Modesto, a significant improvement on anywhere Royal had lived before. As a boy, Royal's only way into a middle-class home was to break and enter. Now, he opened the front door with his own key.

Liz chose bathroom wallpaper with the hippie symbol of giant butterflies. "It's very mod and very nouveau," wrote Royal to Beulah, "rather frightening really, but we're going to brave it and put it up." Royal hung an aquatint of Don Quixote in the dining room.

"I have even, believe it or not, taken to working in the garden," Royal continued. "Not too much, of course. After all, I have other interests." Twice a day, and with some ferocity, he played tennis, a suburban sport he'd first tried with his girlfriend Eleanor while in the army. "I need [competition] on a daily basis," Royal told the novelist James Salter. "If I don't get it in climbing, I have to get it in tennis. Not just exercise, battle."

The Robbinses' world, however, was still built around climbing. Yosemite is about eighty miles from Modesto. Climbers who came to visit were treated to long dinners with wine and conversation about climbing. Harding, Chouinard, and Tompkins were regular guests.

Tompkins had realized that selling goods to climbers would be more profitable than taking them climbing. The North Face, his new store in San Francisco, stocked outdoor equipment, but the three best-selling items were reindeer-skin rugs, bikinis, and cable-knit sweaters. Business was fun. The Grateful Dead played at a store party in the winter of 1968. It was also profitable. By the year's end, Tompkins had sold The North Face for $50,000 (about $392,000 in 2023 US dollars) and left on a protracted climbing trip to South America. Tompkins was just a single success story in a growing industry. Outdoor stores were cropping up all over America, selling equipment for fashionable, low-impact adventure sports like backpacking and climbing.

Royal had always been intrigued by specialized climbing equipment and clothing, and decided to try distributing it. By the end of 1968, Royal's business, Mountain Paraphernalia, owned distribution rights for Galibier boots and Jannu down jackets from France, Snowdon Mouldings' Joe Brown Ultimate Helmet from Wales, MOAC and Peck nuts and Karrimor backpacks from England, Edelrid kernmantle ropes from Germany, and Salewa crampons, carabiners, and Sticht belay plates from Austria.

Royal's gear was mostly either safer, easier to use, or frankly better-looking than what stores had in stock. Edelrid's kernmantle ropes were colorful, smooth to the touch, and stretched less under body weight than the prevalent Goldline hawsers—an equally attractive feature both for big wall climbers and beginners who only toproped. The American hip belay was hard to learn, and stories of rope burns and even failed belays were not uncommon. Salewa's Sticht pattern belay plate gave a secure belay that didn't depend on the belayer's weight or grip. The ropes and belay plates sold out faster than Royal could order them. Helmets, a European invention, were less popular in California and the Gunks, but caught on elsewhere.

"The initial thrust of RR's and Liz's business was modestly scaled wholesale distribution, but climbers actually could stop by Valley Paint and get a fit or pick stuff up, too," wrote Peter Haan, an early employee. "It was a friendly, transitional situation. It did not happen a great deal in comparison to the wholesale receive-and-send-it-out business that was the real activity." Inventory arrived in large shipments, wrote Haan, most of it earmarked for distribution to US retailers; he and a fellow employee would unload the containers parked on the street and bring the items into a vacant building nearby, to then start sending them out "frantically."

Royal's European suppliers struggled to meet the demand. "I am distressed to hear that you will not be able to send any of these [climbing boots] before April 18," he wrote Julien Richard. "If there is anything else that can be done to speed delivery, I would greatly appreciate it." Many items were in a constant state of backorder.

"European companies were eager to get into the American market," said Keith Roush, an early employee. "They trusted Royal, and gave him favorable terms of payment. Galibier would set him up with all their boots to sell in North America . . . and they gave him a lot of time to pay, which was unheard of. Usually, shoe companies made you pay right when you received the product."

Shortages meant that the orders could only be partially filled. Royal placated shop owners as best he could with visits, discounts, and letters of apology, but the scarcity added to the mystique of his product. In the early, idealistic days of the outdoor industry, Royal and his customers shared a passion for climbing that was stronger than their desire for profit.

At first, Royal seemed naïve about business. He was surprised when Chouinard asked to be paid for the distribution rights Royal had given him for RR boots. He created unnecessary chaos by providing every shop owner with their own, tailor-made terms of payment. "Royal never really wanted to be in business," said Roush. "It was the last thing on his mind."

The new business and his job at the paint store cut into Royal's climbing time, but in February 1968, he teamed up with Loyd Price and Galen Rowell for a series of one- and two-pitch new routes in Lower Merced Canyon. Among this haul was the first free ascent of the *Remnant*, first climbed the year before by Ament and Larry Dalke.

Ament had continued to forge his reputation, mostly in Colorado, although many climbers disapproved of his use of rests on pitons and occasional preplaced pitons to push standards. When Royal and Ament climbed *Crack of Doom* together in 1967, Royal told Ament that he had not climbed the route free because his fingers had rested on a piton on the third pitch—here, the compromise Royal had made in vouching for Ament on *Supremacy Crack* would not be repeated.

In 1968, Ament freed the *Left Side of the Slack* at the base of El Capitan and graded it 5.11, the first climb given that grade in Yosemite. Ament described his Yosemite adventures that year in a letter in *Summit*, written in the third person. In a published response, Royal accused Ament of trying to draw attention to himself by pretending to be an impressed, fictional observer; but Royal privately apologized to him for the slight, wrote Ament.

Despite his reputation for indulging young climbers, Royal could also be impatient. In 1968, twenty-two-year-old British climber Edwin Drummond sent Royal a letter declaring his intention to visit Yosemite and do the most difficult routes, including the second ascent of the *North America Wall.* "The brimming self-confidence shown in your letters and elsewhere," wrote Royal, with clanking prose in which his agitation is almost palpable, "borders on audacity and engenders in me irritation."

The second ascent of the *North America Wall* had become something of a fixation for certain British climbers. Ken Wilson even believed that if Drummond or another British team had succeeded, "the international prestige of the route—the pinnacle of Yosemite climbing—would have been weakened," damaging Royal's credibility and that of Yosemite climbing in general.

Royal knew that the British often struggled on Yosemite walls. Mick Burke attempted the *Nose* six times before his successful ascent with countryman Rob Wood. When Drummond arrived in Yosemite, Royal climbed the *Steck-Salathé* with him and suggested that he build up his abilities on other Yosemite features slowly before trying El Capitan. Drummond responded by asking Royal to introduce him to Don Lauria and Dennis Hennek, strong Californians intending to make the second ascent of the *North America Wall.*

Royal declined, observing that Drummond was not only arrogant but prone to dangerous technical errors, like fixing traversing ropes on the *Nose* without tying off the lower end, so that when he had returned, they had blown out of reach. Later that season, Royal reported to the newspapers on the second ascent of the *North America Wall* by Lauria and Hennek. Presumably, he no longer objected in principle to the media reporting on big wall climbs, at least if the reporter was a climber.

In Camp 4 that spring, Royal ran into Dick Dorworth, a ski-racing rival from the 1950s. Dorworth had an illustrious career as a ski racer, but his new obsession was climbing. Their mutual acquaintance, Dougal Haston, had introduced him to climbing in Utah. Dorworth had then befriended Chouinard and Tompkins, now his main climbing partners. With Tompkins, Chouinard, and Tejada-Flores, he was planning a road trip to Argentine Patagonia that winter to attempt the second ascent of Fitz Roy.

Although the icy granite pyramid was only 11,171 feet high, it offered Yosemite-style difficulties in ferocious winds and cold. A big wall specialist like Royal would have been a valuable asset to the team.

Tejada-Flores and Dorworth had no obligations holding them back. Chouinard could depend on his business partner, Tom Frost, to run things while he was gone. And Tompkins had left his wife to look after an infant, a preschooler, and a new business while he was on the six-month trip. But the self-named "fun hogs" knew that Royal would take his responsibilities at home so seriously that there was no point inviting him.

While his friends hit the road for Fitz Roy and alpine glory, Royal attacked tennis balls, and spent the day mixing paints and the evening working on his Mountain Paraphernalia concern with Liz. But circumstances never prevented Royal from staging a surprising and heroic next act, and what he had in mind next, a solo ascent of El Capitan, would be one of his most startling surprise ascents ever.

· · · · ·

El Capitan had seen only a handful of ascents, all of which had been multiday efforts by teams who shared the risks and the work. Shocked crowds clogged the road beneath El Capitan for a glimpse of these adventurers who resembled nothing so much as astronauts on spacewalks. Royal planned to go alone into this arena. A rescue, while not impossible, would have been on a scale never yet attempted in Yosemite.

Royal chose the unrepeated *Muir Wall,* the only El Capitan route he had not climbed. "That would give me a reason to gloat," wrote Royal in the *AAJ,* "if I were inclined to gloat, and secretly, I am." He was, he said, driven to solo by an unrelenting demon inside: "He always asks for more, more, more. He never gets enough. He is insatiable, gluttonous, ever lusting for more of the peculiar meat upon which he feeds." He'd first met this demon when soloing as a boy in the San Gabriel Mountains. "Nice training," he wrote, "if you survive."

Royal saw his solos—the Leaning Tower, the *Steck-Salathé,* Edith Cavell, and now El Capitan—as a progression. Each climb required deeper faith in himself, a greater willingness to suffer, a more fervent devotion to climbing, and greater technical excellence.

May had the most stable weather, but Royal settled for April and risked colder temperatures and spring storms "because," he wrote, "May is a good month to sell paint in the Central Valley." Earl only let him go on the condition that Liz take his place on the sales floor.

Royal climbed no more than 300 feet a day. The slow pace and repetitive tasks took a psychological toll. "The tedium and the loneliness," wrote Royal. "The loneliness and the tedium." He spoke to himself so much he wondered whether he was losing his mind. In the upper dihedral, he tore out the last in a long chain of poor pitons. A piton held and he only fell four feet. He placed a bolt, the third and last he ever added to an established route.

On Royal's second-to-last day on the wall, Liz came to watch from El Capitan Meadow with a pair of opera glasses. Royal had misplaced her binoculars. "Nice move, Royal," she reportedly said. Other climbers who had come to watch were baffled. From that distance, even with binoculars, no one could judge a climbing move, but Liz always saw things about Royal that remained inscrutable to others.

After ten days on the wall, Liz and a few friends met Royal on the summit. "Bathed in my success," he wrote in his report, "I cared not a whit, for the moment, for anything I wasn't." The photo taken of Royal in his white slouch hat, drinking champagne from a plastic cup, smiling, goateed, wearing his Clark Kent glasses, hands scuffed from the wall, with his arm around a beaming Liz, became one of the iconic images of Yosemite climbing.

This time, the press focused on the climber, rather than the climb and its dangers.

"Royal Robbins is a very special breed of human being—an adventurer whose Nirvana is in the conquest of the mile-high granite monoliths of Yosemite Valley," wrote Spence Conley for the *Oakland Tribune* in the article "Ten Days Alone on the Big Rock, Yosemite Chiller, Man versus El Capitan." The next biggest story on the page was the trial of Black Panther Eldridge Cleaver in Oakland.

Even climbers were taken aback by the solo. Royal had reset the benchmark for rock climbing success yet again. Allen Steck, who had once been irritated by a teenage Royal, said Royal's latest effort was unparalleled in the history of climbing.

Royal spent June and July of 1968 selling paint, writing for *Summit*, the *AAJ*, and a few newspapers, and distributing outdoor products coming in from Europe. He returned to the Valley once that season for the uneventful third ascent of the 2,000-foot south face of Mount Watkins, Joe Fitschen's last Valley big wall.

When they got back to their van after their climb, they found a note from Fitschen's wife, Linnea. Fitschen had been offered a job as an English instructor at Lassen Community College in Susanville, a small town in northeast California.

Royal booked a climbing seminar with the British Columbia Mountaineering Club at Squamish that August, and he and Fitschen decided to follow the event with an ascent of Mount Robson, the highest peak in the Canadian Rockies. Their objective was the difficult *Wishbone Arête*. "As with other aspects of climbing," said Fitschen, "we would figure it out." After all, Half Dome alumnus Mike Sherrick had taught himself to climb snow on the *Wishbone's* first ascent.

After a side trip to Mount Shuksan in the Cascades for some practice on snow and ice, they drove to Alberta, only to find Robson shrouded in clouds and rain falling steadily in the campground. The forecast called for a week of bad weather. In Banff, Royal ran into fellow Californians Steve Roper and Joe Faint, and Gunks climber Joe Kelsey. Their season had also been plagued by storms—as Roper put it, "Canada bad."

It's hard to know how much Royal really wanted Robson, but now he left the Rockies, never to return for serious climbing. Back in Yosemite, he threw himself at *Tis-sa-ack*, the object of a more clearly defined, deeply rooted obsession.

"*Tis-sa-ack* was Robbins's idea, mainly. It was on a lot of guy's [sic] minds," he wrote (in the third person) in *Ascent*. "Had been for a long time. . . . Meant more to him than anyone. He already had two routes on the face and couldn't bear to see anyone else get this one. He wanted to own Half Dome."

Royal made his first attempt on *Tis-sa-ack* a few months later with Pratt and Dennis Hennek. Never before had a climb inspired him to expose so many of the emotions and conflicts he usually kept to his private notebooks. Tangled in his hammock, 500 feet up, he unleashed an "explosion of screeching and shouting." "I was amazed that he so completely lost control," said Hennek, according to Royal, "because he always seemed like such an iceberg."

He transgressed his own standards for bolting and enjoyed it. "I had a unique experience," he wrote, " . . . placing sixteen bolts in a row. It was just blank and there was no way around. But it was a route worth bolting for, and after a time, I began to take a perverse joy in it, or at least in doing a good job." Royal had in fact placed all of their bolts, forcing a retreat. They cached hardware for another attempt in the spring.

While Royal released some of his tensions on *Tis-sa-ack*, he enjoyed a period of conventional success that addressed Liz's fears about his capacity to provide. In the summer of 1968, Mountain Paraphernalia became profitable enough for Royal to quit the paint-store floor, but Earl let him continue to use his storage room.

In early October, Royal and German-American climber Fritz Wiessner represented the AAC at the general assembly of the Union Internationale des Associations d'Alpinisme (UIAA) in London. Royal was still bitter about the AAC's former indifference toward California climbing, but when invited to represent American climbing, he answered their call.

In 1968, the assembly would try to establish international norms for symbols for topographical maps for routes, as well as agree on a universal grading system. British and Russian delegates tried to block the proposed UIAA grading system, but it eventually passed. Royal contributed a table equating the new system to other grading schemes that unwittingly made a universal grading system unnecessary. He had contributed the first French-style "topo" guide to the *AAJ* for an American climb and, with the rest of the delegates, welcomed the use of topo symbols that eventually eclipsed written route descriptions as the standard in Yosemite.

Royal returned from London to grim news. In mid-October, Pratt and Chris Fredericks had been stalled by bad weather on the *Dihedral Wall*. They had no radio, and on a rescue attempt, would-be rescuer Jim Madsen had become disconnected from his rope while rappelling and fallen to his death. The climbers finished the wall the next day, knowing nothing of the rescue or the tragedy. The accident exposed the lack of rescue expertise in the Valley, and the need for better communication between climbers on the wall and potential rescuers.

The tragedy was fresh in everyone's mind when Harding and Rowell attempted the first ascent of the 1,900-foot south face of Half Dome a couple of weeks later. The climbers packed a radio and arranged to stay in touch with Glen Denny.

When a storm hit Yosemite, Denny left a potluck supper at the Robbinses', drove to the park, and hiked up Little Yosemite Valley in the rain to get within signal range of the climbers' radio. Harding and Rowell reported that they were about 600 feet from the top, but six-inch-thick patches of snow stuck to the rock. Their ropes were encased in ice. Water flowed down the wall and pooled in their hammocks. They hadn't moved in twenty-four hours, they were hypothermic, and they needed a rescue.

Denny contacted Pete Pederson, the ranger in charge of rescues, and Pederson telephoned a number of climbers, including Royal, who rushed to Yosemite. When he got there, he found Allen Steck, Steve Roper, and Fritz Wiessner already on site. Pederson and climber and seasonal ranger Joe McKeown had begun the rescue. A helicopter summoned from Mount Bullion Airport arrived at dawn.

At noon, Harding heard voices. The helicopter had dropped young climbers Tom Kimbrough and Kim Schmitz on the summit. "We cannot last another night," Harding told Pederson over the radio. "Get us help today! A helicopter if possible. We are very, very cold." Pederson told him that a rescue was underway and the helicopter would return to the summit in a few hours.

Three hours later, Royal was ferried to the summit, where Kimbrough and Schmitz had laid out a 1,200-foot rescue line and were tying together 150-foot Goldline ropes (laid climbing cords) to back it up. Royal volunteered to be lowered to the climbers on the single rope, but the others insisted on using the Goldline as well. When Schmitz commented that Royal was tying into the rope his friend Madsen had fallen from, Royal asked Schmitz if "he had premonitions of disaster." "What a dumb remark," Royal wrote in *Summit*. "I regretted it for hours."

After a final flight at 4:30 p.m., the helicopter returned to the Valley and the climbers were still stranded. Darkness fell at five, but around six, Harding made out someone being lowered on a rope, a hundred feet above. In the gloom neither Rowell nor Harding recognized Royal.

Royal found Harding embarrassed, but undefeated. "Those famous Harding eyes sparkled and flashed in the stark, moonlit darkness," Royal wrote. "Harding, along with Chouinard and Pratt, was one of the great Yosemite Little Men [here Royal refers to their height]. Each one with his own special powers, his own special climbing personality. His strength lies in his bulldog tenacity." Privately, Royal recorded misgivings about Harding, but publicly, he preferred to describe him as mischievous rather than misguided.

"Warren seems to be having a lot of trouble," said Royal over the radio. "His jumars are slipping and his pants are falling off. He's really having problems." He slit Harding's down-insulated trousers and released some of the sodden down ballast. Rowell jumared on his own, and they reached the top an hour later. They camped on the summit; in the morning, the helicopter ferried them to the Valley floor.

The rescue had been launched and completed in a single day, with effective cooperation between climbers, the rangers, and the pilot. Yosemite climbers and the park authorities were beginners at big wall rescue, but they were already outperforming their more experienced counterparts in some parts of the world. The rescue of German climbers on the west face of the Dru in Chamonix in 1966, for example, had been hampered for days by arguments between authorities and climbers.

On November 12, Royal wrote Chief Ranger Claude McClain with his thoughts about the rescue. He warned against what he called "complete reliance on the Helicopter." Even when a helicopter was called to a rescue, Royal said, "four strong climbers should be immediately dispatched." McClain agreed, and his list of "strong climbers" became the nucleus of the famous Yosemite Search and Rescue team.

A few weeks after the rescue, Davie Agnew offered Royal a few weeks' work on a ski film in Verbier in January. Bev Clark bought Royal and Liz tickets so that they could spend the Christmas holidays in London on the way to Switzerland. When Royal and Liz arrived in Brussels to make their connection, however, the tickets weren't there. "We didn't have enough money to buy tickets ourselves," wrote Royal. "Liz saved us by borrowing $50 from a fellow passenger," a task that would have embarrassed Royal. "She really comes through," he wrote Beulah, "when the going gets rough."

In London, Royal came down with the H3N2 virus that had caused a global epidemic, but he recovered in time for Christmas, with its round of parties and visits with friends like Max Gammon and Ken Wilson that reinvigorated Royal's enthusiasm for the British scene.

After a glamorous interlude filming in Verbier, marred only by Royal being jabbed in the chest with a ski pole, they traveled to Izeaux to meet with Julien Richard. Royal, now an important figure in the climbing-boot market, secured exclusive rights to distribute Galibier shoes in the largest western states.

Mountain Paraphernalia's cash flow remained excruciatingly slow, and Royal reconsidered his notion of opening a climbing school to supplement it. In the spring of 1969, he announced that he would address "a tremendous demand for knowledge of [Yosemite climbing] techniques." A small classified advertisement appeared in *Summit*, soliciting clients to attend Rockcraft. Royal was named as the director.

Rockcraft, said Royal, would be "the most extensive climbing school ever initiated in California . . . a more professional, more intensive and complete school than anything that's ever gone before." Royal added that despite these exacting standards, Rockcraft would happily enroll climbers of all abilities. The fee for a four-day session was $150. Food and lodging were included. The first session would begin on June 2, 1969. A second session was planned for June, with another two in late August and early September. Instruction was to be held at Lover's Leap near Lake Tahoe. Accommodations would be in the nearby hamlet of Strawberry.

In 1967, *Ascent* magazine had published a guide to Lover's Leap, but the attractions of nearby Yosemite limited its popularity. Royal chose it partly because it was uncrowded but also because it was in Eldorado National Forest, where he hoped to avoid the regulations that governed commercial activities in Yosemite.

Royal hired Camp 4 climbers as guides and instructors, and it was the first time most of them had made money from climbing. Climbing skills turned out to be an unreliable indicator of teaching talent, but there were many successes.

Dick Erb, one of Royal's first hires, became a senior guide, partly because of his climbing ability and partly because he had a knack for mediating between Royal and the other guides. Michael Covington, twenty-one, had made the fastest ascent of the *Nose,* and unlike most Camp 4 climbers, he was an experienced guide, although Royal found some of his climbing habits in need of reform.

"I was prone to being very vocal and spontaneous when climbing," said Covington. "Royal had asked me to try and be quieter because all the noise was drawing attention. . . . He also felt it was scaring the clients." Eventually, Royal told Covington he'd have to let him go if he didn't tone it down. Covington took the lesson to heart, and it changed the focus of his climbing life from then on. (Covington would go on to form the guiding company Fantasy Ridge Mountain Guides, which took clients all over the world.)

Royal gave his instructors Mountain Paraphernalia products and sent them clients he couldn't accommodate in Rockcraft. He even allowed instructors to send alternates if something prevented them from coming.

"I was staying in some drug den in Washington," said George Meyers, a twenty-one-year-old from New England who had caught the climbing bug and hitchhiked west. "Doug Robinson [a Rockcraft instructor and California climber] had broken his arm. He swung by to ask me to take his place. He didn't tell Royal, so I surprised him when I just showed up at his house. Royal was fine with it, though, and I stayed there and eventually instructed at a number of sessions." Dick Dorworth was also an early Rockcraft instructor. He recalled that although Royal may have been flexible when instructors sent replacements, he was a "control freak" when it came to how things were done. "Royal said, 'Here's how we do it,' and that was that," said Dorworth.

Liz and her friends usually made meals, and the Rockcraft group ate together. In the evenings, there was a campfire with red wine and conversation. Royal enjoyed the verbal sparring common around the fire pits of Camp 4, and expected his clients to enjoy it as well.

"Everyone was relaxing around a campfire," recalled Meyers, "and then Royal said, 'Well, we should legalize marijuana.' Nobody was thinking about that, and now they had to try to figure out the position they would take, and he would make the counterargument. Mostly folks weren't in the mood for an argument. TM Herbert said, 'Royal, we don't need to do this right now,' and he let it go."

Clients' skill levels, age, income, and goals varied. Egon and Johanna Marte, for example, were Midwest-based medical researchers with a respect for guides they had learned in their Austrian homeland. Fifteen-year-old Jim Williams was a starstruck climbing fanatic in the making from San Francisco.

Williams's parents drove him to Lover's Leap, where the scruffy, long-haired staff of Rockcraft awaited him. "My parents," Williams recalled, "looked at these people and thought, 'Oh, my god!' They were still flying by the seat of the pants. We got kicked out of the house we were staying in on the first night and had to get somewhere else to stay." Adult clients may have been annoyed, but Williams learned that hassles with the adult world were part of the climbing game. When the course ended, Williams hitchhiked to Yosemite and stayed there until his mother sent him bus money to return to San Francisco. He later forewent a college career to work with Schmitz, Bridwell, and Dorworth at Exum Mountain Guides in the Tetons, and eventually became Covington's chief guide in Alaska.

Despite full bookings and satisfied clients, Rockcraft failed to generate a profit. Royal paid the instructors $150 (about $1,100 in 2022 US dollars) per five-day session and provided them with room and board. He paid Liz, who cooked and looked after administrative details, the same amount. He had planned on paying himself $250 a session, but took no pay for a session and a half to reduce costs. By season's end, although all the sessions had been filled, Rockcraft was $400 in the red.

Some climbers were pessimistic about the school's future. "Opinion here," wrote Roper, now the editor of Steck's *Ascent* magazine in Berkeley, "says that your school is doomed. I agree, and will be surprised if in five years there is still a school. Poor location, limited clientele, too much money for such specialized training (that is, too much money for the probably poor type of person you hope to attract). Anyway, good luck, dad. We'll all watch with smirking interest." Despite his skepticism, however, Roper, like many Valley climbers, eventually worked for Rockcraft.

· · · · ·

In the late 1960s, a new group of young climbers were establishing themselves in the Valley. "Attitudes toward El Capitan will never be the same again," Royal wrote after Jim Madsen and Kim Schmitz set a speed record on the *Dihedral Wall*. Don Lauria, Dennis Hennek, and Galen Rowell began to repeat the hardest big walls. While El Capitan became a speed-climbing objective, Ken Boche, Jeff Foote, Joe McKeown, and Tom Higgins all pushed free-climbing standards.

As Royal approached thirty-five, he began for the first time to achieve, and more importantly, accept, a kind of eminence that did not require him to be the one creating the latest hard routes. Carlton Fuller invited Royal and Liz to stay with him in Boston and speak to the Harvard Mountaineering Club. Royal was the headline speaker at the annual meeting of the AAC in Philadelphia. He also became the first rock climber to advise high-level government in Washington when mountaineer and Secretary of the Interior Stewart Udall invited him to speak to his department. Royal wrote Beulah from Chicago and told her that Liz, who accompanied him, "was doing very well and is very popular with everyone in the east."

Royal decided that it was time to make the leap from writing articles to authoring a book. In 1969, he produced an outline for a volume on Yosemite climbing with insights into the main players, techniques, and philosophies. He approached one of the only climbers he knew with book publishing experience, James McAvoy III, whose personal letterhead described him as a "Consulting Political Sociologist."

In late November, acting informally as Royal's agent, McAvoy arranged a party at his home and invited Grant Barnes, the sociology editor for the University of California's publishing division. The party was a disaster. McAvoy brought up the size of Royal's advance right away. Barnes, who had assumed the event was a chance to meet Royal informally, tried to make light of the request. McAvoy threw what Barnes described as a "tantrum" and accused Barnes of being afraid of the subversive implications of Royal's book. Barnes left the party.

A few days later, Barnes asked Royal to send the outline and visit him, without McAvoy as a middleman. After reading the outline, Barnes suggested that Royal write the first two chapters, a standard practice in nonfiction publishing, and submit them to a contact of his at Harper and Row. Instead, Royal asked Carlton Fuller for help.

Fuller passed the outline on to James Ramsey Ullman, now a writer of national stature, with several novels and a play that had won a Pulitzer Prize. Ullman commended the project to his publisher at Doubleday, Stewart Richardson, who also asked to see a couple of chapters and asked Royal if he had any idea "how to sell copies in any quantity."

Royal, once again, failed to produce the requested excerpt. Ullman had promised to follow up with other publishers if Doubleday did not work out, but he was on an extended sabbatical. After he returned, he was diagnosed with an aggressive cancer and he died in June of the next year. Bereft of his boyhood literary hero's assistance, Royal gave up on the book idea.

If Royal had signed with a major publisher, his book would have made him America's first nationally famous climber and afforded him opportunities to teach the American public about climbing, elevate its status, and battle sensationalism. A rare surviving snippet from the manuscript gives a tantalizing glimpse of a great American mountaineering book that was never to be. The climbers of Camp 4, wrote Royal to Roper, were "burning mad, unsocial and antisocial." One of the greatest climbing dramas of the age was about to bear out this observation.

9
What Is Acceptable
and What Is Not

BY THE SPRING OF 1969, all of the major Yosemite walls had been climbed at least once, in most cases by Royal. Some thought that the remaining big walls lacked enough cracks to justify new routes. Royal, despite discovering only blank rock on *Tis-sa-ack*, remained curious about whether these walls could be climbed with a tolerable number of bolts at all.

The unclimbed sections of shorter walls offered a less committing laboratory than El Capitan for this next step in technical climbing. The *Prow*, a buttress that divided the south and east faces of Washington Column, was an attractive and accessible example. Its upper dihedrals could clearly be climbed, but the cracks separated by blank sections on the smooth lower part looked too shallow for pitons. In the *AAJ*, Royal would call it "his latest pipe-dream."

With Covington, Royal climbed 300 feet to a bivouac on what they named Anchorage Ledge, continuing the nautical theme. Covington spent much of the next day leading a difficult aid pitch marred, in his opinion, by a large number of bolts. Royal wrote that it seemed like "someone had placed a bomb in Cuv's mind, and after he had placed 11 bolts late the second day, it went off." The young Covington was quite keen to do a big route with Royal, especially since Royal worried he might not have much time left for hard climbing due to encroaching arthritis. But, as they tried to find their way up the largely crackless lower wall, Covington wasn't sure this was the climb. "I was concerned we might be setting a precedent with what looked to be about 200 feet [of bolting] before the climb could really begin," he said; the more Covington drilled, the more he lost heart for the endeavor. "[Royal] offered to take over the lead, and started up only to discover he couldn't reach between my bolts and decided we needed more bolts between the ones I had placed," said Covington. "Royal came back to the belay ledge and we talked some more."

While Royal and Covington discussed what to do next, Roper, Denny, and some friends scrambled up a route below to watch them.

"We saw a serious discussion between Royal Robbins and Mike Covington," wrote Roper. "Then, quick as a flash, Covington tied all three of their ropes together, and jumped into rappel." Covington became the first partner to leave Royal alone on a wall, but Royal wasn't stymied. Royal shouted down to Steve to jumar up and join him, but the route looked difficult and frightening, with Covington's retreat seeming to confirm that it might even prove impossible or at the very least require a distasteful amount of bolting. Roper yelled his response up, "No, no, no, not me, man. No, no, Roy boy!"

"About that time, Glen Denny arrived to take some pictures," recalled Covington, "and I was able to convince him to take my place. So, it worked out for the best. They did the climb and it has become a classic."

Denny nicknamed Royal "the White-Hatted Wall Pecker (*Robbinsis Royalis indefatigabilis*)" and marvelled at his use of hooks and RURPs on what Royal called "the smoothest wall he'd ever been on." Although they used thirty-eight bolts, the same number as on the much longer *North America Wall*, Royal was proud of the climb. He hoped that similarly climbable rock lay beyond his bolt ladder on *Tis-sa-ack*.

Covington, however, had his doubts about whether Royal had made the right choices on the *Prow*. Before the climb, Covington had learned about Royal's arthritis; Royal's sense that he had a limited number of climbs left may have led him to complete his projects quickly and to compromise his publicized views about bolting. He might also have been swayed by the desire to add to his legacy of repeatable routes. The

Regular Northwest Face of Half Dome and the *Salathé Wall* were repeated often, but Royal's dangerous routes like *Arches Direct* and the North Face of Higher Cathedral Spire were ignored. He told Covington he wanted the *Prow* to be accessible.

Other climbers were quick to notice that Royal had strayed from the tenets they had inherited from him. After the *Prow*, TM Herbert, one of Royal's oldest climbing friends, warned him that the *Prow* might open the door for more bolt-intensive walls. According to Roper, some thought Royal was "going downhill." It was an oversimplification, but Royal was certainly at a turning point.

In August 1969, after a drunken fight at Jenny Lake in the Tetons, Gary Hemming shot himself. He had fallen out of love with France, alpinism, and fame, and drifted through the American West, haunted by his alcohol dependency and mental health problems.

In his obituary in *Mountain*, Royal called Hemming's death a tragedy and praised his "unswerving loyalty" and "intensity." "One even feels a bit angry," he wrote, "for in taking his own life, he has taken something from us too."

That summer, Royal faced Hemming's suicide, potentially career-ending arthritis, the first generation of climbers to surpass him, the realization that Yosemite offered no more walls that could be done with a handful of bolts, and the unexpected discovery that he was willing to compromise on climbing style. His writing reflected this new consciousness of the complexities of life.

He assumed the point of view of his partners to critique his own behavior. "Call me Glen Denny," he wrote in his report on the *Prow* in the *AAJ*, borrowing the first line of his beloved *Moby Dick*. He philosophized about the state of humanity: "A man trapped in the anonymity of the crowds," he wrote, "looks upward for a way out and sees in the mountains a way of separating his individuality from the mass."

His comments echoed the darkening mood in America in 1969. A few days before the first ascent of the *Prow*, police had stormed the People's Park in Berkeley and shot peaceful protestors. The Tate-LaBianca murder trials filled the front pages of the newspapers. The Hells Angels, who had been security at The North Face store opening in 1967, killed an audience member at the Altamont Free Concert. News from the war in Vietnam continued to worsen. Idealism of any kind was getting a bad rap.

· · · · ·

In the summer of 1969, Royal took a break from Yosemite and returned to what he called his "alpine hang-up." In 1967, American alpinist David Roberts had deemed Alaska's Cathedral Spires (also known as the Kichatna Spires) "North America's closest equivalent to the towers of Patagonia." Royal had dreamed about Patagonia, but he couldn't afford to be away from his new business long enough for a South American expedition. Alaska, however, could be managed in a month-long road trip, and his friends Charlie Raymond and Joe Fitschen were eager to come along.

"Royal and I sorted climbing equipment in the backyard," wrote Fitschen. "It seemed odd to be considering ice screws. Have another beer and check the check-list that began: 90 pitons, 60 carabiners, 6 ropes. How many ice screws would we need, implements that I had never used?"

Royal's tendency to philosophize found a fertile subject in alpinism. "We read of astonishing Japanese successes in the mountains and dismiss them," he wrote in an *AAJ* article, "subconsciously perhaps, as done by Japanese. After all, they 'climb in a more heroic myth than do Americans.'" Royal was impressed by the almost yearly Japanese successes on 7,000-plus-meter Himalayan peaks throughout the 1960s. He paints a less epic portrait of his Cathedral Spire party: "scions of the Yosemite-Sierra Mother Earth, offspring of sun-worshippers," and asks, "Could we do our thing in the rain and snows and glaciers and cold and harsh conditions of the Alaskan mountainscape?"

The reality of an Alaskan expedition was less intellectual. "We stagger back to camp drenched by a continuing downpour," wrote Royal, "all illusions of the accessibility of summits ripped from our minds. We have been out 41 hours with only one of rest, attempting North Triple Peak, an 8,400-foot tower standing at the head of the Tatina Glacier. Beset by wind and drizzle . . . we fought our way up difficult rock with freezing fingers to arrive on a fog-shrouded hump of snow we thought was the summit. When the fog cleared we could see the true summit apparently 150 feet higher and 400 feet away, but by then it was too late, for snow was falling heavily and we were fatigued. We fought our way to a lower level, where the snow changed to a very cold rain, and thence hour after hour cautiously down in the demoralizing weather to our storm-flattened camp."

During their three weeks of rain and snow punctuated by short breaks of good weather, they retreated a pitch below the summit of Middle Triple Peak but made the first ascents of South Triple Peak, which they named Mount Sasquatch, a peak they called Mount Nevermore, and another they named Mount Jeffers.

"Robinson Jeffers," wrote Fitschen, "was a Californian, as was our group. And he preferred hawks to people and built a stone house. Nevermore was named after the raven who frequented our dump site even in the severest of storms. I am not sure that we ever saw him, though. And Sasquatch was suggested by my father-in-law, an art historian and student of Northwest Indian lore. We were looking for something both formidable and mysterious."

Royal returned in time for his late summer Rockcraft session, but had gained a competitor. The Curry Company, inspired by the apparent success of Rockcraft, overcame their aversion to climbing and opened the Yosemite School of Mountaineering. For tourists too timid to climb, they sold T-shirts printed with the school motto: "Go Climb a Rock." Fitschen, who later taught at the school, speculated that the T-shirts were more profitable than the school itself.

Jim McCarthy accused the Curry Company of trying to commercialize climbing; Royal thought it was a soulless cash grab. The moral distinction between the two enterprises was lost on a number of climbers, however, and even the most idealistic of Valley climbers taught at the Yosemite School on occasion.

A few days after the end of the autumn Rockcraft session, Royal received a letter from the director of the Eldorado National Forest, banning him from holding courses at Lover's Leap, or, for that matter, anywhere on National Forest Service lands.

Royal had felt bossed around by the park service ever since his first visits to Yosemite. He had scoffed at the army's authoritarian culture as unnecessary. Now, like the hero of one of Royal's favorite films, *The Secret of Santa Vittoria*, whose village's wine production is requisitioned by the

Nazis, Royal felt like a little guy whose grassroots enterprise was threatened by unfeeling officials. Despite his nascent libertarian inklings, he had no choice but to search for a new venue for the next year.

In September, Royal made a second attempt on *Tis-sa-ack*. Pratt, anticipating even more bolting, had given up. His absence was a relief for Royal, who hoped to find flakes and thin cracks high on the wall, but was prepared to drill even more if necessary.

Frost was on his way to join British climber Chris Bonington's expedition to the South Face of Annapurna. Chouinard had more or less moved on from Yosemite altogether. Fitschen was teaching English in Susanville, where one of his students would be state prisoner Royal Slagle, Royal's old childhood friend. Dennis Hennek, Royal's closest friend amongst the young Camp 4 climbers, was injured. For once, Royal found himself in Yosemite with only casual acquaintances and strangers to climb with. He asked Don Peterson, a young climber from Colorado who had made a fast ascent of the *Dihedral Wall*, to join him on *Tis-sa-ack*.

Royal submitted an account of *Tis-sa-ack* to the 1970 *AAJ* and *Ascent*, writing in both his own and Peterson's first-person points of view. Using dialogue creation, irony, and story development, he created a unique and original piece that would likely have cost him his friendship with Peterson if it had survived the climb. The piece was published the same year as David Roberts's account of a strained expedition, *Deborah: A Wilderness Narrative*, and both works contributed to a more psychologically realistic American climbing literature.

"I didn't like [Royal's] assumption of superiority," wrote Royal's Peterson. "When we got to the base of the wall he sent me to fetch water. I just don't buy that crap." Peterson brags about the brilliance of his piton placements, which Royal dismisses as "strange maneuver[s]." Royal, on the other hand, "bragged about" the bolt ladder he had placed on his previous attempt, a symbol of his hypocrisy or change of heart, depending on the reader's point of view. Royal admitted that he climbed slowly, placed a lot of bolts, and made Peterson worry that they wouldn't make it. He was shocked by Peterson's arrogance and "dark passions bubbling to the surface." He repressed the urge to shout, "Fuck you, Peterson." The thin cracks and skyhook flakes Royal had encountered on the *Prow* did not appear, and there was even more bolting than he had expected.

Peterson was so impatient to get off the wall that he left all the pitons in the last pitch.

In Denny's summit photograph, Royal and Peterson look angry and uncomfortable. Royal had fallen out with a partner mid-climb for the first time, and when he had dreamed of writing "his initials on the wall forever," it had not been with the 110 bolts left on the face.

But when TM Herbert, who had already been troubled by the bolting on the *Prow*, asked Royal if *Tis-sa-ack* had been worth even more bolts and the possible accusations of hypocrisy, Royal—though he obviously had qualms—didn't apologize. He hadn't even considered giving up the route once he saw how many bolts it would take.

It would be easy, on the one hand, to conclude that like Captain Ahab from his beloved *Moby Dick*, Royal had lost all sense of proportion in the pursuit of his object of desire. On the other hand, you could argue that Royal, who had been an active participant in climbing philosophy in letters and actions, had only temporarily detached from the literal form of his earlier arguments. His moral vision of climbing survived the disintegrating effect of this flirtation with the forbidden, the ethically transgressive. Any argument has two sides, and, for better or worse, although he'd pointed the way toward the next generation of Yosemite big walls, where—as on *Tis-sa-ack*—the cracks would be fewer and farther between, Royal had also explored the outer limits of his own ideals.

As the first autumn snows fell on Half Dome, Royal and Liz began a short lecture and climbing tour in Colorado. Royal added *Tis-sa-ack* to the program, "The Cathedral spires and a wall climb in Yosemite." Attendees at the first lecture, held in a high school auditorium in Colorado Springs, said Royal limited himself to the technical details of the *Tis-sa-ack* climb, keeping the conflicts he described in his *AAJ* article to himself for now.

After the presentation, Royal and Liz met Pratt, Roper, and Roper's wife, Jani, in Moab, Utah. Pratt, Royal, and Roper made an early climb of the 700-foot spire of the Titan in the Fisher Towers and were caught in a rainstorm on the descent. "In the muddy parking lot after the Titan climb," recalled Roper, "the Robbinses forgot that the kitten they had brought along was outside and they ran over the poor thing, but the deep mud saved it. We made a quick run with a howling kitten to a vet in Moab, who said she was fine, but 'she's going to be pretty sore tomorrow.'"

A three-hour, afternoon ascent of the 1,000-foot volcanic plug of Agathlan in Arizona and the second ascent of the 150-foot-high Dark Angel spire in Arizona's Arches National Monument rounded out Royal's single most prolific desert-climbing season.

· · · · ·

Liz and Royal celebrated Christmas and saw in the 1970s in London with John Cleare, Max Gammon, and other friends. Ken Wilson registered his displeasure with *Tis-sa-ack*, which he said compromised Royal's reputation, but Royal appeared indifferent. He knew Wilson was somewhat behind the times. In Yosemite, things were changing quickly and all eyes were no longer on Royal.

The National Park Service had finally tired of the squalid conditions and scofflaw atmosphere of Camp 4. They renamed it Sunnyside Campground. The higher part of the campsite preferred by climbers was closed for environmental regeneration. Royal decried the changes to the "laissez-faire camping" he had known since his first visit, although he blamed "population growth, increased leisure, and four-wheeled 'campers,'"—not climbers—for the era-ending changes, wrote Roper.

The latest wave of climbing talent knew Royal only by reputation; they were impressed but not starstruck. Stanford students Chuck Kroger and Scott Davis made the first ascent of the *Heart Route* on El Capitan in March 1970 without fixed ropes and just a handful of bolts. Kroger combed his hair before topping out—"so Royal, and everyone else on the summit would like me," he reported in the new, Colorado-based *Climbing* magazine. "Then I stepped onto level ground. No one in sight." In climbing, a new negativity about society and its comforts made the summit entourages and champagne picnics of Royal's generation seem sybaritic and self-important. "After the *Heart Route*," wrote Kroger, "we bent under the knowledge that our gods had crashed. Now we were adults without heroes in a large and unfriendly world."

Notable visitors to Yosemite were often less up to date before they arrived, and still hoped to climb with Royal rather than the new generation. In April, Royal climbed the *Steck-Salathé* with twenty-eight-year-old British climber Doug Scott, who would later become one of the world's most successful big wall and Himalayan climbers. Scott, however, ended up being more impressed by Jim Bridwell, then twenty-six.

Bridwell had climbed with Sacherer and most of the climbers from Royal's generation. He had done some big walls and was also one of the best crack climbers in the Valley. With his long hair and handlebar moustache, he looked like a roadie for a rock band. His girlfriend, Beverly Johnson, was the strongest woman climber in Yosemite. In May 1970, Royal, Bridwell, and Kim Schmitz made the first ascent of *Vain Hope*, a 1,500-foot route near Ribbon Falls, on the El Capitan side of Yosemite Valley. On the wall, Royal unwittingly taught Bridwell, who would become the central figure in the upcoming generation, a lesson in charisma.

"I thought it'd be fun doing the route with three people," recalled Bridwell. "Because you'd have someone to talk to at the belays. But when Royal and I were at a belay, he would just stoically stare off across the Valley and never say anything . . . that was him. He had a kind of imposing personality—kind of aristocratic, above reproach."

"I watched Bridwell take on the role of leader from Royal and develop the style of the '70s community," said Yosemite climber Roger Breedlove, "which is probably his most significant achievement, since almost all of the routes done in that time link directly to his efforts to create and support a very diverse community." After *Vain Hope*, Royal referred to Bridwell as the leading figure of the new generation.

Royal's next project was to be the Valley's first solo first ascent of a Yosemite grade V. *In Cold Blood*, a 1,000-foot route on the left side of the north face of Sentinel Rock, took him three days. His report acknowledged changes in the scene. "The renowned American authority on mountaineering, Curtis W. Casewit," Royal wrote in the *AAJ*, "says, 'Solo climbing is insanity.' And Mr. Casewit, of course, is an honorable man. I love to read such fatuous remarks, coming as they invariably do, from the ignorant. It brings back the good old days when climbers were pariahs, when climbing was not 'in,' when there was no room in the game for parasites of

Mr. Casewit's stamp. But now the enemy is within the gates. I confess to lunacy according to Mr. Casewit's ah . . . 'standards.'"

Young climbers didn't get the allusions to Shakespeare's *Julius Caesar* and the satire at the expense of mid-century East Coast mountaineering authorities. They didn't read the *AAJ*.

In a summer when standards were improving in every branch of Yosemite climbing, Royal remained active as he drifted to the margins of Yosemite climbing. He guided his Austrian-American clients, Egon and Johanne Marte, up *In Cold Blood* for the route's second ascent. Royal and Dick Dorworth climbed *Arcturus*, Royal's last new route on Half Dome. "He was displeased with how I had backed up an anchor," recalled Dorworth. "He never said why he wanted something changed, though; he just changed it without getting pissed off. Inside he got really pissed off, but on the outside, no."

Neither *In Cold Blood* nor *Arcturus* became popular, and neither were great challenges for Royal. He continued to climb new routes, but they added little to his legacy. His modest reports seemed to reflect his sense that his earlier successes on El Capitan and Half Dome were too monumental to equal.

Royal's skills remained, however, even as he ran out of projects. Friends were still impressed by his free climbing and his cool head, but in Yosemite, Royal became less comfortable being identified as a leader in a scene he no longer dominated.

"It was also almost impossible for Royal to just show up and climb anywhere without having to play the celebrity," Breedlove recalled. "I remember we were with a group [including Royal] in the Valley and wanted to go to the lodge. We chose the old Mountain Room Bar because it was dark and no one could see who was there."

In the autumn of 1969, Royal had run into Harding, who was with Colorado climber Dean Caldwell, for the first time in a year. "They were getting into Harding's sports car and greeted him [Royal speaks of himself in third person] perfunctorily. There was something in their demeanor, especially Harding's, that struck him as unusual—a certain sense of purpose seemed implied in their smiles and movements, and in Harding's flashing eyes, which gleamed with an inner knowledge."

While Royal had been wrapping up an illustrious career, Harding was still hoping to crown his own with the *Wall of the Early Morning Light*, aka the *Dawn Wall*, right of the *Nose*. The 3,000-foot, slightly overhanging wall was one of the most imposing and unbroken stretches of rock on El Capitan.

Another party had attempted the wall by a crack system that avoided the blank lower section of the wall, but on October 23, 1970, Harding and Caldwell set off straight up the blank rock, bearing for dihedrals high on the face. Drilling hundreds of bolt holes made for slow climbing. Updates from Harding's friends intrigued news editors, who offered daily reports on the lonely little team crawling up the *Dawn Wall*. Before the climb was even completed, reporters had declared it the hardest route on El Capitan.

Some were less impressed. After Harding and Caldwell had been on the wall for two weeks, park rangers decided, with no evidence, that the climbers had become mentally unhinged. Others suggested that they were running out of food. Jim Bridwell, Beverly Johnson, and TM Herbert prepared a rescue. Royal, who was on a lecture tour in the Midwest, turned down their request to come home and join the party.

Harding and Caldwell, tipped off by a bullhorn message from a friend, wrote, "A rescue is unwarranted, unwanted, and will not be accepted" on toilet paper and threw it off the wall in an empty tin. Newspapers touted their refusal as an act of heroism. The rescue was called off.

Royal made extensive notes on the climb and wrote a long, unpublished piece about it in the third person. "And how [the rescuers] must have hated the conquerors of a route some of them had tried and rejected as artificial," Royal wrote, "and being treated by the public as heroes as well! . . . They were mostly, if not totally, composed of men (and a woman) who were opposed to the climb and the way it was being done. They doubtless would have been happy to have hauled the conquerors off. They would have felt righteous. Their values would have been vindicated. It must have been exasperating for them to endure the ant-like but inexorable progress of the indomitable Harding and the neophyte to Yosemite big walls, Caldwell."

A rope guardrail kept back the throng of reporters on the day the climbers reached the rim. A couple of media outlets described Harding's previous rescue by "Royal Bobbins." The *San Francisco Chronicle* called the climb "a heroic achievement in these days when there is precious little adventure left to be had."

Royal, however, who watched the summit event on a motel-room television in Chicago, had reservations. Harding had drilled 330 holes on the *Dawn Wall*, a startling increase in the use of the drill on El Capitan. TM Herbert wrote that he "felt like screaming, 'But they bolted the damn thing and then they sold it to millions on television.'" For his part, Royal had trouble separating his envy and anger at their success from a rational assessment: "His envy was of things he considered more real: of Caldwell's aplomb facing the television cameras on the summit, and of the fact that whatever else might be said, they had stayed on a rock wall almost twice as long as anyone ever had," Royal wrote.

Royal's first public impulse was to bury his darker emotions and defend Harding. In *Summit* in December 1970—less than a month after the first ascent—Royal conceded that Harding had "rejected an easier line to the left," which would have required as many as one hundred fewer drilled holes. But Royal suggested it was "good to have a man around who doesn't give a damn about what the establishment thinks," and, "although this climb may not have been done exactly to our taste, and although we might have fretful little criticisms that envy always produces, we can better spend our time than ripping or tearing, spend it better than denigrating the accomplishments of others."

Harding's more decided opponents were unconvinced. "Can we afford to stand aside and watch our sport being systematically denuded of its risk, character and unpredictability?" frothed Ken Wilson in London. "That this destruction is perpetrated by one who has been lauded as a 'crusty individualist' does not lessen the threat one iota."

A letter from photographer and Sierra Club luminary Ansel Adams first published in the *San Francisco Chronicle* in early December was widely reprinted. Adams described the *Dawn Wall* as a "super-spectacular engineering feat." Although Adams had built his career on publicizing Yosemite, he decried the attention Harding had garnered as "not related to the qualities of Yosemite and the national scene, and I feel that such publicity relates negatively on the National Park Service ideal, the ideals and aims of the Sierra Club and the spirit of mountaineering itself."

When Royal got back to California, he visited Jim Bridwell and Kim Schmitz. Bridwell had rappelled the top few pitches of the *Dawn Wall* and observed bolts placed right next to piton cracks. Royal asked Bridwell if he planned to chop the bolts, but Bridwell suggested that Royal should do it. Royal suggested climbing the route, then chopping only if it was overbolted.

The upcoming release of Royal's book *Basic Rockcraft* overshadowed these deliberations. Predictably, perhaps, the seventy-page paperback had the same number of pages on "Ethics and Style" as it did on the use of pitons and nuts.

"A climb is a work of art," Royal wrote, "a creation of the men who made the first ascent. To make it more difficult by chopping bolts is to insult those who put it up and to deprive others of the joy of repeating the route as the first party did it. It is like taking anothers [sic] painting or poem and 'improving' it. Better to paint our own pictures and write our own poems."

For Royal, however, the *Dawn Wall* was an "outrage," an exception to the rule of respecting first ascents, because it ignored the "mores" of an area. The authors of such outrages were to blame for the removal of their hardware, while those who erased the bolts merely acted on behalf of their communities.

And yet, he wrote, "He was inclined to defend Harding, for although he was an enemy, he was a friend too, and although he hardly shared Harding's sense of climbing ethics, he had great respect for Harding's indomitable individuality. Harding stood alone against the crowd." He surprised many Valley regulars by praising Harding's individuality in the article in *Summit*.

Royal knew that the nuances of his actions and his relationship with Harding would be lost on many climbers. "Obviously," he wrote after he bought two cold chisels for the job of erasing the *Dawn Wall*, "I would have a lot of explaining to do." By January 1971, however, Royal had resolved to chop the climb. Unseasonably fine weather was forecast, and outside of peak season, the Park Service, the press, and climbers were less likely to notice immediately. Wrote Royal, "Whatever others might think, he felt right inside himself about what he was doing. So, he could face the possibility that his action might make him a villain in the eyes of many, that the sale of shoes which he designed and the sign-ups for his climbing school which were based partly upon respect for his name might diminish." Royal also admitted that he was influenced by other climbers who had decided against the route and looked to him to do something about it. "He would be a hero to these elements," Royal wrote, without much enthusiasm.

· · · · ·

Through the Valley grapevine, Royal had heard that experienced Yosemite climber Don Lauria was interested in doing the route and that he was "pro-bolt removal." At the end of January 1971, wrote Lauria, "I drove to Yosemite, met Royal, sorted hardware, and Royal showed me the two cold chisels he had purchased specifically for the bolt chopping. How extravagant I thought. I still hadn't caught on."

"I led the first pitch, using all the bolts for aid," wrote Lauria. "Royal followed and began chopping the first bolt. 'Wow!' I thought to myself, 'I used that bolt. How come he's chopping it? Oh I guess he figures he could have made that move free.' He began to chop the second bolt. 'Hey Royal, I used those bolts for aid,' I yelled. 'Sure you did, but chopping bolts is the name of the game—all of the bolts.' Now I got it, but should I do it? Hell yes!"

They chopped all of the rivets and bolts in the first three pitches, but despite the self-assurance he displayed to Lauria, Royal wrote that "he couldn't repress the guilt . . . he was smashing someone's work." Even recalling the times Harding had embarrassed him with his drunken sarcasm didn't dispel the guilt.

As they climbed higher, Harding's achievement appeared more masterful, despite the unnecessary bolts. In one place, Royal couldn't even make a piton stick in one of the cracks, and reached past it by hooking a rivet with a wired nut.

That night, in his hammock, Royal changed his mind.

"The whole thing," he wrote, "the first ascent, the hullaballoo, the carping afterward, and now their effort—it was all rotten. It was a bad scene."

Harding was to blame for starting the process, but his opponents, including Royal and Lauria, had made it worse. Royal decided to leave the bolts in place on the upper half of the route. For two more days they climbed, passing an overhang that would have made retreat difficult. Royal fretted about "a certain ironic and Olympic justice descending upon them. One shouldn't climb for the wrong reasons. And if there was ever a wrong reason, this was it."

As Chouinard had predicted, the great corner that Harding had been aiming for was devoid of cracks. Harding had climbed most of it with rivets. The last detail that Royal recorded in his unpublished account was an empty wine bottle on the ledge atop the corner, a poignant symbol of the state of his relationship with Harding.

Ten pitches later, Royal and Lauria were on top. They had taken five and a half days, a fast time for the second ascent of a hard El Capitan climb, but no well-wishers waited to congratulate them.

Caldwell and Harding were guests of honor at a Chicago trade show when a journalist told them that the *Dawn Wall* had been chopped. "At the time," wrote Harding, "I was pretty much at a loss to account for such drastic action. I could only assume that it was more of the evangelistic work that R.R. seems to feel called upon to indulge in—sort of an alpine Carrie Nation (substitution of hammer and chisel for a hatchet and expansion bolts for whiskey bottles!)." Yet Harding seemed unfazed, saying that if Royal wanted to go to all the trouble to chop the bolts, it was fine with him.

Ken Wilson praised Royal for "putting his reputation on the line," but also gave him a taste of being at the receiving end of his uncompromising rhetoric when he said that *Tis-sa-ack* was "just a scaled-down version of the *Dawn Wall." Mountain* magazine implied that *Tis-sa-ack* should be chopped as well. Herbert wrote that what he called "the erasure" was "one of the most important events I have witnessed during my years of climbing."

At first, Royal hid his inner conflicts and said that he would rather sacrifice some routes on the altar of style than buck Yosemite tradition. To the disappointment of Herbert and others who had urged him on, however, Royal soon became more ambivalent. In an interview with Allen

Steck, Royal said, "No, I wouldn't do the same thing again. I don't know what I'd do. I guess I'd either climb the route without interfering with it or not climb it at all."

When Rowell, Steck, and others probed Royal about the climb, he could be defensive. "Here was a route with 330 bolts," he wrote, "it had been forced up a very unnatural line, merely to get another route on El Capitan and bring credit to the people who climbed it . . . a distinction between what is acceptable and what is not acceptable had to be made, [and] this was the time to make it."

Ken Wilson, however, accused Royal of inconsistency. "[Your] writing in *Summit* [praising Harding, but not the *Wall of the Early Morning Light*] and [your] wiping the route do appear contradictory—any comments?" he wrote Royal. Wilson was concerned that Royal had changed his mind about publishing an interview he had done with him after the *Dawn Wall*. "I must confess to getting a bit anxious about all this Royal—I hope you haven't gone cool on the idea cos I reckon it's a really good interview."

The *Dawn Wall* incident seemed to have settled little. The protagonists didn't make sweeping exits on opposite sides of the Yosemite stage as enemies. Harding returned to Camp 4, not as a pariah, but as a respected climber and friend. Days after the climb, he and TM Herbert spoke for hours at the campfire.

Surveying Camp 4 on an evening in 1971, Harding called the scene "conducive to mending the soul. It's good to be in such fine company . . . Al Steck and Steve Roper sitting at a table playing checkers, mind and vision too dim to cope with the rigors of chess. . . . Chuck Pratt whiling away the hours conducting some imaginary symphony orchestra."

Royal and Lauria remained friends with Harding.

Rowell, one of Harding's most regular climbing partners, warned that overbolting and route chopping had brought Yosemite's great era to an end. "The creaking door has suddenly closed on the Golden Age of Yosemite," Rowell wrote, "the echo of a rhythmical [drill] tapping is sealing the door for eternity."

Royal believed that John Salathé and Ax Nelson had kicked off the Golden Age with the first ascent of the *Lost Arrow Chimney*, in 1947. For him, the first ascent of the *North America Wall* offered a possible conclusion, as did the *Dawn Wall* saga.

Chouinard predicted a next act for Yosemite climbing when its climbers took their skills to alpine walls. Royal, however, believed that Yosemite climbing, and especially free climbing, had a long future and that few climbers would leave the Valley to make good on Chouinard's chilly and dangerous prediction.

The Golden Age drew to an end not so much on the walls, but in the hearts of those who had climbed them. "We'd spent ten years fucking around," Roper wrote Chouinard, "maybe that was enough. And we didn't like the new group of climbers—even while respecting their talent. Too many people for one thing. They didn't love the mountains, etc., etc."

That summer—1971—Royal rarely visited Yosemite. In May, at the Buttermilk Boulders on the East Side of the Sierra, he frightened Roper by free soloing a number of new routes and, in nearby Pine Creek Canyon, leading the vertical offwidth of *Pratt's Crack*. "RR leads the two pitches," wrote Roper in his notes, "and I can barely follow." In August, with Roper and Covington, Royal made an early repeat of *D7* on Colorado's Diamond. He wrapped up the season on the conglomerate towers of Pinnacles National Monument, where he made a rare ascent of John Salathé's unprotected 1946 route, *The Hand*.

None of these climbs added much to Royal's legacy. There was a playfulness about his climbing now that hadn't been there since the mid-1950s. He seemed, at last, to have been climbing for the sheer fun of it. He had weathered Harding's last and greatest challenge. He no longer had one eye on the next big Yosemite wall.

There were, however, other challenges in life, and a few weeks after the *Dawn Wall* ascent, Royal received news from Liz that disoriented him in a way Harding never could have: she was pregnant.

10

There Is Only One Eminence

"I CAN'T PROMISE THAT I will be a good father," Royal told Liz. He shared the sentiment with his friends, who responded that his biggest fear was the loss of his freedom to climb. His life history and his journals portray a more painful reality. In his journals, he conjured the main specters of his troubled childhood, the two father figures who had broken under the weight of parental responsibility. He mused on the disorienting experience of the child born during his first marriage. The physical act of birth also terrified Royal.

"I was dragged screaming from the warm, tight security of my mother's womb into the bright lights of the operating room," he wrote in an unpublished essay, in an apparent attempt to recreate the events of his own birth. "They handled me. The nurse and the doctor both passed their hands over my body, cleansing me of the slime which had accompanied my appearance. It was a shocking and revolting scene from which I have never recovered."

Royal actually came into the world in his mother's bedroom, and there was nothing clinical about the Appalachian midwives in attendance. His allusions to slime, nakedness, vulnerability, the loss of the mother as shelter, and the unwanted touch of strangers might have been symptoms of what later became classified as tokophobia, a fear of the act of birth that also manifests in depression and social withdrawal. Some psychologists popular in the day, notably Alfred Adler, framed fatherhood as a mighty burden, and for Royal, it was.

It wouldn't be the first newborn in Royal's circle—the Herberts' son, Thomas, had been born in 1969; the Fitschens' daughter, Lorca, in 1970. Nonetheless, Royal's sense of disorientation was exacerbated by his friends' skepticism about his prospects as a father. One Camp 4 wag gave Royal two pages of cartoons forecasting triplets and showing Royal throwing himself off El Capitan with a rock tied to his ankle.

Royal withdrew from Liz and reversed his recent retirement to cobble together two wild, new climbing goals: the first solo of a new route on El Capitan and the second ascent of Cerro Torre in Patagonia.

Both ideas had a whiff of improbability about them. Royal had his eye on the overhanging wall right of the *North America Wall*, which looked even harder and smoother than the *Dawn Wall*. The Cerro Torre trip was proposed by Chouinard, Tompkins, and Jack Tackle, all more experienced alpinists than Royal. Success would catapult Royal to the top of the world of alpinism, but most parties were turned back far from the summit by Patagonia's notorious high winds. "The weather down there is so terrible," he admitted to Beulah, "that it is very unlikely that we will come even close to success. We may not even come close to the mountain."

Royal began his 1971 climbing season in the Granite Dells, Arizona, with Rusty Baillie, now an outdoor education instructor in Prescott. They protected both their climbs, *Mecca* (5.9) and *Siege*, the area's first 5.10, with Peck Crackers chocks. It was the last time Royal boosted the standards of a climbing area by simply showing up and climbing.

Before Royal could attempt his El Capitan solo, Yosemite climbing standards took several rapid leaps forward. Bridwell and Schmitz made a spectacular first ascent near the West Buttress of El Capitan that May. The *Aquarian Wall* demanded the latest hard aid- and free-climbing skills in a committing big wall setting.

The scene Royal had once been part of no longer existed. Young climbers adopted Bridwell's hippie hairstyle and bandana, and infused free climbing with an ostentatious countercultural glamor that wasn't Royal's style. Free-climbing talent seemed to trump experience, even on big walls. Young climber Peter Haan soloed the *Salathé Wall* that summer, before he had ever even bivouacked on a climb. His report hinted that the big walls of Royal's generation weren't such a big deal.

"Neediness that brusquely races past the humble realities of rest places," wrote Haan in the *AAJ*, "large ledges, good protection and fun climbing" falsely amplified the difficulties of the *Salathé Wall*.

Thin-crack specialist Barry Bates, wide-crack expert Mark Klemens, and out-of-state climbers like Jim Donini and the East Coasters John Bragg, Steve Wunsch, and Henry Barber increased the free-climbing gap between Royal and themselves almost weekly. "From 1971 to 1972 some appalling new routes were conceived," wrote Bridwell in an article for *Mountain*, describing "esoteric exercises as well as unique boulder-ballet problems" that epitomized the best in Yosemite climbing. In the same article, Bridwell reported on a new system in which Tahquitz/Yosemite Decimal System grades from 5.10 upward would be further subdivided into four subgrades of a to d, marking an intensification of the focus on short, hard climbs.

Royal found the new generation obsessive in ways that contrasted with the easygoing nature of his own. He loved to eat and drink, and never trained. He referred to the young climbers as "yogurt-eating health faddists." As the new climbers pushed further into extreme free climbing, Royal dismissed some of their routes as impossible "unless you're Jim Bridwell or someone."

Royal seemed eccentric and haughty to young climbers. "I thought he was full of himself," wrote Dale Bard, who came to Yosemite from Los Angeles in the early 1970s, "and at the time he and another climber who I respected also, were running around and soloing easy routes in sneakers called Tretorns. I was not impressed, nor did I like the elevated way they considered themselves." Many of Royal's solos, including the 1,000-foot East Buttress of El Capitan, which he climbed in Tretorn sneakers, were not easy, but such was the perception.

Between 1970 and 1972, more first and first free ascents were made than at any other period in Yosemite's history, with Royal all but absent from the credits. "Climbing had moved on," said Roger Breedlove. "Bridwell had redirected himself [from big wall climbing] to free climbing to keep up with Klemens and Bates. I recall that Royal's response was to solo up and down the crack climbs at the base of El Cap in tennis shoes. The gap between Royal's natural pulling-back and the more pronounced change in direction within the new climbing community widened."

As soon as Liz went into labor, Royal's need to rise to a challenge outshone his inner anguish. "Royal was magnificent," said Liz. He timed her contractions and drove her to the hospital in the middle of the night. Royal, like most men of his generation, waited outside, safe from the events that he had obsessed about. On September 20, 1971, Tamara Shannon Robbins—the third generation of Robbinses to bear the name Shannon—was born. "Royal thinks she's beautiful," wrote Liz to Steve Roper. Royal brought Liz dinner with wine in her hospital bed every night. Four days later, the exhausted and bewildered new family returned to Durant Street. Climbing friends, once again, had left it in a mess.

In early October, Royal attempted his new route on El Capitan. The climbing was overhanging and strenuous. After two pitches, he encountered extreme climbing where Copperheads—wire swages pounded into shallow seams—and pitons in shallow cracks barely held his body weight.

After four days, he estimated that at his present pace, he would arrive on the rim fourteen days later—several days after he ran out of water and food. The fifth pitch would traverse up and left above a roof. The rock above looked even steeper and smoother. On *Tis-sa-ack*, he had lost his confidence that cracks would always appear. Retreat from above the roof would have been difficult.

Royal could have gone down for supplies and returned, or blamed his retreat on his other responsibilities. But instead, he judged himself as too weak for the task, rappelled, and never tried the route again.

"I wasn't good enough," said Royal, in an interview decades later, "and I lacked courage. If I had held out with that route, I probably would have done it, because it turned out that there were cracks up there. . . . And it would have been more honorable to have pushed it higher, too. I didn't. I'm a little ashamed of that frankly. It was a moment of weakness." The next year, the route would receive its first ascent by twenty-year-old

Charlie Porter and Jean-Paul de Saint Croix, who gave the wall the new-school psychedelic moniker *Tangerine Trip*.

· · · · ·

After a brief stop in Modesto, Royal gave a presentation in Vancouver sponsored by the British Columbia Mountaineering Club. Anderl Heckmair, the German climber who'd led the first ascent of the Eiger Nordwand in 1938, gave him a standing ovation, but Royal noted with some bitterness that he hadn't made enough money to justify the trip. Few students could afford the $2.50 ticket. After a short visit to the crags of Murrin Park near Squamish, Royal went home.

Parental responsibilities, disappointment on El Capitan, and the rigors of the lecture circuit made Royal nostalgic for the less structured life he'd shared with Liz just a few years before. Liz, weighed down by the expectations of 1960s motherhood, had similar feelings.

A couple of months after Tamara's birth, Liz and Royal indulged in a spontaneous, nostalgic adventure. Leaving their daughter with her grandparents, they met Steck, Roper, and other friends for dinner in Berkeley. Roper recorded the rest of the evening in his diary, beginning with the portentous opening line, "At 10 pm, a drunken crew ends up at the freight yards in Oakland; there is an AAC annual meeting in Portland and we decide to take the freight train" to the event. On the chilly morning of December 3, 1971, the crew of six arrived in Dunsmuir, California, where it was snowing and the train was delayed four hours. Roper and his wife, Jani, bailed on the meeting, taking a Greyhound home to Oakland. The Robbinses, however, stayed the course, attending the cocktail reception in the same wet clothes they'd worn on the six-hundred-mile flatbed ride from Oakland.

Despite Royal's nostalgia for less structured times, he was more in demand than ever as an importer and retailer. The Salewa hardware and Edelrid rope companies brought him to Europe, where they entertained him and talked business. In the weeks following Tamara's birth, Royal and Liz had begun fitting out an outdoor store in Modesto. The demands of Royal's status as a businessman and new father might have bred inertia in some men, but his resolve to attempt Cerro Torre only increased.

Italian climber Cesare Maestri's claim that he and Toni Egger had made the first ascent in 1959 was widely doubted. (Maestri also claimed that Egger had died on the descent, swept away by an avalanche, taking with him the camera that had images supposedly snapped on the summit.) In 1968, Royal's friends from Leysin, Dougal Haston and Mick Burke, turned back high on the southeast ridge after they ran out of bolts. In 1970, Maestri returned with a gas compressor and a drill and bolted the southeast ridge to a point sixty meters below the summit. Climbing luminaries decried Maestri's effort as an outrage against climbing style.

Climbs tainted by the unscrupulous use of bolts turned some climbers off, but they had a special magnetism for Royal. "The beauty of the Torre is that it defies technique, it confounds technology," Royal wrote in an unpublished journal article. "No other mountain so lays it on the line against the mountaineer's spirit."

Tompkins had discovered a talent for business, and his and his wife Susie's casual clothing company, Esprit, had made him a millionaire. He sometimes rode a skateboard to work, but he arrived at Durant Street for a meeting in a Ferrari and a sheepskin jacket, turned down a glass of wine and asked for orange juice instead, enthused about the Cerro Torre climb, and complained about the AAC old guard, with whom Royal had finally reconciled after decades of feeling ignored.

"There has always been an edge between Tompkins and me," Royal admitted. "I have always resented his brassiness, his confidence and his proneness to success."

Chouinard, who had become synonymous with climbing hardware in the United States, arrived at the house soon afterward. "The Fox," wrote Royal, using a nickname for Chouinard, "wants to sound us out on how fanatical we are about the [sic] Tory, how willing we would be to give it up if it looks hopeless." They agreed to carry through with the climb only if the summit ice mushroom fell off, letting them reach the top via rock climbing. As Chouinard remembered it, they had "no particular route in mind—we went to check it out and pick the route."

In January, Royal and Steve Miller flew to Patagonia with Tompkins in his Cessna 210. Chouinard was skeptical of the tiny aircraft and flew commercial. Unfortunately, the climbers spent most of their time in a rented *estancia*, waiting for the wind and rain to let up enough to climb. Tompkins tied his plane to a cattle fence to keep the winds from blowing it away.

Miller and Royal attempted a new approach to Fitz Roy, only to be blocked by a broad icefield and, as Chouinard put it, "freaked out partly by the danger and partly by just being overawed by the area. Another case of 'reality-itis.'" Chouinard and Tompkins set out to scout a new approach to Cerro Torre, also without success. That trip, none of the climbers ever set foot on the peaks.

After the Fitz Roy reconnaissance, Royal began to suffer severe pain from kidney stones. For two weeks, he could hardly eat, let alone climb or hike.

"He was determined," wrote Chouinard, "to have battle with this disease-pain business." Royal bore the protracted physical discomfort of big wall climbing without complaint, but acute pain from illness or accidents sometimes overwhelmed him. He had always made up the difference between his prodigious talent and his physical attributes through discipline. He decided to face down his pain without medicine. Wrote Chouinard, referring to the gaunt American poet, "Robbins, in his agony, was looking more and more like Ezra Pound."

The endless days of pain and waiting in Patagonia seemed to liberate Royal. After his return to health and home, he devoted himself to his family and his business with new passion. For the first time since 1956, he had no serious plans for the Yosemite season. He traveled to England on business, played with Tamara, worked in his new store, played tennis, and soloed moderate routes in Yosemite, savoring the beauty of the Valley for its own sake. During a guided trip down the Green River in Utah, the beauty of the canyons and the excitement of running rapids drew him into a whole new form of outdoor adventure.

In 1972, after thundering in defense of Yosemite climbing traditions in *Mountain* for half a decade, Ken Wilson finally visited the Valley. Royal had lost the urge to be a tour guide and suspected that Wilson could find his own way around. Yosemite, Royal wrote, was "the arena of competition, of mangled hands and knees, exultation and despair, arrogance and sycophancy, where the sun shines SO HOT. A tight, noisy place. Actually, most of that rather suited Ken."

Wilson was hard at work on his upcoming book, *Hard Rock*, a compendium of classic climbs in England, Scotland, and Wales. He asked Royal to contribute the essay for *A Dream of White Horses* at Craig Gogarth in Anglesey, a route they'd climbed together. Royal's description of the rock at Gogarth in *Hard Rock* is at once tactile and imaginative: "Dalinian rubble, rubble gone soft like Dali's watches, rubble which had melted and then refrozen, a great, dripping morass of melting vanilla ice cream refrozen into its slopping and plopping descent into the sea. Frozen magically hard."

In December 1972, Mountain Paraphernalia finally moved out of the Valley Paint storage room. Royal needed help, and instead of hiring young climbers who left during climbing season, he put a classified advertisement in the *Modesto Bee*. The notice caught the attention of clean-cut local kid Loren White.

"I went in for the interview," recalled White, "and [Royal] was this hairy mountain man, but the interview was pretty straightforward." Royal's vast vocabulary had amused some climbers, but it impressed White, especially his avoidance of expletives. "He used words carefully," said White, who would later learn Royal had given him the job despite White's not having any outdoor-sport experience because he wrote that he was a Boy Scout second class on his application—and Royal himself had been a Boy Scout. White also recalled Royal's careful, studied decision-making and his commitment to environmentally friendly practices in his business.

In 1969, the Santa Barbara oil spill, pervasive smog in Los Angeles, and the Cuyahoga River fire in Ohio were just a few of the events that confirmed the warnings of the fledgling environmentalist movement. American outdoor businesses began to advertise their commitment to environmentalism. Even Republican president Richard Nixon introduced the Environmental Protection Act.

Royal was, for some, an unexpected skeptic. "As much as I credit getting out-of-doors and escaping the city streets with saving my life," Royal wrote to Doug Tompkins, "as much as I love nature and recognize that we must have it to be sane, as far as my priorities go, the environment is second and the health of our society is first."

"Saving the earth will do no good unless our children are taught how to think straight," he wrote. The relaxation of traditional morals led to "sacrificing our children on the altar of selfishness." For Royal, John Muir's most valuable achievement was conserving the wilderness for—rather than from—society. Royal had once seen climbing as an escape from the demands of society. Now he saw the outdoors as a source of health and clear thinking.

Royal's drift toward more conservative attitudes was by no means unusual. In the sixties and seventies, California had given rise to the New Right. Millions of migrants to California from Appalachia and the Midwest, including Royal's family, had brought traditional views of marriage and society and a libertarian distaste for government interference in their affairs. Royal wasn't the only one who decided he'd been ill counseled by his own times. Former Black Panther Eldridge Cleaver, whose trial had shared the front page with the first ascent of the *North America Wall*, also joined the cause.

Royal began to see himself as a patriarch: Fatherhood and business became opportunities to support his kin, as well as earn an honest paycheck. He encouraged a troubled nephew to take up tennis. His sister, Peggy, whom he alone called by her given name, Helen, came to Modesto with her kids often. "We had fun running loose in the warehouse," said his niece Shelley Aros, "but I'm not sure if [Royal and Liz] thought that was fun. They were always so gracious and comforting. They looked out for everyone." He sent Beulah money and urged her to go on holidays. He hired the kind of working-class people with no outdoor experience he had grown up with.

"He was quiet and went about doing good in ways few people knew about," said White. "After me, he hired a woman who had come out of prison after five years for drug possession. She was a mess, and Royal gave her a chance to work in the warehouse. . . . When an ex-employee had trouble, Royal visited him to talk to him about it. He was just wonderful, and I came to respect him and even see that he exemplified Christian values." Royal, however, was not yet a Christian—that conversion would come later in life.

. . . . .

Advanced Rockcraft was published in 1973. The book was about 50 percent (thirty pages) longer than *Basic Rockcraft*. In the introduction, Royal states for the first time that success in climbing depends on "spiritual discipline," and the book's contents include practical advice as well as philosophical musings and opinions.

Readers looking for technical information would not be disappointed. The "Nutcraft" chapter from his previous book was expanded and renamed "Chockcraft." The book also contained the most coherent description of the Yosemite method for climbing big walls yet in print. Aid climbing, what gear to bring, and, importantly, what not to bring, the use of jumars, and hauling were all clearly described and illustrated.

The "Solo" section was the first treatise on free soloing in American rock climbing. "Control," wrote Royal, "comes only from mastery of the rock and oneself," although "accomplishments lead to praise" and tempt the climber to attempt harder solos.

Royal expanded the paragraph on "The First Ascent Principle" from his first book into a three-page treatise. Whoever creates a new climb, he wrote, however badly, sets the standard for how many pitons and bolts there are on the route in perpetuity. "Though we may find a painting exe-crable, we respect it as a creative effort," he wrote. He saw the addition to or removal of the first ascentionist's bolts or pitons as a major source of route degradation.

Then he added a section on "Outrages" to explain why and how cer-tain routes do not deserve protection under the first ascent principle. According to Royal, every "climbing center" had "mores" that protected the rock. Tuolumne Meadows, for example, allowed bolting, but only on lead: "preplacing of bolts is held contemptible." He alluded to the recent removal of a Tuolumne route with preplaced bolts. "That route is gone, and no one is weeping," he wrote, although there were in fact complaints about its removal.

Some saw contradictions in Royal's ideas. On the one hand, he granted anyone the right to place or remove bolts, and on the other hand, sug-gested that local tradition should be the arbiter. In a review of his book in

Mountain Gazette, Dick Dorworth pointed out that Royal's partial erasure of the *Dawn Wall* was hard to reconcile with "The First Ascent Principle." Royal, who could so easily forgive friends who failed his expectations in other ways, was stung by written criticism and remained annoyed with Dorworth for years.

Advanced Rockcraft sold four hundred thousand copies, but its homey layout, typewriter font, and Royal's well-known views made it look a little old-fashioned next to the previous year's Chouinard Equipment catalogue. The longest document in the catalogue is the now-famous essay "The Whole Natural Art of Protection," by California climber Doug Robinson. "Make the Rock Happy, use a nut," wrote Robinson, ". . . . the full rewards of clean climbing will be yours. . . . relax your mind, relax your mind, you've got to relax your mind."

Despite Royal's coolness deficit, his reputation as the climber who'd pioneered everything from big wall climbing to the use of nuts grew. The 1971 and 1972 Rockcraft schools filled up quickly. Courses were held at Wamello Dome near Fresno, Donner Summit, and a quartet of domes in southern Yosemite that Royal called The Balls.

Royal grew and defended his gear business with initiative and energy. He had asked Recreational Equipment Incorporated (REI), his largest account, to charge the same price for his Galibier boots as other stores. When the company's CEO, Jim Whittaker (the first American to summit Mount Everest), found out a small local store was undercutting him, he complained to Royal that "by following your suggestions [in pricing], we get screwed."

Royal's reply was swift. He compared REI to "an elephant running amok at the sight of a mouse. It does rather seem that power and paranoia go together. As a further example there is your hysterical reaction at an AAC meeting to the suggestion that Mountain Paraphernalia [and not just REI] distribute AAC books. And on the basis that we were a competitor! It is amazing how with some companies, the larger they get, the smaller they grow." Whittaker dropped the matter.

Royal and Liz branched out from technical clothing to the handmade British wool sweaters popular with British climbers. In 1975, the entire Robbins family, plus a babysitter for Tamara, traveled to the Lake District in England to meet with the weavers. John Cleare was hired to take photographs for the marketing campaign, and some of his photos of Tamara and Royal together show a side of Royal that was tender and playful and rarely seen by his climbing friends.

In 1973, New Hampshire climber Henry Barber, then nineteen, had made the first unroped ascent of the *Steck-Salathé* and the first ascent of *Butterballs*, a 5.11 thin crack on the Cookie Cliff. Royal admired Barber, an Anglophile obsessed with climbing style who shared Royal's preference for a white slouch hat. Most of the next generation of Yosemite climbers, however, were less amenable to their elders.

In Yosemite, a new group of tanned, fit, longhaired California climbers took the lead. The self-styled Stonemasters spent hours training in Camp 4, where they installed gym apparatuses. They free soloed casually at high standards and adopted Bridwell's habit of wearing bright clothing and bandanas during photo shoots. Soon, every young climber on the planet wanted to look and climb like a Stonemaster.

"Royal was impressed with John Bachar," said Dale Bard. "But at the time he was more impressed with himself. The rest of the Stonemasters really could not and did not want to relate. We all respected him for his contributions . . . in the early sixties, but he was too aloof for us to relate to."

Nineteen-year-old Mike Graham free climbed the first ten pitches of the *Salathé Wall* in 1975 and chopped Royal's bolt ladder on the fifth pitch. When he handed the chopped equipment to Royal in Camp 4, Royal couldn't do much besides accept the attempted humiliation.

In 1975, Warren Harding's book, *Downward Bound: A Mad! Guide to Rock Climbing*, was published, not by a tiny press like Royal's books but by the major publisher Prentice Hall. Harding satirized Wilson as the "Penthouse Pundit," dressed in bell-bottoms and butterfly lapels, screaming and pointing his finger in judgment from his "well-appointed London flat." Royal became "Mr. Clean Climber." Harding claimed that Royal had done his own big climbs because he was insane. His book ends as Mr. Clean Climber enjoins Penthouse Pundit to help him "in erasing Batso!"

Harding meant his book only half-seriously, if that. After numerous jokes at Royal's expense, Harding acknowledged Royal not just as the leader of the Valley Christians but as "simply Numero Uno—truly the theanthropic climber," a climbing god. He also recommended Royal's Rockcraft courses and his books to beginners.

Royal saw Harding's book as harmless satire. He was less forgiving of Chris Jones's history of North American climbing, *Climbing in North America*, copublished a year later by the University of California, Berkeley and the AAC.

Jones acknowledged Royal as one of the leading climbers of the 1960s, but he also included gossip that made Royal seem petty and at times dishonest or pretentious. He called Royal "a remote, hard-to-fathom figure who took himself seriously and liked to appear well-read." He reported on the push-up contest in the Tetons Royal had supposedly secretly trained for, although Royal denied that it had happened. He also described how a starstruck Liz pointed out a mouse to Royal, who corrected her and said that the mouse was an elephant. According to Jones, Liz replied, "Oh Royal, you know everything." Liz described the story as ridiculous.

The male infantilization of Liz, a talented climber in her own right and important contributor to Camp 4 culture in Yosemite's Golden Age, was a sad moment in climbing literature. Royal shared his criticisms with Jones, who republished the same stories in subsequent versions, stating in the foreword that "Robbins points out several stories about him are misleading."

"As one who has long savoured the diversity of mountain writing," Royal wrote in the introduction to the 1976 Robbins Mountain Letters catalogue, "I feel our catholic offering is in keeping with the varied interests of those who delight in alpine literature. Although our collection is liberal, we have culled the misleading, the inaccurate, the meretricious." *Climbing in North America* failed to make the list. When Royal was made an honorary member of the AAC in 1977, he suspected, without proof, that it was to make amends for the damage done by Jones's book.

In late summer of 1976, Royal returned to the Kichatna Spires with Geoffrey Coates and made the first ascent of the South Ridge of the West Face of Archdeacon Peak. It was a footnote to a glorious season in Alaska when Yosemite-trained climbers put up hard big wall routes in the Cathedral Spires and Valley big wall expert Charlie Porter, then twenty-five, soloed the massive *Cassin Ridge* on Denali. It was also Royal's last alpine foray.

· · · · ·

In 1976, Lito Tejada-Flores invited the Robbinses to visit him in Telluride, Colorado. Royal and Liz fell in love with the little mountain town and the nearby canyons full of unclimbed cliffs and uncrowded ski slopes. Royal decided to offer a Rockcraft course there the next summer.

The previous year, New York novelist and screenwriter James Salter, stung by the lukewarm response to his latest novel, left New York for Aspen. He let his hair grow, wore a bandana, and looked for a new idea. He had been disgusted by the 1975, Clint Eastwood–helmed, spy-cum-climbing film *The Eiger Sanction*. "Idiot machismo with airline food," he raged, "a playboy film, a television film, plastic and life destroying." He decided that he could do better.

Salter discovered Gary Hemming's story in *Straight Up*, Ullman's book on Harlin, and quickly drafted an entire storyline that he showed to actor Robert Redford. Redford turned it down, but Salter decided to turn it into a novel. During his research, Salter began a lively correspondence with Royal, whom he soon trusted enough to ask for feedback on his first draft.

"You've got the Chamonix flavor quite well," Royal wrote. "The slip on the ice scene seems a bit implausible. The bit about Carol and Dix after the death of Coy [in which a dead climber's partner propositions his surviving girlfriend] is insightful. Something like that did happen (not to me)." Salter ignored the advice about the fall on the ice.

On April 7, 1977, Salter visited Royal in Modesto. He had intended only to interview him for background, but Royal made an unexpectedly strong impression. As he listened, Salter noted words that struck him in Royal's speech—"assail, strive"—and his own impressions of Royal, including "arrogant," which he later struck out and replaced with "aggressive." He describes Royal as "low-voiced, almost diffident, disinterested."

"One thing Royal has always gotten from climbing is battle," noted Salter. "Not just exercise; he needs to compete. It is so much a part of him that in games, of which he is fond, if he cannot find someone to play against, he plays against himself."

As they climbed *After Six* in Yosemite, Salter observed "a certain reluc-
tance to [Royal's] speech which makes the occasional unhindered remark
seem overwhelming." When Salter returned to Aspen, he decided to write
an article about Royal for *Quest* magazine that would later be entitled
"Man Is His Own Star." In the margin of the longhand draft, he wrote,
"There are other climbers; Harding, Chouinard, Whittaker, Powell. But
there is only one eminence."

Royal's first reaction to the article was that Salter had used the word
"infers" when he meant "implies." "Rest assured that I am very pleased
with the article," Royal wrote, "and that I agree with the editor that it
is impeccably written." Salter's first disappointment with writing about
climbing was his $225 paycheck from *Quest*, a fraction of what Salter called
"their going rate."

Salter climbed with Royal again in Colorado, and took Royal and Liz
to Chamonix for research. On the plane, Salter produced a large Thermos
full of martinis. When they landed in Paris, Liz was sick in the taxi. "The
only time," she said, "I can remember being like that."

Salter sent Royal the final manuscript before publication in 1978.
"Everyone want[ed] to read it . . . " Royal wrote Salter. "I enjoyed it greatly.
It should get an excellent reception. . . . I found the ending extremely well
done—lovely haunting, poetic, and I appreciate the tribute to Emerson
that runs through the entire work. Good job, Jim. I hope you sell thousands and thousands."

The book in question, *Solo Faces*, was something of a disappointment
to Salter. In the *New York Times*, Vance Bourjaily wrote that its strained
technical devices were not "good servant[s] of narrative drive," but conceded that "perhaps I have made too much of this." Other reviewers found
it exciting but clumsily constructed. Salter had said, "I'll be crushingly
disappointed if [*Solo Faces*] isn't cherished." The book was a cult hit with
some climbers, but literary critics and the book-buying public were ambivalent. Salter never wrote about climbing again, and didn't produce another
novel for thirty-three years.

Royal didn't ask Salter for a professional opinion on his articles, or for
an entrée into the world of publishing. His experience with the Stanford

Press and his literary hero, James Ramsey Ullman, had convinced him that the publishing world, outside of what he called "mountain letters," wasn't for him.

In September 1977, Liz and Royal bought a house in Telluride. Royal brought Chris Vandiver, an employee from the Modesto store and Rockcraft, to Telluride to join him, Tejada-Flores, and Bill Kees on the nearby cliffs, although psoriatic arthritis had begun to slow Royal down.

That summer, severe joint pain and raw skin curtailed Royal's climbing. Kayaking offered a less painful alternative, although his arthritis prohibited him from rolling his kayak, which meant he would have to ditch it if he capsized in a river. Liz started paddling with him, although after an overhanging tree branch caught her helmet strap and temporarily trapped her under a tree on the Mokelumne River in Northern California, Royal became more nervous about her on the water than he'd been on the rock.

In the mid-1970s, Royal helped design the Salewa Royal Robbins Superlight. At forty-four grams, it was the lightest carabiner available at the time. Royal was optimistic about the demand, and his first order was for ten thousand carabiners.

Shortly after it hit the market, employees in a Jackson Hole climbing store jumped up and down in a sling hooked over the noses of open carabiners, deliberately holding the gates open to reduce their break strength. They eventually broke a Royal Robbins Superlight, which ended up in a display at the Jenny Lake Ranger Station intended as a warning to climbers. They also wrote Royal and asked him for a refund for the broken carabiner. When Royal learned that the breakage had occurred from a deliberately improper use, he wrote Grand Teton National Park's chief ranger, accusing those involved of "extremely bad judgment and carelessness with a citizen's reputation and integrity." The superintendent apologized, and the display was removed.

A month later, Royal received a letter from a young climber who'd fallen fifteen feet on a single-pitch aid climb and broken a Superlight. Royal wrote Hermann Huber, his contact at Salewa, asking him to halt production and shipping of the carabiner until Salewa was able to conduct a "prompt and thorough investigation." Salewa's tests showed that the carabiners were reliable and that the breakage had been due to the carabiner being stressed along its minor axis, an avoidable and improper deployment.

By the late 1970s, several carabiner brands competed in the American market, including American-made options the Seattle Manufacturing Company (SMC) and Chouinard Equipment. On November 11, 1977, Royal wrote Huber, telling him, "Frankly, it's difficult to picture importing carabiners as being a workable proposition in 1978." Liz and Royal decided to slowly reduce their dependence on hardware sales by expanding their clothing line.

"I told Susie Tompkins what we wanted to do," said Liz, "and she said, 'Come on over.'" Their goal, Liz told the Tompkinses, was to produce a functional, aesthetic garment for the Royal Robbins brand. Working with the Tompkins' pattern maker, Liz came up with the rugged, canvas Billy Goat shorts, which resembled, more than anything, the shorts worn by Royal's boyhood crush, Nyoka the Jungle Girl. The shorts sold out six months in advance, which Royal took as a sign for the company's future direction.

"Gratified and encouraged by the reception given our British Wool sweaters, our handknit Shetland wool hats and our 100% wool turtlenecks," declared the 1978 Robbins Mountain Threads catalogue, "we have expanded the line to include some exciting new items. Among these are wool sweaters and shirts from South America, cotton shorts from the Orient, and wool sweaters and hats made in the United States."

Company staff, including Royal, modeled the clothes in the catalogue, which had no fine art plates or essays about the "Whole Natural Art" of anything. Lito Tejada-Flores and Keith Roush shot the photos. The cuts and fabrics were sturdy, practical, American.

Royal had now worked with American outdoor stores for a decade and knew that they lacked the skills for effectively displaying and selling clothes. "We had to teach all of these climbers and backpackers how to sell clothes," said Roush, "like physically show them how to display them, how to do the retail math on sizing." They invited staff from the stores to Telluride, where they introduced them to climbing and, in Roush's words, "showed them how to make a living."

In 1979, Earl and Carrie Burkner, now retired, moved out of their home on Magnolia Avenue. Royal and Liz purchased it and kept the house in Telluride as a summer residence. Against all expectations, in a period of 18 percent inflation, Royal and Liz had become wealthy.

In November 1979, Liz and Royal's second child, Eric Damon, was born. This time, Royal showed none of the ambiguity and fears that had preceded Tamara's arrival. Business flourished. Royal, who had always been frugal, spent money on luxuries. His favorite new indulgence was the ballet.

Liz and Royal volunteered on the board of directors of the Central West Ballet, a small company that performed in the Gallo Center for the Arts in Modesto, and eventually helped bring Canadian René Daveluy and Oregonian climber and dancer Leslie Ann Larson to direct the company. Through his friendship with Daveluy and Larson, Royal developed a deeper understanding of dance and its similarities with climbing. "He especially loved the lifts and other maneuvers," said Daveluy. "They reminded him of the way climbing partners relied on one another."

Twice in his life, Royal had come to the verge of dancing. He had pushed his body to the limit on the most public rock walls in America, but the intimacy of the stage intimidated him. With Daveluy's encouragement, he finally arrived on the dance floor in 2014—as the narrator of the story of *Peter and the Wolf* for the Central West Ballet.

In some ways, Royal was happily, conspicuously unaware of middle-class aesthetics of restraint. "That was Royal," said Liz, "a dreamer, not practical; he did things on impulse." He once bought Liz a white Mercedes she'd seen and commented on en route to the airport for a business trip to Hong Kong, picking her up in the airport in it after her voyage. And he'd lavish jewelery upon her, including a "really big" diamond he asked Liz to design the setting for.

One Christmas morning, Tamara came downstairs to find a new saddle beside the Christmas tree and a pony tied to a tree on the front lawn. If Damon saw a toy he wanted on television, Royal drove him to the store and bought it for him. Royal and Liz purchased a cabin in Pinecrest, set amongst trees on a small lake near Lover's Leap, only about eighty miles from Modesto. Royal kayaked on the lake, explored the hills for crags, and learned to windsurf.

Royal mixed business with recreation when he could. At the annual ski trade show in Las Vegas, he spent hours playing tennis with Chouinard. Sometimes, he went skiing with shop owners and left Roush to do the marketing. "He liked numbers and going to banks and figuring stuff out," said Roush. "Sales, not so much."

Success gave Royal the opportunity to invest in what he called "mountain letters." In 1978, young Valley climber George Meyers pitched Royal on the first topo guidebook to Yosemite to replace what Meyers called "Steve Roper's hopelessly narrative book." Royal thought the market was small but offered to print it and give Meyers a dollar for each copy sold.

Meyers also pitched Royal on a book of photos and essays about the scene of the moment in Yosemite, which intrigued Royal, who had once tried to publish his own book about the Valley scene. He teamed up with Ken Wilson's Diadem Books, which had published the lavishly illustrated and well-received *Hard Rock*. *Yosemite Climber*, subtitled "Action photographs from the world's leading rock climbing area," was a glossy, hardcover, ninety-six-page coffee-table format book.

Yosemite Climber ignored Royal's legacy and the Golden Age, and focused instead on contemporary scenes and concerns. "Three bodies arise quickly [for the first one-day ascent of the *Nose*]," wrote John Long, " . . . they dress in costume for the occasion, à la Jimi Hendrix." Big wall evenings had once been spent in thirst and silence, worrying about what lay above. Now, per Meyers's book, climbers took "the energizing music of Hendrix or Pink Floyd" and "plentiful supplies of beer, or drugs."

"There was no question [Royal's generation] got short shrift," said Meyers. "It was implied that they used any way to get to the top, that they were presumptuous and arrogant to call themselves 'Golden Age.'" In 1979, Royal and James Salter stared together at a new 5.12 climb at the base of El Capitan. Royal admitted that he could not even get off the ground on it. Salter didn't believe him, but Royal knew and accepted the truth. For the moment, he was unimportant to Valley climbing.

A longtime Valley climber called Meyers's book the high school yearbook of Camp 4. It also inspired a generation of climbers to make the pilgrimage to Yosemite, to dress and act and speak like the climbers on its pages. Camp 4 became a state of mind for climbers, a country of dreams. Climbing became a global movement, with Yosemite at its center.

Perhaps it's just the color photographs, but in some ways, the scene in *Yosemite Climber* actually looks more suburban and better-funded than it did in the 1960s, with better camping equipment and plentiful sophisticated climbing hardware. Royal knew that for all the talk of a new age in the Valley—the funny clothes and high grades—he and his friends had forged the lifestyle depicted by Meyers: sacrificing everything for climbing, wearing your clothes until they fell apart, starving or stealing food to climb, pushing your body and mind to the limit on the walls, and smoking marijuana. For Royal, underwriting Meyers's book was an act perhaps not quite of love but at least of acceptance of Valley climbing's present form, and with that recognized the need of generations of Valley climbers to tell their stories. Royal, too, had dwelt in that paradise—in its earliest, most unspoiled days.

11

Rivers and God

"I'D BEEN KAYAKING SOMEWHAT," wrote Royal in 1980, "but I didn't consider myself an expert by any means." He paddled in a stiff, upright position with his arms next to his body to minimize arthritis pain. Some of his friends thought he looked as if he'd rather be climbing. Others observed that he hit a few too many rocks, but the new plastic kayaks were forgiving. "We rejoiced at plastic boats," said Royal, "because we could throw them down cliffs."

Doug Tompkins had become an expert kayaker. Esprit now sold a million dollars' worth of clothing a day in the United States alone, but Tompkins's interest had dwindled with its success. He had fallen in love with Patagonia and spent months in Chile, making first descents of wild rivers. Royal, unlike most young whitewater fanatics, had the time and money to accompany him.

In February 1980, Royal and paddler Jim Sims flew to Santiago in Tompkins's Cessna. They made the first descents of the lower and middle Rio Maipo, a class V on the whitewater scale (with VI being the most difficult), and the lower Rio Cachapoal and Rio Pangol in the Santiago region, at grade IV. In the South Central Andes, they were the first to run Rio Cautín, with its complicated grade III rapids; Rio Trancura, which varied from IV upward; and the upper and lower Rio Maichín. On the hardest river they ran, the lower Salto del Soldado Canyon of Rio Aconcagua, escape by portage was almost impossible. Some of these descents were not repeated for fifteen years.

In early summer 1980, the Robbinses returned to Telluride. Lynn Hill and John Long, members of the Stonemasters group, stayed with them and tried to start a guiding business, but there were few clients, and they spent the summer doing hard new routes in Ophir Canyon and guiding Royal's salespeople. "Royal cast a long shadow on climbers of my generation," said Long. "He really was, and wanted to be, and worked hard to be the man people saw him as, almost like a Knight Templar of climbing."

Hill had just made the first free ascent of *Ophir Broke*, one of the hardest routes in North America, and Royal wanted to climb with her. He suggested a 5.10d, at the upper end of his abilities at the time. She shouted out advice on how to climb the crux, but he still couldn't do it. "I felt embarrassed that I might have insulted the dignity of this climbing legend," wrote Hill. "Perhaps he was distracted by my comments or maybe he was concentrating on avoiding painful movements in his arthritic wrists. . . . Royal's polite silence in the face of my ignorance spoke louder than words."

In 1980, Tompkins offered a paddling trip on Chile's Bío Bío River to a group of high-performing Esprit employees. Royal and Liz came along, bringing nine-year-old Tamara with them. Tompkins hired Sobek Tours, some of whose guides had made the river's first descent, to provide the rafts, equipment, and leadership. For once, Royal was destined to have a low profile on an outdoor adventure. The river was not without danger. Even after watching from the shore as her mother's raft was stuck for more than an hour in a rapid, Tamara was intrigued enough to later become a whitewater guide.

In January of 1981, Royal, Tompkins, and California kayakers Reg Lake and Newsome Holmes flew to Chile for the first descents of Rio Lincara, upper and lower Rio Fuy, and the lower, upper, and middle Rio Tinguiririca. Back in California, Royal began running steeper rivers. On the Merced, one of his first Sierra rivers, he dislocated both his shoulders. The injury could have ended his kayaking, but after getting medical attention, he adjusted his paddling style to accommodate the decrease in mobility.

Instead of taking the injury as a warning, Royal dreamed of more undescended rivers. He searched maps and guidebooks for thin blue ribbons that snaked through closely bunched contour lines; rivers that traversed mountain ranges attracted him the most. For Royal, portages with technical climbing and hikes through alpine terrain weren't a distraction from paddling, but part of the adventure.

He scouted rapids from the shore like a climber considering a hard pitch, a process he compared to "chickens looking at a python." He brought a rope to rappel if the river was too steep to run or to climb cliffs that blocked a portage. He carried his boat as far as necessary and camped out for days at a time to continue the descent.

Kayakers, whose primary goal was boating the river, not descending it on foot or with ropes, were surprised by Royal's methods. "It didn't factor into [paddlers'] consciousness that carrying [kayaks] was a proper part of wilderness river running," said Royal. "Boating is a part of it, but not the whole thing. We were willing to carry [the boats] all the way if necessary."

Reg Lake found Royal's sense of mission infectious. "Before I started going on trips with Royal and Doug Tompkins," said Lake, "paddling was mainly social. Until that time, there wasn't as much overnight exploration with loaded boats on classified rivers. It was pretty much unheard of." Lake welcomed the new approach: "The opportunity to paddle with [Royal and Tompkins]," he said, "was irresistible."

For their first difficult Sierra river, Royal, Tompkins, and Lake chose the Middle Fork of the San Joaquin. The gorge held rapids where Royal thought a mistake would be fatal, but the trio safely descended the river in a thrilling six days. "If I had to give up all the climbs I've done except for one," said Royal, "it would be the *Salathé Wall.* If I had one river to keep, I would choose the Middle Fork of the San Joaquin, because of the scenery, the adventure, the friendship, the beauty and everything it involved."

And yet Royal and Tompkins, despite their teamwork on the river, began to grow apart in other ways. Tompkins had immersed himself in the environmental philosophies of David Brower and Norwegian climber and ecologist Arne Naess. Naess argued that the world's problems were caused by human intrusion into ecosystems and that a decrease in the number of humans overall and in wilderness areas generally would solve many of these issues.

Royal, however, gleefully described cliffs "swarming with climbers—folks living on the sharp end—burning, alive, loving outdoor action, loving the earth and its beauty, loving life and all it has to offer." He thought access to the outdoors would improve attitudes toward the environment, and he saw no conflict between using the landscape for industry and conserving it.

"I'm not a lover of dams," Royal told a newspaper, "but I couldn't help wondering why no one had used [the Middle Fork of the San Joaquin River] for hydro—it seemed like the perfect place." Royal knew that the Sierra Club had made advocating against damming western American rivers a central issue of their environmental program since the 1920s. He worried, however, that people would be left behind, the public remaining unconvinced by what he saw as the misanthropic, anti-progress tone of contemporary environmentalism. The bluntness and tendency to play the devil's advocate that had exasperated Royal's friends around the campfire puzzled the general public, who expected an at least more-cautious view from an eminent figure in the outdoor scene. Royal, however, seemed not to have taken his own comments very seriously, and continued to revel in the wild California whitewater that would no longer exist were damming to proceed uncontrolled.

At dinner the night after the San Joaquin River, Royal produced a sheaf of documents and asked Tompkins and Lake if they could keep a secret. "I said, 'No,' and he put the maps back in the drawer," said Lake, "but he eventually couldn't help himself and brought them out anyway." Royal's secret file turned out to be maps of the Upper Kern, another much-discussed but unrun Sierra river.

The main obstacle to paddling the Upper Kern was that the river began in Junction Meadow, high in the Sierra, twenty-one miles from the nearest road. Tompkins removed the doors and rear seats from his Cessna to accommodate kayaks, and with Royal and Lake in the backseat without seatbelts, flew over the starting point, but there was nowhere to land. The trio turned back.

Royal suggested carrying kayaks and supplies over the 8,374-foot Whitney Portal to the Kern headwaters. Lake and Tompkins agreed, and Esprit employees were enlisted as porters. Portaging kayaks up snow slopes on Whitney Portal proved an exhausting task, made more dangerous by the porters' slippery basketball shoes covered in plastic bags to keep their feet dry. Only Tompkins and Royal had climbed on snow before, and they had no ice axes for self-arrest. As they neared the top of the pass, it began to snow. Lake slipped and lost his footing. His kayak dragged him hundreds of feet down the slope, leaving him with painful scrapes for the rest of the trip.

· · · · ·

After the Kern, Royal began to imagine a trio of hard Sierra rivers akin to his three great climbs on El Capitan: the *Salathé Wall*, the continuous ascent of the *Nose*, and the *North America Wall*. After the Middle Fork of the San Joaquin and the Kern, only the Middle Fork of Kings River remained to complete what became known as the Sierra Triple Crown—but it was the hardest of the three, and most kayayers doubted it could be run.

The Middle Fork of Kings River surged through canyons so deep that there was no way to see from above whether they could be run. In several places, the river dropped more than 500 feet over a mile. Even before the river had been attempted, kayakers knew it would be more technical and dangerous than anything else in California. Speculation about who would run it first was inevitable.

In the early 1980s, friendly competition had arisen between Royal's group and the experienced kayaking trio of Chuck Stanley, Richard Montgomery, and Lars Holbek, nicknamed the Hipsters on the Move. Holbek and his friends dubbed Royal, Tompkins, and Lake the Billy Goat Crew, after their shorts. The competition was friendly, but the Hipsters judged Royal and Tompkins in the same way that Royal had judged Yosemite dabblers. "We viewed Reg Lake," said Holbek, "as the only real paddler of the [Billy Goat Crew]."

But some of Royal's strength as a paddler came from his experiences as an outsider and a climber, able to—with his well-honed reflexes—quickly resolve any mishaps. In 1980, Royal, Tompkins, and the latest addition to the Billy Goat Crew, athlete and kayaker Newsome Holmes, made a weeks-long descent of Chile's Rio Tinguiririca. Halfway down the river, a powerful current trapped Royal under a rock and pulled him out of out of his cockpit. Swept downstream, Royal was sure he was going to drown. The thought of his children and Liz gave him a sudden burst of energy. Just before a second rapid finished him off, he saw a rock hold, grabbed it, and clambered out unharmed. Some might have been chastened, but the spill proved Royal could survive a whitewater bailout, and so he decided to try the Middle Fork.

"Many paddlers had their eyes on the Middle Fork [of Kings River], myself included," wrote Stanley. "I mentioned my interest to Royal, but Royal said the river was much too steep. At that instant I just knew he was going to run it."

In early 1981, Royal and Tompkins returned to Chile, where they made the first descent of the Rio Laja and were later joined by Holmes for more whitewater. By 1982, Royal and his friends were ready for Kings. As with the Upper Kern, Esprit employees again helped portage to the put-in, but in addition to carrying his own equipment, Royal packed a typewriter to record the descent for an article.

Holmes broke his paddle in the first hour. They ran some of the hardest rapids they had ever done and scrambled on technical rock where they couldn't run the rapids. Holbek and Stanley had put in half an hour after Royal and his friends, but soon gave up.

A few days later, the Sierra Triple Crown, a trio of rivers as significant to the history of whitewater kayaking as Royal's first ascents had been to climbing, was completed. After Kings, the Hipsters and the Billy Goats bonded over their shared experiences. Holbek, Stanley, Montgomery, their friend John Armstrong, Tompkins, and Royal joined up to make the first descent of the Tuolumne River, the last and easiest of Royal's big first descents in the Sierra.

At age forty-six, Royal was finally free of ambitious climbing and paddling plans. He now climbed and paddled for the pleasure of movement and his surroundings. His final first descents were mostly of creeks only runnable after rain or in the spring. "Flash-boating," as Royal dubbed these excursions, emphasized that, for him, the charm of these descents was partly that they were ephemeral.

Perhaps the absence of ambition at this point in Royal's life opened him up to unexpected insights and experiences. As he floated down the

Middle Fork of the Salmon River in Idaho, Royal felt what he described as "the unmistakable presence of God behind my right shoulder." Royal, who had been skeptical about—and occasionally hostile toward—religion, began a years-long attempt to come to terms with the experience.

Royal's experiences with religion had begun as a child with the fiery Appalachian fundamentalism of the Christian Church of Christ in Point Pleasant and continued at the Sunday school of the same denomination in Los Angeles. The Scouts had enjoined a kind of muscular, practical Christianity, but Royal was more interested in hiking and camping.

When Royal was a teenager, he discovered Jean-Paul Sartre, Albert Camus, Søren Kierkegaard, and Fyodor Dostoevsky and called himself an existentialist. And yet, a number of his favorite writers and composers were Christian, or at least theistic. His beloved Emerson believed God revealed his presence in the natural world. Whitman had his own image of God. Tolkien sublimated his Roman Catholicism into the hierarchical and moral universe of Middle Earth. One of Royal's favorite climbing authors, Roger Frison-Roche, bestowed his conservative Roman Catholicism on his fictional mountain guides. Many of Royal's favorite composers had written their most profound works for the Christian liturgies. Recently, Bob Dylan, the popular musician Royal esteemed the most, had undergone his own Christian conversion.

Royal had always battled his weaknesses, reformed his morals, and taken strong views on issues. Sometimes, he had taken the side of the establishment; more often, he had rebelled against it. His friends had always seen a religious fervor in his ideas about climbing, dubbing him the leader of the "Valley Christians." Religion, at least potentially, had attractions for a man who had always survived not by his strength but by his capacity for discipline. After the Salmon River, Royal blamed the existentialists for convincing him faith was a kind of weakness. In his youth, he had been as pleasure loving and self-involved as those around him, at times incautious in the way he spoke, lived, wrote, and even climbed. Why should the philosophies of those days of anarchy, precious as they were to him, suffice for his mature years?

At home, Royal said grace before dinner, read the Bible before breakfast every day, and spoke of himself as a man of faith, although not yet a Christian. Some of his friends said Royal had become a "born again" Christian, an understandable oversimplification. Royal's own life furnished possible foundations for a more idiosyncratic personal faith. Raised by a mother who would suffer anything for her children, he had survived by summoning discipline, overmastering fear and pain rather than simply ignoring them; Royal had found a code to live and climb by that was beautiful and, if inexact in its strictures, at least not incoherent.

He eschewed fundamentalist services and attended mass at Our Lady of Fatima in Modesto. "He liked the Catholic Church," said Liz, who did not share Royal's newfound faith, "because there weren't sermons about recent events, and there was a timelessness about it, like classical music." After sitting in the pews and watching for a few months, he introduced himself to Father Michael Kelly, an Irish priest with an interest in chess and theology who became Royal's spiritual confidante and prepared him for baptism and first communion. Royal, however, remained unorthodox. "With all the variations of people," he told Dick Erb, "somehow a virgin birth could happen as a scientific fluke."

In London, Royal's friend Max Gammon had undergone his own conversion. After a personal crisis, he dropped his work as a surgeon, lost his flat at Chilton Court, moved into a garret in a friend's house, and became an ordained minister. Gammon was delighted that his friend now shared his faith, although he admitted that despite Royal's "abiding awareness of the transcendent, awareness of God," he "wasn't religious in the conventional sense, thank God."

By the mid-1980s, Royal and Liz's business was so successful that they turned down two offers to buy it. "We just couldn't see parting with something that has become part of us," said Royal. He put a poster of the *Salathé Wall* up in his office and wrote in the names of some of the features, with sales projections that increased with the height of the wall. He compared his greatest climbs with his company. He believed both were built on integrity and adventure, but some did not.

"Might I remind of your earlier, and if I may say so, more brilliant period," Tompkins wrote Royal, "railing against the climbing world for distorting adventure and turning it into a sport. My God, Royal, you seem to have fallen rather heavily into the same trap. 'Business is the big adventure.' My God, Royal, what has happened to you, old chap?"

Royal politely reminded Tompkins of the wealth he had accrued through his own enterprises. "I hear you live in a magnificent house," responded Royal in a letter, "which doesn't surprise me, as you were never good at mediocrity."

Royal and Liz had built their company on savings from Liz's family, a taste for hard work, and the belief that people's lives were improved by the outdoors. He resented being judged by his friends for his increasingly conservative economic and political views. "I have noticed," he wrote Roper, "that my liberal friends (most of my friends happen to be liberals) who value diversity and autonomy will forgive me all sorts of immoral or dishonest acts except holding a different political philosophy."

In 1986, Royal faced the first existential challenge to his business, and it came not from his critics but from the old source of trouble, carabiners. A climber who had broken an RR Superlight in a leader fall filed a suit for damages against Mountain Paraphernalia. Testing showed that the carabiners broke at 1,000 pounds above their advertised strength. Engineers suggested that a load-limiting sling was to blame, and the plaintiff ceased litigation.

In June 1987, Liz's mother, Carrie, died. A year later, Earl Burkner, who had always been close to Liz, and who was the only paternal figure Royal had ever looked up to, also passed away. Burkner's death was a stinging emotional blow. It was also a reminder to the whole family that Royal Robbins, the company, was a precious family enterprise that overlapped three generations. From now on, Royal and Liz agreed that they would no longer sell climbing hardware to protect it from litigation.

12

A Mountaineer Is Always Free

IN OCTOBER OF 1986, French climber Jean-Baptiste Tribout climbed the sheer, vertical wall of *To Bolt or Not to Be* at Oregon's Smith Rock, America's first 5.14, without even visiting Yosemite on his trip. Tribout was the product of the nascent European sport-climbing scene, in which climbers placed bolts on rappel, hung on the rope to try moves, and occasionally even chipped holds on blank rock. Young climber Kurt Smith summarized American objections to this new style of climbing, "It's cheating—even my grandma could climb it that way." Nonetheless, Tribout's achievement inspired a small but growing cadre of American sport climbers to follow his lead, and more traditionally minded climbers to protest, sometimes by removing bolts, but more often by accusing their opponents of ruining climbing.

The AAC hosted a debate in Boulder about the controversy. Stonemasters Ron Kauk and Lynn Hill defended the new tactics. John Gill and Royal joined the side of the traditionalists. Gill said he "wasn't going to compete with some anorexic little f——t in tights." Hill felt grilled by McCarthy for hanging on the rope on a new route. Royal accused Kauk of having roughed up the opponents of rappel bolting. Royal's tone throughout the fracas remained authoritative, but never quite respectably official. Both sides believed they had won, and for now, went their different ways.

In 1988, Royal, Chouinard, and Tompkins became the first Americans invited to Russia to descend the Bashkaus River, for what would be Royal's last major river expedition in a foreign country. Back home, when he wasn't attending to business, he paddled, played chess, and indulged his obsession with the San Francisco 49ers football team by traveling to home games. His kids remember him staying up late to watch taped games.

Royal had attended his first Rotary Club meetings with Earl Burkner, mostly to help Earl with his waning mobility, but after two decades as a nervous public speaker, Royal was intrigued by the club's emphasis on speeches. He joined and received his first formal training as a presenter. "Rotary was just as important to Royal as the Boy Scouts had once been," said Liz. He threw himself into meetings, adopted the club's principles, and even changed his voice—becoming smooth, like a "radio announcer's," said Glen Denny—to suit his new public-speaking style.

On a single page in his journal, Royal pledged himself and his business to the first two lines of the Nicene Creed; he affirmed Jesus Christ to be the son of God and the word made flesh, the Ten Commandments, and the Golden Rule (the royal law from Epistle of James in the New Testament to love your neighbor as yourself); and he endorsed the Rotarian four-way test of truth, fairness, goodwill, and benefit, Christian principles in general, and unlocking the creative potential of his employees. "His deliberateness," said Tamara, "was the foundation of his every move—the painstaking daily affirmations, detailed bookkeeping, dedication to reading, and learning or growing every day."

To Royal's disgust, sport climbing appeared in Yosemite in the late 1980s. Bolts were chopped and replaced, and the leading lights of American rock climbing squabbled in parking lots and on the pages of *Rock and Ice* and *Climbing*. Royal himself penned an article for Michael Kennedy, the editor of *Climbing*, with the hopes of seeing it published in that magazine. "As a has-been," he wrote to Kennedy, "who am I to meddle in new directions and hinder those who carry the banner of the new age?" But meddle he did. The piece's title, "Vandals in the Temple," reflects Royal's religious preoccupations of the moment. He called the sport climbers "barbarians at the gate," against whom traditionalists should "hold the fort."

Kennedy and Royal engaged in a spirited back-and-forth in the editing notes in the story's margins. When Royal boasted that visitors to Yosemite came "to feed at the springs of a set of values handed down from the leading exemplars of the past," Kennedy scribbled, "blah. people go there to climb." Next to Royal's complaint about sport climbers "chiseling holds until it's possible to climb," Kennedy wrote, "simplistic and unfair" and "this implies that all bolters chip," although most did not. Then, wrote Royal, "[Sport climbers] violate the spirit of friendship in climbing by knocking down anyone who gets in their way." "Oh yes," wrote Kennedy, "every one of them." Finally, continued Royal, "Climbing publications should refuse to publish information on new routes done in a style that shows poor environmental citizenship," by which he meant sport climbing. "You gotta be kidding," Kennedy scribbled.

Kennedy told Royal that he wouldn't change many minds with his arguments and that climbers were tired of arguing about sport climbing. He also called his polarization of "eurostylists" and "traditionalists" simplistic. Wrote Kennedy, California traditional climber John Bachar had "ruthlessly toproped" routes before soloing them, and, in Colorado, Christian Griffith had done "incredibly bold leads" as well as sport routes. "Chopping gets us nowhere; besides damaging the rock even further," wrote Kennedy, who also supported preserving some areas for traditional climbing.

Royal took Kennedy's response as "a very friendly and kind rejection slip," but became more ardent than ever. "This is like the Battle of Britain," Royal wrote. "Are we going to stand idly by and see rock climbing as we know it disappear forever?" He said the issue was "white hot," and he intended to "breath new life into it." He predicted that far from ignoring the article, climbers would "read every word, and there will be a response such as [Kennedy] would have never seen before"; it was a "shout of alarm" that Kennedy had "something like a moral obligation to publish."

On August 31, 1990, Royal sent a longer version of "Vandals in the Temple" to *Mountain* and *Rock and Ice* "with the intention of weighing the

treatment each magazine will give the piece before deciding who will publish it." If anything, his position had become more extreme. He mostly
blamed Stonemaster Ron Kauk "and his pugnacious subalterns" for an
"apostasy" that had introduced sport climbing to the Valley. "Let me state
the matter plainly," he thundered. "We are talking about the death of
American rock climbing." He said that if sport climbing flourished unim-
peded, there would be a "Eurostyle" route right up the *Nose*, with bolts
every six feet and chipped holds the whole way.

"It might seem, from my above remarks," he wrote, "that I am against
sport climbing. I'm not." He conceded that it could be all right at an "otherwise useless" crag, but its methods are "garbage."

"Chop all rapbolts," wrote Royal, evincing none of the tentativeness
he had shown before chopping Harding's bolts on the *Dawn Wall*; "I know
this sounds a little extreme." He struck out the next sentence, but left it
legible: "So, I say, chop, chop, and don't stop chopping until the Euroboys
say, 'Enough already.'" "I am suggesting," he wrote, "that we designate
Yosemite National Park a Eurostyle-free zone."

On this latest draft, Kennedy wrote, "'LET'S SAY 'HELL, NO.' I tried
reading this again and it seemed so absurd that I couldn't finish. I think it
would be a mistake for us to publish it."

Royal sent a letter on December 11, registering his disappointment
in Kennedy's decision to not publish his article and instead run a piece
supportive of sport climbing. The article was eventually published, in an
abridged form, in *Rock and Ice*. Royal accused Kennedy, the veteran of
numerous hard alpine ascents, of having gone over to the sport-climbing
side of the dispute and suggested he change the name of his magazine to
Sport Climbing.

Before publication time for the February 1991 issue of *Climbing*, Royal
wrote a letter that was eventually published. "It's been a year since I've
been moved to write a letter to the editor of a climbing magazine," Royal
began, although it had actually only been weeks. He proposed that the
magazine had made concessions to hold chippers.

The letter ended his American campaign against sport climbing, but he
continued the fight, briefly, in the United Kingdom. In March 1991, he joined
Ken Wilson in Manchester for a debate about "in-situ" protection. Wilson

and Royal would champion traditional British ethics in a debate with sport climbers Jerry Moffatt and Chris Gore at the Buxton Adventure Festival.

Wilson's picture of a future in which sport climbing was not banished from Britain was as dystopian as Royal's had been for Yosemite. "There'll be bolts all up [the Idwal Slabs, a popular moderate crag in Wales]," he wrote, "bolts on the stances, bolts halfway up the pitches. That is the spectre we are facing." He railed at a speaker at an Alpine Club meeting that was part of the event, "All over Europe crags are being covered with bolts, and what we have to decide in this country is: do we want it to happen here?"

Royal and Wilson carried the day. British climbers were overwhelmingly committed to traditional climbing; many hadn't even seen bolts. Some were shocked by the number of bolts they'd encountered even in Yosemite. Wilson soon returned Royal's favor of coming to the aid of British traditional climbing by launching a campaign of correspondence with American climbing magazine editors. He boasted of a "dawn raid" to remove 33 bolts, and another event in which he played a role where 140 bolts were removed. He even told American editors to "STOP APPEASING" bolters and accused them of a lack of morals.

In 1992, Royal was invited to join the AAC's newly formed Access Fund to assist with their program of securing the right to climb at crags across the country, many of which were, by now, equipped for sport climbing. In the process of promoting the fund, however, Royal had been singled out as a threat to climbing because he was in favor of chopping some bolts. With considerable forbearance, Royal nonetheless accepted the invitation, but explained that his position was now "against rap-bolting in Yosemite," clarifying, in correspondence with Access Fund President Armando Menocal, that the notion that he'd issued a "clarion call to ban all bolts" was false. He conceded that a compromise had been struck between sport climbing and traditional climbing, although the "unseemly simian chest-thumping and hosannas of triumphs" by the sport climbers continued. Menocal apologized to Royal, admitting that he had become "an attention-getting foil," and they worked together to secure access rights for American climbers, regardless of their preferred climbing style.

Royal's predictions about chipped routes up El Capitan did not come true, and sport climbing remained a fringe activity in Yosemite, partly because its main proponents hadn't truly intended it to be anything else. Royal came to live with sport climbing. Whether his campaign against it played a role in limiting it to appropriate areas or inflaming its proponents to even more bolting is impossible to tell.

· · · · ·

This last anti-bolting crusade had left Royal ambivalent about taking on the role of climbing's moral leader again. He'd lost interest in the present battles of rock climbing and began to think more about his past. Royal had always been loyal to old friends, and now he began to reach farther back into his past to reconnect, and to exchange and gather stories with them.

The cabin in Pinecrest became the setting of many reunions. In 1992, the Robbinses hosted alumni of the Leysin American School. Among the guests were Kathleen Galvin and Kathy Gaylord. Pat Ament, who had begun a biography of Royal, came to Pinecrest. Jerry Gallwas, Jim McCarthy, Tom Frost, and Ken Yager stayed and discussed the creation of a Yosemite climbing museum, which eventually came to fruition with Royal's support.

Royal's oldest friend, Bill Derr, visited. "Royal, another guest, and I got up quite early and drove up to Sonora Pass," remembered Derr, "and hiked north to Stanislaus Peak. On the way down, I dislodged a boulder. I vividly remember Royal put a hand on the boulder, pushed it back in place, and closed a gap in the trail. When we got back to cabin, he got on his wind-surfer . . . then he attended a Rotary meeting. He didn't slow down—he was still training youths to rock climb near his cabin."

Royal got in touch with his childhood partner in crime, Roy Slagle, who now called his prison years "a healthy life." "I had a similar experience when I was drafted into the Army," Royal wrote to Slagle. "I didn't like it, but afterward I had to admit it did me a lot of good. In other words, I really appreciated civilian life after being in the Army." And yet, although Royal had taken to quoting Winston Churchill's more bellicose lines when discussing climbing ethics, he wasn't a jingoistic supporter of American intervention abroad. A letter to a friend's son, a soldier headed to the Gulf War in 1991, conspicuously lacked patriotic encouragements, comments about the rightness of America's cause, or enthusiasm for the adventure.

Royal's curiosity about the past brought him back to Point Pleasant, where the dramas at the root of his life had occurred: the absent father, the flood, the journey north and then west. He mused on the West Virginia state motto: *Montani semper liberi*—"Mountaineers are always free." He met with a relative who knew someone who'd seen Royal's father box and been impressed. The idea gave him some solace, as if the fight revealed some grace hidden in the brutality of the man who had abandoned him as a child.

In the early 1990s, Royal organized the first annual rafting trip for family and employees on the Middle Fork of the Salmon River. Damon remembered his father's yodels echoing off the walls of empty canyons. Here, Royal could be himself in the sanctuary the American wilderness had always offered him.

On the way home from a trip in 1993, Royal set up a toprope on a small crag in Nevada, noting and avoiding a flake on the wall that looked loose. When he flicked the rope at the base of the climb, however, he dislodged the rock, which struck him on the right shoulder and back. In shock, he made it down to the car, where he was situated in the back seat. Liz and Damon drove him to the hospital in Reno as he screamed with pain at every bump in the road. Damon, who was eleven years old, was shocked by the sudden vulnerability of his father, whose outdoor heroics were a legend. Royal had broken several ribs, but escaped serious organ damage. Though Royal made light of the incident afterward, the falling rock could have killed him. He was prescribed painkillers, and after a few days left the hospital for a sales-team meeting at Pinecrest.

Royal usually entertained the team with elaborate treasure hunts featuring hidden clues and challenges, but this time, Damon and a friend had to set it up for him, as Royal could barely move from his chair. That evening, powered by painkillers and alcohol, Royal was the master of ceremonies at a party on the deck, seated in a chair, dressed as Gandalf, laughing so hard that he wheezed with pain.

Although disarming and gracious in small groups, Royal could still seem socially awkward on lecture tours or with strangers. At a presentation in Squamish, Jim Sinclair, who had climbed *Tantalus Wall* with Royal in the 1960s, entered the room where Royal was making final touches to his slideshow. Without looking up, Royal said he did not want to be disturbed. Sinclair tried to break the ice and said, "You dragged me up *Tantalus Wall* a while back." Royal responded, "I'll accept that." Royal was always nervous before presentations and may have meant his response as a dry joke, but the impression was one of indifference.

When American mountaineer Ed Webster returned from the first ascent of the Kangshung Face on Mount Everest in 1988, he was the keynote speaker at the AAC annual meeting in New York City. He introduced himself to Royal, although they couldn't shake hands because Webster's fingers were heavily bandaged.

"I got frostbitten on Everest," said Webster, who was excited to finally meet one of his heroes. "I was on a small team. We climbed a new route up the mountain without bottled oxygen. I froze my fingertips and several toes."

"Well, congratulations on your effort and your new ascent," replied Royal. "The Himalaya. That's the one kind of climbing I never did."

Webster wondered what Royal could have meant and, inevitably, what impression he had made on America's most celebrated climber. In an interview late in his life, Royal admitted that he had always wanted to climb Everest—something he'd hinted at obliquely to Webster.

· · · · ·

Despite his natural awkwardness, Royal remained dedicated to self-improvement. In the late 1980s, he discovered the books of Lou Tice, a Seattle football coach, motivational speaker, and close associate of Jesuit leadership guru Robert Spitzer. Tice, like Royal, had grown up poor in the forties on the West Coast, had a background in sport, was broadly supportive of America and business, and connected to the Catholic faith. Royal was compelled by Tice's belief that carefully monitored thought processes led to better outcomes. Royal participated in several seminars at Tice's Pacific Institute in Seattle.

Royal could be a creative and indulgent father. When Damon decided to echolocate his way around the house, Royal indulged him. When Damon abandoned his position in the outfield in a T-ball game and climbed up a tree, Royal didn't coax him back to his position but pointed out ways he could climb even higher. The mother of one of Damon's friends was surprised to find Royal, Damon, and her son sixty feet up the backyard redwood tree. For the Fourth of July, Royal spent hundreds of dollars on fireworks only to hand them all over to Damon and his teenage friends to do with as they wished.

"It simply didn't occur to Dad," said Damon, "not to do this kind of stuff."

Royal startled his kids with his compassionate responses to the plight of almost anyone who asked for his help. Friends asked for money, and he gave it to them. "He picked up this family of hitchhikers," said Damon, "and gave them my ski holder for some reason. Maybe that was all there was in the car, but I was a kid and I was pissed. When he dropped them off, he gave them a hundred bucks." Family members and acquaintances suffering from bad luck stayed at Magnolia Avenue for weeks.

Insecure young men who came into Royal's life mainly through climbing received his emotional support and encouragement. He patiently listened to their laments about relationships, their place in climbing, and the world. He advised them and defended them, and gave them work if they needed it.

Ament's biography, *Royal Robbins: Spirit of the Age*, came out in 1992. Reviews in the climbing media were positive, and Royal resolved to begin an autobiography, although his efforts, at first, were sporadic.

In 1998, Royal and Liz celebrated thirty-five years of marriage. He wrote her a letter revealing his joy at having achieved so much together and expressing faith in God, as well as espousing his undying love. "We will grow in love for each other," wrote Royal, "grow and grow in love, until our love envelops us totally and conquers any negative thing that threatens to come into our lives, for God will be with us because we are trusting him through this. We will do all of these things. I see us doing them now."

By the spring of 1999, Royal and Liz owned Royal Robbins factory outlet stores in Modesto, Sacramento, Berkeley, and on Hilton Head Island, a resort and golf town in South Carolina. Their clothing was sold in eighteen countries. "The company had never lost money," said Loren White. "We were focused on financial goals and pretty darn successful. Our profits were up to 7 percent."

"We're little," said Royal, "but we're light on our feet. Our goal isn't to be big or even to make a lot of money. It is to be a company that lasts."

When they considered expansion, Royal and Liz approached Dan Costa. A member of their trusted council of business advisors since 1996, Costa was a self-made man and successful entrepreneur who had built and sold a restaurant chain and was looking for new ventures. According to some former employees, Royal brought Costa into the business quickly—and managers and staff liked him—but as the process of securing capital continued, Royal began to doubt his decision. Royal was ready to cancel the deal, but lawsuits were discussed and Royal asked the managers if they would stay on if he sold 51 percent of the business. "Some had realized that their fortunes would grow," recalled White. "There was a real motivation for growth, and if we couldn't get capital, they would have to look for greener pastures."

Royal and Liz sold 51 percent of their company to Costa and, as a compromise, stayed on as brand ambassadors. "I would not have considered this," said Costa, "without the long-term commitment by Liz and Royal to be involved."

Royal, Costa said, was "the first to tell you he'd rather be climbing. . . . As the Robbinses aged, so did the line. People respected Royal and Liz and what they accomplished, but they had to sell clothes." Royal withdrew from his management role to begin work in earnest on his multivolume autobiography.

He was late to this task. Harding's climbing memoir had come out in 1975, and Steve Roper's history and memoir of 1960s Yosemite had been published in 1994. Royal was in his sixties, and remembering the details of some of the numerous great ascents of his life was difficult. Some of his fellow climbers had already passed away; others were disinclined or unable to recall details from events that had occurred decades ago. Royal had to learn how to use a word processor, which baffled him at first. "Writing was never easy or fun" for Royal, wrote Tamara, but with the help of Pat Ament, Glen Denny, and others, he persevered.

Royal described the project at first as "halfway between the Hardy Boys and the comic strip *Terry and the Pirates*. It's different." He explained, "It's never been done this way. It'll be used as a marketing item, so the more [product] you have, the better." The main similarity to comic books would be serialization and a handful of drawings of climbing scenes and boyhood antics.

"I want to capture an era and all the players in it," Royal wrote Roper. "I am, as I said, very ambitious. I don't know if I told you, but I plan on about ten volumes, each about the size of my *Rockcraft* books. In other words, the opposite of fancy. I want to educate on the craft of climbing and on the characters of climbers as well as entertain. I may be overreaching, and if you are right, I am doing so."

The promotional function of the memoir project was dropped in 2001, when the Robbinses sold the remaining 49 percent of Royal Robbins Inc. to Costa. Royal gave a farewell speech to his employees and said he intended to stay involved, but his enthusiasm for the business was gone. Asked by a newspaper what he felt when Costa sold the company in 2003, he said, "When I sold that thing, it was gone. I don't have any thoughts." "We weren't involved one way or the other," said Liz. "What is there to say?"

"We sold the fucking company," Royal wrote Roper, "and my fucking name."

With more time on his hands, Royal visited old friends and climbing haunts. A climbing trip to Tuolumne Meadows, he wrote Roper, was "just wonderful. I felt like a kid again. Wonderful is a good word. I wondered at it. The camaraderie of our times was more than a wishful word."

Ed Drummond was now suffering from Parkinson's disease. Royal invited him to Pinecrest and gave him some money to continue the writing work that Royal admired. Steck, Roper, and a host of others visited Pinecrest and competed against Royal at darts or foosball, which Royal had taught himself to play one-handed as an extra challenge.

Those close to Royal said the death of Chuck Pratt in 2000 struck him with an unexpected flood of nostalgia and grief. "Chuck, Chuck, so lately here, so soon gone," he wrote in the obituary in the *AAJ*. "How can I be writing this? You, gone? Yes, irrevocably. Your death sudden and shockingly unexpected. It seems not real. Somehow . . . wrong." Writing of a climbers' reunion in Yosemite in 1994, Royal reflected, "It all came back; it all came back in the laughter. My friends, now as before, took life and its tears, and turned them into laughter. And it was so wonderful, so refreshing, so freeing! And I remembered why my best friends were climbers, why I loved them. Because in them burned the joy of life."

In February 2002, Royal visited Warren Harding, who was ill and still living in his mother's house in Anderson, California. In an email to Roper, Royal reported that Harding "can't thumb his nose at his critics by doing another blank wall—he is frustrated and would like to not be seen as the bad guy, the persona he has always gloried in. So he is stuck, and probably disproportionately out of joint at anything he sees as criticism, or as damaging him in the eyes of history." And yet, "[Royal] would have done anything for Warren," said Liz, "without thinking about it." His relationship to Harding, whom he called his "Mephistophelean friend," had always defied simple rivalry. It came to an end a few days later, on February 27, when Harding died.

· · · · ·

At the crags of Gianelli Edges and Burst Rock, near Pinecrest, Royal, accompanied by Tom Frost and a crew of local climbers, put up a couple of dozen new lines. He organized Boy Scout climbing events and an annual "Climb-in" at the Gianelli Edges for AAC members and old friends. The event was, wrote Royal in an invitation, "a sterling example of what we used to call 'the brotherhood of the rope'"—which he updated to be the brotherhood and sisterhood, or even fellowship, of the rope. He also stressed how climbers were one big, crazy family: "And, like a family, we have our black sheep. We have our oddballs and curmudgeonly uncles and nutcases, our elders and youngsters, our loners and flockers and givers and takers and care-givers and care-needers," he wrote.

The new millennium saw a renaissance of interest in the Golden Age of Yosemite climbing and even added a new shine to it. Yosemite climber and guide Ken Yager had collected thousands of climbing artifacts, including hardware, clothing, and documents. In 2003, the Yosemite Climber's Association was founded to build a climbing museum, and Royal was made an unofficial patron of the association.

Royal was invited to contribute an essay to the latest, photo-rich book on Yosemite, *Yosemite: Half a Century of Dynamic Rock Climbing*, cowritten by Heinz Zak, Alexander Huber, and Jim Bridwell. Magazines and newspapers profiled Royal and his contemporaries, and asked them about their views of the past and present in climbing and their tastes in music and books. In photographs, Royal smiles and looks pleased. Having become measured in his comments about climbing, he came across as wise.

In 2006, Royal had a hip replacement. "For some reason, he didn't want them to do it," said Tamara. "There was something about going inside him that did a number on him. I flew from Oregon to be with him . . . he was a different person; he did not want the surgery. He went into a fetal position and screamed."

"Royal," said Liz, "was stoic, but he had an honest response to pain—he had no compunction expressing it; he screamed." Apparently, even Royal's ability to summon deep resources of self-discipline in the face of pain was occasionally, and dramatically, exhausted.

On the fiftieth anniversary of the first ascent of the *Regular Northwest Face* of Half Dome, the first ascentionists—Royal, Jerry Gallwas, and Mike Sherrick—and their spouses met in Yosemite. The first day was spent at the Ahwahnee Hotel. Nick Clinch, a leading American Himalayan climber from the 1970s, came to an evening presentation during which Gallwas wore a Tyrolean hat from his climbing days. A photograph shows the group on the hotel patio in the gathering shade, enjoying a bottle of white wine. Outside the frame is the northwest face of Half Dome, the wall Royal had climbed so many times he'd once said he wanted it as his tombstone. Liz is beside him; on the lawn behind them, children are playing.

The AAC, which had hardly noticed the climb in 1957, sent a letter of appreciation. The next morning the veterans of Half Dome had coffee in Camp 4 at an event organized by El Capitan expert Tom Evans and climber Linda McMillan. They were presented with Yosemite Search and Rescue T-shirts. In one photo, Dean Potter, a leading Yosemite climber of the moment, stands between Gallwas and Royal. Royal smiles politely. Potter's intense gaze recalls Royal's from the days when his mind was high on the walls, even when he was down in the Valley. A visit to the "Granite

Frontiers" exhibition at the Yosemite Museum, curated by Ken Yager, rounded out the weekend.

· · · · ·

Royal had achieved peace with climbing, but his turmoil over religious matters and the meaning of life and society itself continued.

Royal had begun to blame America's problems on a loss of moral and spiritual direction, often ascribed to the two bugaboos of America's entertainment industry and counterculture. This critique had its historical roots: Immigrants from the Midwest and Appalachia had brought their conservative views of family, society, and religion with them when they migrated west. This change allowed a conservative political culture in California to flourish, one that gave rise to Republican president Richard Nixon, whom Royal defended against criticism from his friends, and California governor and later president Ronald Reagan, who'd been raised in the Midwest. The Christian Coalition linked conservative, "small-government" politics from California with Southern, fundamentalist Christianity.

Royal defended the Christian Coalition's aims and donated to the Republican Party. He wrote to friends about the importance of "religion, family, church, local government, and community," as well as his loathing for "dumb regulations." In 1968, he had lambasted the Pope for his regressive stance on birth control. Now in a letter to Doug Tompkins, he bemoaned "unrestricted access" to abortion as "a culture of death." "Kids see an adult world unwilling to make sacrifices to the welfare of children," he wrote, "and they, in their heart of hearts, know that it is they who are being sacrificed. . . . We have the slaughter of the innocents and the sacrifice of innocence." He wrote the *Modesto Bee* regularly, decrying violence on television, the removal of God from the Boy Scout oath, and the lack of sexual morality, and backing the call for parental permission for teenage abortions.

Royal championed the value of religious faith, but he seemed, at times, to hold back from fully embracing it. Tompkins sent Royal a copy of Portuguese novelist José Saramago's *The Gospel According to Jesus Christ*, a secularist treatment of the birth of Christianity. "I appreciate the thought," Royal wrote, "and your attempt to keep me from going off the deep end by pointing me in the direction of a more humanistic Christ. Sorry, to me Christ is more than a philosopher. You see, I really believe in all of that stuff." But he also wrote, "I am still an aspiring Christian and have to get rid of a lot of debris of my soul before I can properly call myself one." But Royal never revealed the nature or scope of that spiritual debris.

In the spring of 2007, Royal's religious confidante, Father Michael Kelly, was accused of abusing children in his care between 1984 and 1986. Members of his parish supported him, and some called him a martyr. Kelly denied the allegations. Royal reserved judgment on the matter until the upcoming trial.

Later that summer, Max Gammon visited California, and he and Royal climbed *After Six*. Gammon took a less political approach to religion than Royal. "I am confident that this will not be our last climb together," Gammon wrote, quoting St. Paul: "Our happiest times on earth are simply foretastes of what our Heavenly Father has in store for us. 'Eye has not seen, nor ear heard, nor have entered into the heart of man, the things which God has prepared for those who love Him.'"

Royal continued to work on his autobiography with feedback from his friends. Roper warned him to avoid moralizing and pointed out historical errors. Ken Wilson encouraged him to include more social and historical background. Glen Denny and Pat Ament read numerous proofs and returned suggestions.

To Be Brave, the first volume, was published in 2009, when Royal was seventy-four. It covered his childhood and youth, and began and ended with reflections on his solo of Leaning Tower and friendship with Warren Harding. He dedicated it to "my beloved mother, who has taught me so much and who has stood by me all these years." It received a Special Jury Mention at the Banff Centre Mountain Film and Book Festival in 2009 and a positive review by Jim McCarthy in the *AAJ*.

"I was the only speaker at the Banff Festival to wear a tie," Royal wrote to Steve Roper. "(When the subject was brought up at a panel, I asserted, 'I have always been a non-conformist.') At the AAC meeting in 1964, I was the only one without a tie."

Canadian writer Geoff Powter interviewed Royal at Banff. Royal still looked powerful and broad shouldered. The high point of the festival for Royal was shaking hands with German climber Anderl Heckmair, the leader of the 1938 first ascent of the Eiger Nordwand—one of the few climbs Royal regretted not having made—as well as the great Italian mountaineer Riccardo Cassin.

In his foreword in *To Be Brave*, Steve Roper called Royal "a wilful visionary who didn't merely see things differently; he also saw different things." He reminded Royal of the lines Royal had once written in the *AAJ* about the *North America Wall*: "Some people are bothered by thoughts of decay and death. Not me. Rather I am obsessed." "I urge him to get to work on the remaining volumes," wrote Roper. "Time flies!" Roper had already urged Royal not to undertake a multivolume project for the same reason.

In 2009, Royal's typical day included writing, walking his dog, and going out for lunch. After an occasionally wild youth, Damon had become a restaurateur. His Camp 4 wine bar in the old Royal Robbins warehouse on Needham Street was Royal's favorite lunch spot. The décor included huge Glen Denny prints of life in Camp 4 during the Golden Age. Royal also frequented Stonehenge, the climbing gym in Modesto. He continued his habit of filling small notebooks with his thoughts:

> *"For a man to feel like a man is the greatest happiness he can know, but he can only know it by <u>enormous effort.</u>"*
> *"It doesn't matter if your blood flows, if it flows in support of a great cause."*
> *"The reason that people buy mountain climbing boots is that they know mountain climbers are free."*
> *"The lover takes his mountain with love, not with hate, a feeling of thankfulness, not conquest."*
> *"The reason that I am what I am is that there is something in me that keeps pulling me upward."*

· · · · ·

Fail Falling, the second volume of Royal's memoirs, came out in 2010. It begins with his discovery of climbing and ends with his first ascent of Half Dome in 1957. Elite American climber Tommy Caldwell wrote the foreword. Caldwell was impressed by what he called the "upper-crust" atmosphere of Royal's home and the stately presence of Royal himself: "classy, detailed, thorough." Shaking hands, Caldwell "felt like the white-trash kid on the first day of East Coast prep school," a feeling Royal could have related to from his own experience as a white-trash kid.

Producing several books with individual prefaces, introductions, acknowledgments, appendixes, and covers continued to slow down the project of getting Royal's story out. He began to be more selective about what he would include, leaving out more than he had in the earlier volumes, sticking to the most important climbs.

In 2010, Royal began to have difficulty speaking, and his natural good balance failed him; he suffered two painful falls. He was diagnosed with progressive supranuclear palsy (PSP), an incurable brain disorder. At the time, the average life expectancy for PSP sufferers was six or seven years.

Royal impressed the doctors by continuing to hike, write, and play a role in family life. In 2011, Ken Yager organized a presentation by Tom Frost and Royal in celebration of the fiftieth anniversary of the first ascent of the *Salathé Wall*. "You could see the love, concern, and respect between them," recalled Yager. "Royal had trouble speaking, and there was a sense of the onset of the disease."

Beulah had moved to a nursing home in 2006, but she still wrote Royal long, detailed letters, often about family history, in perfect longhand. On May 11, 2011, she died peacefully at the age of ninety-five. By that time PSP had severely affected Royal's speech and so he let his nephew, Brian Aros, and niece Nancy Boyd speak at the funeral. Beulah had always been the pillar of the family and the central figure in Royal's life; he'd never lost an opportunity to thank her or express his love and respect.

Royal's acceptance of death as a natural conclusion to life only partly explains his relative calm when Beulah died. While she lived, he had openly expressed his love for and dependence on her, and she had shown her love for and approval of him. Boys are often brought up to feel independent, despite their reliance on their mothers, but Beulah raised Royal to freely acknowledge his dependence on her. The stability of her love had freed him to pursue his unique and adventurous path in life. In fact,

Royal's open need for his mother, and for the women who were partners in his life, allowed him to sidestep the fantasy of machismo and unleash his power to live creatively.

. . . . .

The third volume of Royal's memoirs, *The Golden Age*, was published in 2012. It describes events through his first visit to Europe to the first ascent of the *North America Wall* in 1964. He dedicated it to "my beautiful wife, Liz. Thank you for letting me lean on you during all of life's challenges." The foreword was by Ron Kauk, a former target of Royal's complaints about sport climbing who had become a close friend.

At age seventy-seven, Royal reduced the number of projected volumes to seven. If he maintained his present rate of a volume every two years, he would complete the opus in 2020, at age eighty-five. Volume four was to cover the remainder of the 1960s, including Royal's time in the Alps and the United Kingdom, as well as Yosemite climbs from the last half of the 1960s, a formidable era of complicated events that could have made for the longest volume. The fifth volume was to cover the start of Royal and Liz's business and the history of the Rockcraft school. Volume six would cover Royal's kayaking career. The seventh volume would chronicle Royal Robbins Incorporated.

In 2011, another child abuse claim was made against Father Michael Kelly. In 2012, the court found him guilty of three counts of sexual molestation of a child. Rather than stay in America and likely face prison time, Kelly fled to Ireland. Running from danger and abdicating personal responsibility were affronts to Royal's sense of honor. Royal remained uncertain of Kelly's guilt, but there were no more prayers before meals or salutations of "God bless you" in letters. He even stopped going to mass.

In April 21, 2013, a giant from Royal's heyday, Layton Kor, died after suffering from cancer and kidney failure for years. He was seventy-four. Kor had once said that all Royal and he possessed was climbing, which was true to the end for Kor, who died almost penniless. Royal was heartbroken again, as when Pratt died.

In 2014, Peter Mortimer and Nick Rosen's film *Valley Uprising* was screened to acclaim at mountain film festivals around the world. The film was breathtaking, humorous, and broad in its scope. It added to the rebirth of interest in Yosemite's Golden Age and the men and women who had gilded it. Despite his illness, Royal attended the premiere at the Chautauqua Auditorium in Boulder, Colorado. He could no longer speak without difficulty, but he confided in Tamara that he was unhappy with the film's oversimplification of his relationship with Harding.

On his last visit to Royal in 2016, Roper found his old friend playing chess with his caregiver, but no longer able to speak. "I don't know much about chess," wrote Roper, "but I told him to move the rook. He did, and lost the game. It was the first time I ever saw him capitulate. I went to look at some old photos with Liz, and when I came back, Royal had gone for a rest. The chessboard and the pieces were back in their starting positions."

By 2017, Royal's health had declined dramatically. As he lost more and more control over his body, he rarely complained. Many people can talk about their obsessions with death and decay, but few can live them out with the same style as Royal. "That stoicism remained throughout his illness," said Tamara. "The last few months, he needed help with even the most basic things, but he never apologized and never got angry."

On Damon's frequent visits, when Royal felt a little better, their interactions could take a serious turn. Royal told Damon that he had two main regrets in life. First, unlike his father, he hadn't learned to defend himself physically. He acknowledged the fragility, the fear of pain that others had rarely seen and that had seemed so unlikely in a man who had chosen a life of danger and effort in the mountains. He also said that he wished he had had more children, which perplexed Damon, who had thought him an awkward father.

Although he no longer had faith, Royal found consolation in the words of the Lord's Prayer, which he repeated every day with Liz or his aide until he could no longer speak.

"In his last months, he struggled to walk," Damon continued. "He struggled to eat, to breathe. He struggled. But honestly, you never really knew it. He was so graceful. He insisted until his last day that he was dressed every morning: button-up shirt, dressed in sharp khakis—never jeans . . . nails clipped, hair combed, and his beard trimmed. He never allowed the struggle to take his dignity. . . . Living and dying well is something he thought about often. . . . His last ascent, I like to think, might have been his greatest."

Royal had reflected often upon death, even as a young man. As Liz observed, he neither surrendered to nor resisted its inevitability, but acted like death was a kind of summit that could be reached by digging deeper, trying to make it just a few more feet, to live through another day.

When he could no longer speak, Royal continued to read. Max Gammon, who knew nothing of Royal's loss of faith, sent him regular letters. "I said to him that he needed to look at what was happening as a difficult climb," said Gammon, "and that the last move was utterly impossible, unless he trusted in Christ's rope." What Royal thought of this advice will never be known.

Royal wrote one of his last missives on a postcard of the *Salathé Wall* that he sent to Max Gammon's young son, Matthew. "Live, so that when you die," wrote Royal, "you are a great loss."

"It had always been so important to Royal to die well," said Liz, "[and] in the act of dying, to not be cowardly but honorable. We all know you're going to have to do it, and very deeply within himself, Royal knew he wanted to do it well."

And so, on March 14, 2017, at 10:10 in the morning, in his bedroom on Magnolia Avenue, with the California sun shining on his face through the branches of the giant redwood, the light slipped from Royal Shannon Robbins. He went off to some place none of us have ever seen, and it was a great loss.

"His greatest climb," wrote Liz, "was to die in the manner that he did . . . so stoic."

Epilogue
The Fanatic

Royal was interred at the family plot in Modesto with a small number of family members and friends in attendance. A local carpenter and friend had built the casket, on which Tamara carved "Keep on Climbing" and Royal's initials.

The *New York Times* had published an obituary calling Royal "The Conscience of Rock Climbers." The *Washington Post* called him "the celebrated climber who left no trace of his ascents." "If Royal had learned that he merited a half-page obit in the *New York Times*," wrote Joe Fitschen, who learned about his friend's death from the morning newspaper, "I imagine that he would have responded with a wry smile."

Outside magazine's obituary declared, "Anyone who has ever climbed outdoors owes a debt to Robbins." Swiss newspapers, reflecting the national interest in such matters, noted that Royal had entered the select list of deceased historic figures who'd left dormant bank accounts in the country. Most of the world's greatest news outlets covered his death. The Sierra Club called him a "climber and environmentalist," despite his dislike of the latter term. The hagiography Royal had feared began to rear its head. People had wanted Royal to like them, but he'd usually been indifferent. He was no longer around, so his legacy belonged to everyone.

After months of mourning, the family decided on a memorial that would allow the wider community a chance to grieve with them and to celebrate

Royal's life. They set the date for March 14, 2018, the one-year anniversary of Royal's death. Tamara, Damon, and Liz tracked down the names and contact information of hundreds of Royal's friends and associates.

Tamara had helped Royal with his biographies and was already familiar with his extensive collection of letters, photographs, and documents. She had scanned and transcribed hundreds of documents for electronic storage, and selected certain originals to display on the walls of the hall they had rented for the event.

Early climbing friends Frank Hoover (now in a wheelchair), Mike Sherrick, Jerry Gallwas, and Bill Derr came. Gallwas and Derr gave speeches. Friends from the Golden Age of the Valley included Glen Denny, Jani Roper, Dick Dorworth, Harding's former girlfriend Beryl Knauth, Don Lauria from the *Dawn Wall*, and Russ McLean; Joe Fitschen and Yvon Chouinard gave short addresses. From the Rockcraft years, Dick Dorworth, Dick Erb, Gary Colliver, Joe McKeown, and Michael Covington came. Royal's European years were represented by Davie Agnew, while LAS alumni John Feasler and Kathy Gaylord gave addresses. Janie Levy (née Taylor) and her husband, Daniel, came. The Royal Robbins business was represented by dozens of people, including Keith Roush and Loren White. Royal's paddling friend Newsome Holmes was the MC. The greater business environment in Modesto was also saddened by the loss. Ryan Gallo, of the Gallo winemaking family, came to pay his respects. John Long, Peter Croft, and Ron Kauk represented recent generations of climbers.

Kauk, in his address, summed up what many felt when he said Royal "touched me so deeply because there is something in the humanness of Royal, through his evolution of youthful enthusiasm and competition . . . to recognize the humility of it all. . . . There is a momentum of his energy along with the other ones of that era that I think deserves to continue to go with the story we want to promote for the future."

Chris Jones attended. Some of those who could not come, like Pat Ament, whose health was poor, sent encomiums. In Ament's obituary for the *AAJ*, he called Royal "a man who stamped us with his elegance and class."

Guests were struck by Tamara's displays of Royal's documents. There were letters from Boy Scout camp, pages from his unpublished journal article about the *Dawn Wall*, a blueprint for the RR climbing shoe. John Long, one of climbing's most influential writers, was moved by this fresh glimpse into one of his heroes as a human being. "It confirmed in me," said Long, "the suspicion that Royal had always struggled against himself to be 'The Man.'"

"Royal was a very complex person," wrote Joe Fitschen in a presentation he later gave at the Oakland Climber's Festival. "Not a chameleon, not one who changed his personality to suit the occasion like one might change clothes, but one who couldn't be put in a box, one whose behavior was not a function of habit but was an attempt to deal honestly with the situation at hand." Max Gammon compared Royal to a massive, multifaceted rock wall: all routes were difficult; all routes were mysterious.

"Our road trips, his love of adventure," wrote Tamara, "Tintin and Asterix, the way he would laugh, his sportsmanship. These are what we who knew him miss. I think his story is less about the forces which shaped it and more about how consciously and deliberately he shaped it. That is an unusual thing."

"One is never hard at the center," Royal wrote in his notebooks, bringing us closest to the source of his being. "At the center is that little boy, open and flower-like, who screams to be listened to, who cries to escape, to be let out, to not be so deeply imprisoned, who would prefer to submit before God, yet is forced by the repeated blows of life to retire deeper, safer from the wounds, to retire so deep and so safe that he appears to be not there at all."

The notion that American climbing's greatest moments can be traced to the aftermath of unresolved childhood trauma inflicted by toxic father figures and poverty bears consideration. Abuse not only failed to extinguish Royal's hunger for joy, transcendence, and ecstasy but heightened it to a perhaps unusual level. But recent historians have shown that in America, the line between being outdoors recreationally and out of necessity (i.e., homeless because of poverty or mental health issues) is much thinner than many might suppose. Squalor revealed that Royal, more than most people, was built for wonder. The inhumanity of his tormentors convinced him of a personal superiority that often served him well on his chosen path, even if it annoyed others. And not all were annoyed, as his lifelong partnerships with the greatest climbers of his age showed.

But more important to Royal than Pratt, Chouinard, Frost, Fitschen, McCarthy, and the rest was Liz, a kindred spirit, a wanderer who helped him become the Royal Robbins of history, who created with him a home, children, inspiration, and love. They were in each other's arms within hours of first meeting; their attraction overthrew propriety and reason, and lasted until Royal died. In Yosemite's Golden Age era and beyond, male climbers who were aware of the effect their sexuality had on women—and for that matter, men—were revered. If they also drank, slept around, or neglected their families, they became known as lovable rogues. For her part, Liz was aware of and welcomed the attentions of men—the list of smitten young men from Camp 4 and elsewhere was long. The historical negativity toward women like Liz who deliberately rejected these macho narratives can be seen as punishment for undermining male climbers' fragility. A life with Liz proved that Royal's weaknesses never added up to any such fragility. A devoted husband, he always saw and appreciated how Liz engaged with the world.

Royal's closest connection in life, however, was with Yosemite, where he found wonder, shelter, and a place to be seen and heard and to interrupt history. When Royal was the leader of Camp 4, Yosemite, formerly an also-ran in American climbing and an obscurity in the global scene, blossomed into a world center, even eclipsing the Alps. His ethics were meant to guard both the game and the wonder of climbing; most of the time, they did both. The little boy who'd found freedom in climbing shared it through hundreds of articles and presentations plus thousands of pitches of often-visionary climbing, curtailed only by the illness that eventually killed him.

"To a climber," Royal wrote, "a mountain is a symbol of all of the frustrations of life, and the true climber, the fanatic, can never be satisfied"—because for him, climbing itself was life.

Author's Note
A Remote, Hard-to-Fathom Figure

"In Yosemite, there are other climbers,
but there is only one eminence."

—*James Salter*

Royal Robbins is everywhere in modern rock climbing. His name is almost as synonymous with Yosemite as John Muir's. Discourse about his obsessions, triumphs, and fiascos continues today. Modern big wall climbing, the use of clean gear instead of pitons, the Yosemite Decimal System, and the concept of a "first ascent" all bear his mark. Few have achieved his degree of climbing fame.

I wrote this book principally out of admiration for Royal's visionary climbs and the writing with which he supported, explained, and described his craft, both publicly and privately. This material may comprise the largest body of literature created by any climber, at least in North America.

Royal remains most alive in the popular imagination in stories of his rivalry with fellow climber Warren Harding over the use of bolts and fixed ropes. In various iterations, Royal plays a dour, sanctimonious, and sometimes authoritarian Zeus against Harding's wine-swilling, fun-loving Dionysus.

The truth is more complex. Royal's friend Harry Daley told Royal "he was the most hated climber in America." The historian Chris Jones described Robbins as "a remote, hard-to-fathom figure who took himself seriously and liked to appear well-read, he constantly put himself on trial to maintain his position." His friend and biographer Pat Ament called him a "doer, prime mover, teacher," "simply magic," "a most worthy hero." Any number of his closest friends spoke of how his loyalty overlooked even their most obvious flaws. Some of Royal's acquaintances described him as a man worthy of Hadley Richardson's description of Hemingway, with "so many sides to him, he defies geometry." But through all the change and adventure, patterns emerge, clues to why and how Robbins became America's greatest climber.

In addition to the numerous tools available to the modern biographer, with the help of the Robbins family, and particularly Tamara Robbins, Royal's daughter, I perused some forty-six thousand archival items. Without Tamara's ongoing input, it would be hard to imagine this book ever coming into existence. In Modesto, Tamara and her mother, Liz, graciously helped me navigate hundreds of other pieces of correspondence and documents from Royal's friends, business partners, and associates. Tamara also helped immensely by reviewing drafts and offering suggestions. The Robbins family has been crucial to the completion of this portrait of Royal, and I thank Liz, Tamara, and Damon for spending time discussing their father with me and welcoming me into their homes.

I had hundreds of conversations and communications with people who knew Royal or engaged his legacy. In particular, I would like to thank Rick Accomazzo, Davie Agnew, Shelley Aros, Rusty Baillie, Dale Bard, Eric Beck, Ken Boche, Audrey Borisov, Roger Breedlove, Patrik Callis, Malinda Chouinard, Bev Clark, John Cleare, Gary Colliver, Ed Cooper, Michael Covington, Peter Croft, René Daveluy, Glen Denny, Dick Dorworth, Ed Douglas, Sid Eder, Dick Erb, Tom Evans, Joe Fitschen, Jerry Gallwas, John Gill, Alessandro Gogna, Dennis Gray, Steve Grossman, Peter Haan, John Harlin III, Tom Herbert, David Hopkins, Thomas Hornbein, Katie Ives, Michael Kennedy, Jane Levy, John Long, Jerry Lovatt, Jim McCarthy, Roy McClenahan, Bernadette McDonald, Dougald MacDonald, Doug McKeown, Russ McLean, Cindy Merry, John Middendorf, Jon Popowich,

Geoff Powter, Dave Rearick, Damon Robbins, Liz Robbins, Tamara Robbins, Doug Robinson, Chris Rogers, Steve Roper, Keith Roush, Jan Sacherer Turner, Katie Sauter, Jim Sinclair, Chris Vandiver, Larry Ware, Loren White, Jim Williams, Ken Yager, and Pete Zabrok.

Finally, I confess to having come to this work as a climber who has repeated some of Royal's routes. My sense of what they involve is tactile. Some of my strongest memories were forged on walls he first explored. I write from the partisan point of view that Royal's choices and beliefs are significant because his climbs were significant. It's a perspective I believe he would share.

Notable
First Ascents

Note: The route names listed below are the ones in use at the time of writing. FFA means first free ascent.

Tahquitz, California, *Long Climb* (5.8), with Don Wilson, May 1952.
Tahquitz, *Open Book* (5.9), FFA with Don Wilson, 1952.
Tahquitz, *Human Fright* (5.10), with John Mendenhall, June 1952.
Tahquitz, *Lower Royal's Arch* (5.10), with Don Wilson and Chuck Wilts, May 1952.
Yosemite Valley, California, Higher Cathedral Spire, *Robbins Variation* (5.9), with Roy Gorin, May 1952.
Tahquitz, *The Swallow* (5.9), with Chuck Wilts, June 1952.
Tahquitz, *Upper Royal's Arch* (5.8), with Jerry Gallwas and Chuck Wilts, 1953.
Tahquitz, *Gallwas' Gallop* (5.9), with Jerry Gallwas and Chuck Wilts, 1953.
Tahquitz, *The Flakes* (5.8 A2), with Don Wilson, July 1953.
Tahquitz, *Frightful Fright* (A2), with Don Wilson, July 1953.
Tahquitz, *The Blank* (5.8 A2), with Jerry Gallwas, May 1954.
Tahquitz, *The Hangover* (A3), with Jerry Gallwas, Frank Martin, and Mike Sherrick, August 1954.
Tahquitz, *Northeast Face East* (5.7), with Don Wilson, September 1954.
Tahquitz, *The Reach* (A2), with Mike Sherrick, September 1956.
Yosemite, Liberty Cap, South Face (IV 5.8 A3), with Mark Powell and Joe Fitschen, September 1956.
Tahquitz, *The Step* (5.8 A1), with Jerry Gallwas, 1957.

Yosemite, Half Dome, *Regular Northwest Face* (VI 5.9 A3), with Jerry Gallwas and Mike Sherrick, July 1957.

Tahquitz, *Whodunit* (5.8 A1), with Joe Fitschen, September 1957.

Tahquitz, *The Unchaste* (5.9 A1), with Mike Sherrick, September 1957.

Tahquitz, *The Innominate* (5.10), FFA with Jerry Gallwas, 1957.

Organ Mountains, The Wedge, *Direct South Face* (5.9, some aid), with Pete Rogowski, 1958.

Hueco Tanks, Texas, North Mountain, Front Side, grade unknown, 1958.

Tahquitz, *The Consolation* (5.9), FFA with TM Herbert, 1959.

Tahquitz, *The Illegitimate* (5.9), with TM Herbert, and FFA with TM Herbert, May 1959.

Tahquitz, *The Vampire* (5.9 A1), with Dave Rearick, June 1959.

Tahquitz, *The Jam Crack* (5.8), with Don Wilson, September 1959.

Yosemite, *The Crack of Dawn* (5.9), with Chuck Pratt and Tom Frost, September 1959.

Tahquitz, *Dave's Deviation* (5.9), with Tom Frost, 1960.

Tahquitz, *Dave's Deviation, extension* (5.10), with Tom Frost, 1960.

Yosemite, Lower Cathedral Rock, North Face (V 5.9 A3), with Chuck Pratt and Joe Fitschen, June 4, 1960.

Yosemite, *Arches Direct* (VI 5.8 A4), with Joe Fitschen, June 1960.

Yosemite, Rixon's Pinnacle, *East Chimney* (III 5.10), FFA with Dave Rearick, June 16, 1960.

Yosemite, Half Dome, North Ridge (III 5.9 A2), with Chuck Wilts, June 24, 1960.

Yosemite, Nevada Falls, *Left Side* (5.6 A4), with Lin Ephraim, June 1960.

Tetons, Wyoming, Middle Teton, a new route on the north face (IV 5.10 A1), with Joe Fitschen, July 30, 1960.

Tetons, Garnet Canyon, a new route on Big Bluff (5.9 A3), with Joe Fitschen, August 12, 1960.

Yosemite, El Capitan, the *Nose* (VI 5.9 A3), first continuous ascent, with Tom Frost, Chuck Pratt, and Joe Fitschen, September 13, 1960.

Yosemite, Bridalveil East, *Aqua Variation* (5.8), with Rich Calderwood, 1961.

Yosemite, Slab Happy Pinnacle, *Center Original* (III 5.9 A4), with Tom Frost and Harry Daley, May 1961.

Yosemite, Slab Happy Pinnacle, *Dihardral* (III 5.10), with Tom Frost, May 1961.

Yosemite, Higher Cathedral Spire, Northwest Face (VI 5.8 A4), with Tom Frost, June 8, 1961.

Yosemite, Sentinel Rock, *Direct North Face* (VI 5.9 A4), with Tom Frost, July 4, 1961.

Tetons, Middle Teton, Northeast Face, *Taylor Route* (IV 5.9 A4), with Janie Taylor, August 16, 1961.

Tetons, Teepe Pillar, Northeast Face (IV 5.10 A3), with Janie Taylor, August 24, 1961.

Yosemite, Sentinel Rock, *Steck-Salathé* (V 5.9 A3), first solo ascent, September 1961.

Yosemite, El Capitan, *Salathé Wall* (VI 5.9 A4), with Chuck Pratt and Tom Frost, September 24, 1961.

Tahquitz, *El Camino Real* (5.10), with Harry Daley and Janie Taylor, November 1961.

Tahquitz, *Lizard's Leap* (5.9), with Harry Daley, November 1961.

Yosemite, Slab Happy Pinnacle, *Left* (III 5.8 A3), with Jack Turner, May 1962.

Yosemite, Little John, *Right* (5.8), with Jack Turner, May 1962.

Valley of the Gods, Utah, Mexican Hat, *Robbins Route* (A4), with Jack Turner, June 1962.

Chamonix, France, Aiguille du Dru, *American Direct* (VI 5.9 A2), with Gary Hemming, July 26, 1962.

Calanques, France, *Voie Americaine* (5.9), with Gary Hemming and John Harlin II, July 1962.

Calanques, *Machine a Sécher* (A3), with Gary Hemming and John Harlin II, July 1962.

Yosemite, El Capitan, *Salathé Wall* (VI 5.9 A4), first continuous ascent, with Tom Frost, October 13, 1962.

Yosemite, Leaning Tower, West Face (VI A4), first solo ascent, May 1963.

Yosemite, *Misty Wall*, (VI 5.9 A3), with Dick McCracken, May 23, 1963.

Yosemite, Rixon's Pinnacle, *Far West* (III 5.9 A3), with Dick McCracken, June 1963.

Yosemite, Half Dome, *Direct Northwest Face* (VI 5.9 A5), with Dick McCracken, June 13, 1963.

Cirque of the Unclimbables, Northwest Territories, Mount Proboscis, Southeast Face (VI 5.9 A4), with Jim McCarthy, Layton Kor, and Dick McCracken, August 8, 1963.

Rocky Mountain National Park, Colorado, Longs Peak, The Diamond, *Jack of Diamonds* (V 5.10 A4), with Layton Kor, August 13, 1963.

Rocky Mountain National Park, Mount Meeker, Ship's Prow, *Gangplank* (III 5.7 A4), with Pat Ament, August 1963.

Yosemite, Bridalveil Falls, East Buttress (III 5.8 A3,) with TM Herbert, September 6, 1963.

Yosemite, Goodrich Pinnacle, *Right Side* (III 5.9), with Liz Robbins and TM Herbert, May 1964.

Wind River Range, Wyoming, *Cirque of the Towers Traverse* (V 5.8), with Dick McCracken and Charlie Raymond, July 16, 1964.

Wind River Range, Watchtower, South Buttress (IV 5.9 A2), with Charlie Raymond, July 18, 1964.

Wind River Range, Mount Hooker, North Face (VI 5.9 A4), with Dick McCracken and Charlie Raymond, July 25, 1964.

Lumpy Ridge, Colorado, Sundance Buttress, *Turnkorner* (5.10), FFA with some falls, with Bob Boucher, July 1964.

Needles, South Dakota, Cerberus aka Tricouni Nail (5.8), with Liz Robbins, Dick Laptad, and Sue Prince, August 1964.

Needles, Sandberg Peak (5.8), with Liz Robbins, August 1964.

Needles, Queenpin (5.9), with Liz Robbins, Dick Laptad, and Sue Prince, August 1964.

Needles, Tent Peg (5.7), with Liz Robbins, August 1964.

Devils Tower, Wyoming, *Dance Macabre* (5.10), with Peter Robinson, August 19, 1964.

Devils Tower, *The Window* (IV 5.6 A4), with Peter Robinson, August 20, 1964.

Boulder Canyon, Colorado, Castle Rock, *The Final Exam* (5.10), with Pat Ament, August 1964.

Boulder Canyon, Castle Rock, *By Gully* (5.9), with Pat Ament, August 1964.

Boulder Canyon, Castle Rock, *Athlete's Feat* (5.10), FFA with Pat Ament, August 1964.
Eldorado Canyon, Colorado, *Yellow Spur* (5.9+), FFA with Pat Ament, August 1964.
Big Cottonwood Canyon, Utah, *Amphitheater Overhang Left* (A3), August 1964.
Big Cottonwood Canyon, *Amphitheater Overhang Right* (A3), August 1964.
Little Cottonwood Canyon, Utah, The Thumb, *Direct South Face* (5.9), with Ted Wilson, August 1964.
Little Cottonwood Canyon, The Thumb, *Robbins Crack* (5.10), with Ted Wilson, August 1964.
Yosemite, El Capitan, *North America Wall* (VI 5.8 A5), with Tom Frost, Yvon Chouinard, and Chuck Pratt, October 31, 1964.
Joshua Tree, California, The Blob, *Buissonier* (5.7), with Mark Powell, 1965.
Yosemite, Wawona Tunnel, *Eat at Degnan's* (5.9), May 1965.
Yosemite, The Slack, *Left Side* (5.10), with Chuck Pratt, May 1965.
Leysin, Switzerland, Sphinx d'Aï, *Petite Diagonale* (5.11), with John Harlin II, 1965.
Leysin, Switzerland, Diamant, Tour de Mayen, *Voir de Diedre* (5.10), with Layton Kor and Don Whillans, 1965.
Chamonix, Petit Dru, *West Face Direttissima* (VI 5.9 A3), with John Harlin II, 1965.
Yosemite, *Boulderfield Gorge* (5.8), with Liz Robbins, Mike Dent, and Victor Cowley, September 1966.
Yosemite, *Reed's Pinnacle Direct* (5.10), pitches one and three, with Gordon Webster and Terry Burnell, September 1966.
Yosemite, The Pulpit, *Notch Route* (5.10), FFA, 1966.
Shawangunks, New York, *Grim-ace Face* (5.9), with Jim McCarthy, 1966.
Yosemite, Manure Pile Buttress, *Nutcracker* (5.8), with Liz Robbins, May 1967.
Yosemite, Manure Pile Buttress, *Nutcracker, Direct Finish* (5.9), with Yvon Chouinard, May 1967.
Yosemite, El Capitan, West Face (VI 5.9 A4), with TM Herbert, May 1967.
Yosemite, Half Dome, *Regular Northwest Face*, with Liz Robbins, first female ascent of a Yosemite Grade VI, May 1967.
Kings Canyon, California, Grand Sentinel (V 5.10 A3), with Yvon Chouinard, May 1967.
Sugarloaf, California, *Self Abuse* (5.10), summer 1967.
Sugarloaf, *Fat Merchant Crack* (5.10), summer 1967.
Canadian Rockies, Mount Geikie, North Face, (V 5.10 A3), with John Hudson, July 15, 1967.
Canadian Rockies, Mount Edith Cavell, North Face (V 5.7), first solo ascent, July 1967.
Yosemite, *The Vendetta* (5.10), FFA with Galen Rowell, 1968.
Yosemite, The Remnant, *Left Side* (5.10), with Loyd Price, February 1968.
Yosemite, The Cookie, *Left* (5.10), with Loyd Price, February 1968.
Yosemite, The Cookie, *Right* (5.10), with Loyd Price, February 1968.
Yosemite, *Meat Grinder* (5.10), with TM Herbert, March 1968.
Yosemite, El Capitan, *Muir Wall* (VI 5.9 A4), first solo ascent of El Capitan, April 1968.
Yosemite, Washington Column, *The Prow* (V 5.9 A4), with Glen Denny, May 1969.
Kichatna Spires, Alaska, Mount Nevermore (III 5.7), with Joe Fitschen and Charles Raymond, July 18, 1969.

Kichatna Spires, Mount Jeffers (IV 5.8 A1), with Joe Fitschen and Charles Raymond, July 22, 1969.

Kichatna Spires, Mount Sasquatch (IV 5.8 A2), with Joe Fitschen and Charles Raymond, August 2, 1969.

Yosemite, Half Dome, *Tis-sa-ack* (VI 5.9 A4), with Don Peterson, October 7, 1969.

Lover's Leap, California, *Craven Image* (5.7), with Steve Roper, 1969.

Lover's Leap, *Crud Gully* (5.8), with Steve Roper, 1969.

Pigeon Cliff, California, *The Robbins Route* (5.9), with Joe Fitschen and Steve Roper, 1969.

Mount Woodson, California, *Robbins Crack* (5.10), FFA, free solo, 1969.

Yosemite, Sentinel Rock, *In Cold Blood* (VI 5.8 A4), first solo first ascent of a Yosemite big wall, May 27, 1970.

Yosemite, Half Dome, *Arcturus* (VI 5.7 A4), with Dick Dorworth, July 1970.

Yosemite, Tuolumne Meadows, Lembert Dome, *Interrogation* (5.10), with Dick Dorworth and Lance Poulsen, July 1970.

Yosemite, Tuolumne Meadows, *Gray Ghost* (5.9), with TM Herbert, July 1970.

Yosemite, Ribbon Falls, *Vain Hope* (V 5.7 A3), with Kim Schmitz and Jim Bridwell, October 5, 1970.

Yosemite, Tuolumne Meadows, The Lamb, *Passover* (5.9), with TM Herbert and Jim Bridwell, June 1971.

Prescott, Arizona, Thumb Butte, *Mecca* (5.9), with Rusty Baillie, summer 1971.

Granite Dells, Arizona, *Siege* (5.10), with David Lovejoy and Rusty Baillie, summer 1971.

Squamish, British Columbia, Sugarloaf, *Thriller off the Void* (5.11), toprope, October 1971.

Squamish, British Columbia, Murrin Park, *Mr. Crabbe* (A3), October 1971.

Lover's Leap, *Incubus* (5.10), with Steve Roper, 1972.

Lover's Leap, *Fantasia* (5.9), with Ken Wilson, 1973.

Donner Pass, California, Snowshed Wall, *Karl's Gym* (5.10d), with Chris Vandiver, 1973.

Queen's Throne, California, *Coronet* (5.8), 1973.

Queen's Throne, *Scepter* (5.6), 1973.

Southern Yosemite, The Balls, various multipitch routes, 1973–1974.

Fresno Dome, California, *Watership Down* (5.7), with M. Sorenson and R. Baum, 1976.

Kichatna Spires, South Ridge of the West Face of Archdeacon Peak (III grade unknown), with Geoffrey Coates, August 1976.

Cracked Canyon, Colorado, *Chewbacca* (5.8), with Bill Kees, 1977.

Ophir Wall, Colorado, *Arachne* (5.10), with Dan Langmade, May 26, 1978.

Ophir Wall, *Adam's Rib* (5.9), with Allen Pattie, May 30, 1978.

Ophir Wall, *Adagio* (5.9), with Bill Kees, June 8, 1978.

Ophir Wall, *Rickety Split* (5.8), with Bill Kees, June 8, 1978.

Ophir Wall, *Rickety Split variation* (5.8), with Bill Kees, June 8, 1978.

Ophir Wall, *Chestnut* (5.9), with Bill Kees, June 9, 1978.

Cracked Canyon, *Cello* (5.10), with Chris Vandiver, 1978.

Cracked Canyon, *Javelin* (5.11), with Chris Vandiver, June 14, 1978.

Cracked Canyon, *The Crock* (5.10), with Chris Vandiver, June 14, 1978.

Cracked Canyon, *Thor* (5.10), with Bill Kees, June 15, 1978.

Cracked Canyon, *Detour* (5.8), with Chris Vandiver, June 22, 1978.

Cracked Canyon, *Nid D'Oiseaux* (5.9), with Chris Vandiver, June 29, 1978.

Cracked Canyon, *Where the Wild Things Are* (5.9), with Chris Vandiver, June 30, 1978.

Cracked Canyon, *Iago* (5.8), with Jim Sweeney, 1978.

Cracked Canyon, *Othello* (5.9), with Jim Sweeney, 1978.

Cracked Canyon, *String of Diamonds* (5.10), with Kevin Cooney, 1978.

Cracked Canyon, *Attica* (5.9), with Jim Sweeney, 1979.

Gianelli Edges, California, *Bright Light* (5.6), with Tom Frost, Brad Young, and David Harden, October 2000.

Gianelli Edges, *Solo* (5.1), October 2000.

Gianelli Edges, *Crackside* (5.7), with David Harden and Brad Young, October 2000.

Gianelli Edges, *Lani's Leap* (5.9), with Lani Holdener and Tom Frost, September 2001.

Gianelli Edges, *Jamcrack Joe* (5.8), with Tom Frost, September 2001.

Gianelli Edges, *I Can't Believe It* (5.9), with Tom Frost, September 2001.

Gianelli Edges, *Easy Finish Corner* (5.10), with David Harden, September 2003.

Gianelli Edges, *Frosty Fingers* (5.9), with David Harden, September 2003.

Notes

Chapter 1: Ride the Trail in Style

p. 14 **In the rented second floor:** Beulah Bowen's birth certificate records her birth year as 1915, but the 1920 Census records it as 1916, a mistake repeated in the 1930 Census. Census takers were permitted to estimate dates and probably just repeated the error. Sourced from the United States Department of Commerce, Bureau of the Census, Fourteenth Census of the United States, 1920, East District 51, sheet 3, National Archives; and United States Department of Commerce, Bureau of the Census, Fifteenth Census of the United States, National Archives. US Census, Ohio, Gallia, 1930, Sheet 13A 27-7.

p. 15 **Shannon left school at six:** Sourced from the US Census, 1930, Mason County, West Virginia, Point Pleasant Town, sheet 1A.

p. 15 **The attraction was mutual:** Sourced from the Marriage Record, Royal Shannon Robbins, Beulah B. Bowen, July 3, 1934, County Records, Mason, West Virginia, United States, Number 296.

p. 15 **And although Royal's father:** Royal Robbins is listed as Jimmy Chandler, for instance, in the US Census, 1940, Richland, Ohio, sheet 25-B.

p. 16 **The family lived off the wages:** An exaggeration Chandler made on his draft-registration card. Jimmy Lee Chandler, serial number 2519-2279, Mansfield, Ohio, Draft Registration Cards, World War II draft cards, National Archives.

p. 16 **For his own protection:** Sourced from the US Census, 1940, Richland, Ohio, sheet 25-B.

p. 16 **Jimmy's older brother:** William Bruce Chandler, serial number 2011, 235, Los Angeles, California, Draft Registration Cards, World War II draft cards, National Archives.

p. 17 **As he wrote in *My Life: To Be Brave*:** "Children throughout the ages," wrote 1940s psychiatrist Lauretta Bender, "long before Superman existed, have tried to fly. . . . Certain children with certain emotional problems are particularly preoccupied with the problem of flying, both fascinated by it, and fearful of it." Sourced from the "Testimony of Dr. Lauretta Bender, Senior Psychiatrist, Bellevue Hospital, New York, N.Y.," thecomicbooks.com/bender.html, last accessed December 19, 2021.

p. 18 **Through her retail job:** Sourced from the City Planning Commission, Los Angeles, California, *Distribution of foreign born, US Census data, 1940–1943.* Maps were made for fourteen national, ethnic, and racial groups.

p. 20 **By April 1940:** Sourced from the US Census, April 18, 1940, Nankin, Michigan, sheet 45 B. Residents of the poorhouse did not list themselves as inmates, unlike Robbins. Eloise had both a poorhouse for unemployed and homeless persons, as well as a notorious mental hospital.

p. 21 **His spelling was poor:** Royal's backwardness in reading and writing is evident in his letters from this time. For more on his problems with mathematics, see *To Be Brave,* pp. 85–86.

Chapter 2: Anarchy and Aimlessness

p. 23 **In 1947, however:** This would be about five hundred dollars in 2022 currency.

p. 25 **Although Royal had been a Scout:** Only Life Scouts with eleven merit badges could undertake the qualification for Eagle Scout. To upgrade from Life to Eagle Scout required ten more merit badges and the completion of various other projects.

p. 26 **He scrounged money to buy:** Accounts from Mendenhall, Gallwas, Dawson, and others describe piton prices ranging from 5 cents to $1.50.

p. 26 **At the library:** Henderson's book was tarnished by racism. He advised avoiding "Indian [sled] dogs," for example, as they "have usually been mistreated and are apt to be vicious."

p. 29 **At eighteen:** Some sources state that Wilson was three years older than Royal. Wilson was born on October 6. So he was still eighteen in the spring of 1951.

p. 29 **I liked its precision . . .:** Sourced from Robbins's memoir *Fail Falling* (p. 44). Royal's first LP records included Bach and Vivaldi by Russian violinist David Oistrakh and Polish-American violinist Isaac Stern, as well as Tchaikovsky and Mozart symphonies. Early purchases included Nikolai Rimsky-Korsakov's "Scheherazade," Opus 35; Antonín Dvořák's "Symphony Number 9 in E Minor, The New World," which reverberated with the composer's awe of the American wilderness; and Sergei Rachmaninoff's torrential "Piano Concerto Number 2, Opus 18." The weekly live broadcast by the New York Opera Company on Saturday afternoon aired when Royal was at the cliffs. The only opera amongst his earliest recordings was Sergei Prokofiev's *The Love for Three Oranges,* in which a prince dying from reading too much sad poetry can only be revived by the love of a woman.

p. 30 **Because he was the only member:** Joe Fitschen describes the car as a 1941 Chevrolet with "three carbs and a racing cam" (*Going Up,* p. 92). Robbins describes it more modestly as a "souped up" 1950 Mercury.

p. 31 **The RCS took Royal:** Mount Williamson in the Sierra is a different peak than Mount Williamson in the San Gabriels.

p. 32 **In 1951, Beulah moved the family:** Sourced from the *Los Angeles Street Address Directory* (Los Angeles: Pacific Telephone and Telegraph Company, 1951, p. 72).

p. 33 **One day, on the way:** Joe Fitschen and Royal give differing accounts of this event.

p. 34 **Qualified climbing leaders:** By 1954, only 849 people were qualified to lead climb in Yosemite. Sourced from the United States Department of the Interior, "Summary of Annual Mountaineering Reports from Areas Administered by the National Park Service, 1955," June 12, 1956, Yosemite Central Files, Mountain Climbing 1957–1969, L3423-L48.

p. 38 **The RCS made Wilson:** Many climbs and names of formations used by climbers in the 1940s and 1950s in Joshua Tree have been lost.

Chapter 3: Rotten Lucky Bastards

p. 41 **At that moment:** Royal left the first ascent of the world's highest peak out of his memoirs. As he wrote in *Fail Falling* (p. 99): "Those mountains [the Himalaya] were very far away, and I didn't know how to reach them. I knew it took a lot of money, and I didn't have any. But I had a thumb, and one of the world's best climbing areas was only a few hours away."

p. 41 **The ascent of Everest:** Permission to climb without registration was secured by Richard Leonard. Richard Leonard to John C. Preston, May 25, 1954, Yosemite Central Files, Mountain Climbing 1957–1969, L3423-L48.

p. 42 **That night it rained:** Gallwas says the bivouac was unplanned. Gallwas to author, April 4, 2021. Royal recorded it as his first planned bivouac in *Fail Falling* (p. 73).

p. 42 **Apparently, [Wilson] approached [Steck]:** Fitschen confirms this event as well.

p. 42 **He didn't know it:** The north face of the Locomotiv in the sandstone towers of Saxony in East Germany, climbed in 1948 by Hans Michael, as well as a few other climbs in the same area by Hans Gonda and Herbert Wünsche, matched or exceeded the difficulty of *The Innominate*, although in East Germany resting on bolts and standing on other climbers' shoulders were accepted as free climbing. The closest achievements would be by British climbers. Joe Brown's 1952 route *Cenotaph Corner* in North Wales, *Right Eliminate* on gritstone in northern England, and that summer, the first free ascent of a long offwidth crack on the Aiguille Blaitière in Chamonix were the closest comparisons in terms of style and difficulty.

p. 45 **Gaunt, unshaven, and clad in black jeans:** Steve Roper recalled that Harding wore the more common army surplus pants dyed black—not jeans.

p. 46 **But their priorities remained their careers:** Lin Ephraim was an actor, editor, and producer. His greatest credit when Royal Robbins met him was editing the television show *Mars and Beyond*, 1957, Wide World of Disney.

p. 46 **The third week of June 1955:** Parties of four climbers were considered optimal for big walls. The technique of fixing the rope for the second to ascend with prusik slings had not yet been invented; instead, the second climbed from piton to piton while belayed by the leader, so neither climber got to rest. Supplies were carried in packs by the second, or hauled hand-over-hand before the second climbed.

p. 47 **Both Royal and Harding believed:** Robbins later recalled that Gallwas also wanted to descend. Gallwas, however, said that he sided with Wilson not because of the difficult climbing or loose rock, but because they only had one more day's worth of food and water.

p. 50 **If you wish to contact your father:** A letter from the Office of Veterans Affairs, Detroit, to Royal Robbins, December 20, 1956.

p. 51 **For gear:** The impression that most of the equipment was designed or collected for the climb was inadvertently created by Mike Sherrick. See Mike Sherrick, "The Northwest Face of Half Dome," *Sierra Club Bulletin*, November 1958, Vol. 43, No. 9, pp. 19–23.

p. 54 **Half done [sic] . . .:** Jerry Gallwas to Lois Gallwas, telegram, June 29, 1957 (incorrectly dated 1956). Sourced from Gallwas, Jerry, ed. *Half Dome, First Ascent of the North West Face* (commemorative pamphlet for the fiftieth anniversary of the first ascent), 2007, p. 24.

p. 54 **In the July *Mugelnoos*:** For some time, the wall was referred to variously as the North West, Northwest, and North Face of Half Dome.

p. 55 **They eloped to Las Vegas:** Sourced from the Marriage Register, Clark County Recorder's Office, Clark County, Nevada, July 14, 1957, 052-83889.

p. 55 **Later that day:** Fitschen says that Rearick introduced himself at the campsite the night before (August 24, 1957).

p. 55 **Sherrick was ill:** My source for this is Joe Fitschen's *Going Up* (p. 206). Other accounts state that the climb had been planned solely for Royal and Fitschen all along.

Chapter 4: The Big Daddy

p. 59 **In February, Grace gave birth:** Sourced from State of California, *California Birth Index, 1905–1995*, Sacramento, California, USA: State of California Department of Health Services, Center for Health Statistics. Registry of birth: Lawrence M. Robbins, February 26, 1958.

p. 59 **At Fort Ord:** Sourced from US Army, Fort Ord Yearbook: Company A, 3rd Battle Group, 1st Brigade, 3 March 1958–26 April 1958, p. 34.

p. 62 **That September, they climbed:** Royal Robbins wrote in his memoirs that he met Pratt in 1960, but they climbed together in September 1959.

p. 63 **Royal's first written response:** Royal Robbins to Yosemite National Park chief ranger. Sent from Fort Ord after November 1958, when Powell quit Harding's party.

p. 63 **I am writing to request:** The letter also proves that neither Royal Robbins nor Powell yet saw Powell's injury as permanent.

p. 64 **Fitschen says Tetons climber Dave Dornan:** Either Yvon Chouinard counted incorrectly or another member was intended. Steve Roper favors the first explanation.

p. 65 **They stayed up talking:** Royal Robbins wrote that he first met Janie Taylor in August 1960 (*The Golden Age*, p. 18). Taylor wrote that they first met on

Thanksgiving weekend 1960. Sourced from Levy (née Taylor), Janie, "Climbing History," unpublished article, October 29, 2020, p. 1.

p. 67 **He was genuinely proud of her abilities:** This observation is from Jan Sacherer's essay "Girls Can Be Dirtbags Too," published in Lauren DeLaunay Miller's *Valley of Giants.*

p. 68 **He hated them:** This is taken from an unpublished article by Royal (ca. 1970, unpaginated), mostly concerning the *Wall of the Early Morning Light.*

p. 68 **I heard a small ping . . .:** Joe Fitschen wrote that the fall was caused by rope drag pulling out a piton (see *Going Up*, p. 370). Steve Roper wrote that a flake popped off (see *Camp 4*, p. 114). Royal Robbins wrote that he fell when a piton he was placing came out (see *The Golden Age*, p. 33).

p. 69 **In early April:** Aid climbing was still graded 6.0 to 6.9, but a year later, Powell's aid-climbing system was adopted, grading pitches A1 to A5. This system is still in use, both in Yosemite—and for the purposes of clarity—in this book.

p. 69 **He ended the 1960 spring season:** This attempt, however, was not on June 14, as recorded in *The Golden Age*: when Joe Fitschen was on Half Dome, but likely in the last week of June.

p. 69 **The Valley would soon be too hot:** Ament states in *Spirit of the Age* (p. 36) that Taylor accompanied Royal and Joe Fitschen to the Tetons in 1960, but Fitschen's account suggests that she did not.

p. 70 **He had found Judith:** Hemming's biographer, Mirella Tenderini, does not know— or at least provide—Judith's last name.

p. 71 **Royal did not make:** The Tetons season of 1960 is one of the few months-long climbing episodes Royal Robbins omitted from his memoirs.

p. 71 **Pratt has a white patch:** The eye healed by the day of the climb.

p. 72 **He closed with a bientôt,:** At least two of these notes are preserved in the Robbins family records.

Chapter 5: Poste Restante, Chamonix

p. 76 **The wall was known as the Southwest Face:** The naming of the *Salathé Wall* also introduced the confusing Yosemite practice of naming climbing routes "walls."

p. 76 **In addition to ticking off classic itineraries:** In the mid-sixties, rockfall destroyed part of the *Taylor Route*, but it has since been free climbed at 5.11.

p. 77 **Today Tom and i climbed Sentinel north wall:** The previous record for Sentinel had been set that summer by Steve Roper and free-climbing ace and physics graduate student Frank Sacherer, both of them twenty years old at the time. After their climb, Royal gave them a bottle of champagne and his congratulations. He and Frost broke their record the next day.

p. 79 **Leaning Tower was the last:** Harding's three siege routes were the West Face of Leaning Tower, the East Face of Washington Column, and the *Nose.*

p. 80 **Florence Elizabeth Burkner:** Sourced from Florence Elizabeth Burkner, June 22, 1938. San Joaquin County, State of California. California Birth Index, 1905–1995. Sacramento, California, USA: State of California Department of Health Services, Center for Health Statistics.

p. 81 **Her coworker Herb Swedlund and his friend:** Swedlund had placed seventeen bolts next to cracks on a new route; Steve Roper chopped the offending hardware (see *Camp 4*, p. 121).

p. 83 **Royal followed Kerouac's example:** Passenger fare on a Jugalinija liner cost $120—about a third of the price of airfare.

p. 85 **His travel expenses were mounting.:** Camping cost seventy-five cents a night, and a loaf of bread cost twenty cents. A hundred dollars went a long way.

p. 88 **That autumn, Royal and Frost:** Royal Robbins left the fall season of 1962 out of *The Golden Age*, although he included a photograph of himself on the East Face of Washington Column.

Chapter 6: We've Got Nothing Else But Climbing

p. 97 **At the bivouac:** Glen Denny wrote that Steve Roper showed the chopped bolt to Royal in Camp 4.

p. 99 **After a rest day:** The song "Jack O'Diamonds" was recorded by John Lee Hooker in 1949, Odetta in 1956, and the Fendermen in 1960. The facts were better known to Kor, who probably named the route, than to Royal.

p. 99 **Kor returned to Boulder:** The photo in *The Golden Age* (p. 110) is captioned "Liz with her arm in a cast outside a hut in the Tetons." The same photograph is reproduced in *Spirit of the Age*, with the location described as "the shelter cabin (on Longs Peak)." The ashlar wall and doorway behind Liz match that of the Agnes Vaille Shelter on the Longs Peak Boulderfield.

p. 100 **Royal paid back their affection:** Curiously, Royal did not include this Colorado visit, with its considerable successes, in his memoirs.

p. 101 **In September of 1963:** In *The Golden Age*, Royal says filming began in early 1964, but Yvon Chouinard was still in the army at the time.

p. 106 **They made plans to return after Labor Day.:** Royal Robbins left the spring season of 1964 out of his memoirs, possibly because he made no major first ascents.

p. 107 **Piton cracks were rare.:** The first recorded climbing activity in the Needles was in 1937, when New York–based German-American climber Fritz Wiessner dropped by. Wandering climbers Herb and Jan Conn came ten years later and began to develop the area in earnest.

p. 109 **Royal invited Chouinard:** Royal wrote that he invited Pat Ament as Denny's replacement, but that Ament couldn't come.

Chapter 7: When the Saints Come Marching In

p. 113 **With investment from:** Sourced from a flyer, International School of Modern Mountaineering, 1965.

p. 115 **Chouinard and Royal also climbed:** A photograph, usually published flipped in the wrong direction, shows Yvon Chouinard leading the Cassin Traverse on that route.

p. 115 **From there, they saw the bolts:** The Scoiattolli, or Squirrels, were a climbing club based in nearby Cortina d'Ampezzo.

p. 117 **Royal, whose French comprised:** John Harlin, letter to Royal Robbins, August 1965.

p. 117 **I recall being struck:** Sourced from Sid Eder, *Rearview Mirror*, vol. 2, *Once Upon a Time in Switzerland*, unpublished, p. 271.

p. 118 **The next day:** This was sourced from a letter Royal wrote to his mother, Beulah, dated August 7 but likely written after August 14, when Royal returned to Leysin from Chamonix.

p. 120 **The Vag (with a hard g):** Sourced from Abby Rand, "Leysin: For the Young and Frugal," *Ski Magazine*, January 1971, p. 96. According to Rand's story, breakfast cost 40 cents; a multicourse dinner, including wine, cost $1.25; and a shot of whisky was 50 cents. After paying $1.25 for a membership, visitors were entitled to rent a bed in a dormitory room with three to ten others for $2.50 a night. (Prices listed in 1971 currency.)

p. 123 **In a demanding:** Sourced from a letter Royal wrote to the Dean of Admissions, Colorado School of Mines, March 5, 1967.

p. 128 **On the gritstone crags of northern England:** In 1961, Briton John Brailsford produced the first commercially available, purpose-made metal climbing nut: the Acorn. These were quickly followed by a variety of other models like the Peck Cracker, made of aluminum stock; the Ny Chuck, slung on tape; and, eventually, units slung with swaged wire loops.

p. 130 **Royal had started climbing in basketball shoes:** He wore the Kronhofer Zillertal, a flexible, light suede boot, before he switched to the stiffer, narrower Pivetta Spider, which was better for edging. He also climbed in the Cortina, which had an upper that protected the feet in wide cracks.

p. 130 **Jim McCarthy called the RR:** Sourced from Jim McCarthy to Julien Richard, reviewing the Royal Robbins climbing shoe, undated.

p. 131 **After visits to Seneca Rocks:** Royal climbed no new routes in either Seneca Rocks in West Virginia or the White Mountains in New Hampshire.

p. 132 **Royal was happy:** The first foreign ascent of El Capitan was made in April 1966 by Chamonix guides André Gaunt and Jacques Dupont.

Chapter 8: To Engrave My Initials on the Face Forever

p. 142 **He named it *Tis-sa-ack":*** *Tesa'ak* or *Tis-sa-ack*, meaning "cleft rock," was the Paiute Ahwahnechee name for Half Dome itself.

p. 142 **I need [competition] on a daily basis:** Sourced from James Salter's notes for "Man Is His Own Star," article on Royal Robbins in *Quest* with notes, drafts, typescripts, and correspondence, March–April 1978. "Man Is His Own Star," James Salter Papers, 1953–2000, Henry Ransom Center, University of Texas, Austin.

p. 145 **The brimming self-confidence:** Royal Robbins's letter is cited in Edwin Drummond's "Out of the Mid-day Sun: Lost Arrow Chimney," *Summit*, 15, Number 3, April 1969, p. 23.

p. 145 **Later that season:,** Sourced from Royal's article "Yosemite Climbers Nearing Record on El Capitan Wall," *Oakland Tribune,* September 6, 1968. Royal's photos and commentary were used; Dennis Hennek's name was misspelled in most articles on the climb as "Hennig."

p. 146 **But the self-named fun hogs:** Yvon Chouinard and Malinda Chouinard to author, September 4, 2021.

p. 152 **A small classified advertisement:** The name Rockcraft was an homage to one of Royal's favorite books, Geoffrey Winthrop Young's at once idealistic and practical *Mountain Craft.*

p. 154 **By season's end:** Source: Royal Robbins, "Rockcraft, Financial Statement—1969," January 7, 1970.

Chapter 9: What Is Acceptable and What Is Not

p. 160 **In 1967, American alpinist David Roberts:** The Cathedral Spires later became better known as the Kichatna Spires.

p. 163 **Peterson was so impatient:** Charlie Porter retrieved the pitons on the climb's second ascent.

p. 170 **In one place:** Peter Zabrok, who has climbed El Capitan sixty-six times, made the following comments about the difficulty of Harding's climb: "Harding most assuredly did not overbolt or put in 'chicken bolts' or dowels when he got scared. He was a master at piton craft and had balls the size of grapefruits, and when you climb his route, you know this. He did the best that could possibly be done at the time. The bolt count on other routes in the area would be comparable, when measured on a 'need-to-use' basis. For instance, you are climbing a crack, and it ends. There is another crack up above or to the side, so you have to drill a rivet ladder to connect. Example: Texas Flake to Boot Flake. Harding made a strange choice on the diagonal, but there is never anywhere he drilled a rivet where you thought, 'Why did he drill that? He could have used a piton instead.'" Source: Peter Zabrok to author, February 2, 2021.

Chapter 10: There Is Only One Eminence

p. 177 **I wasn't good enough:** Royal Robbins, interviewed by Geoff Powter, Banff Centre Mountain Film and Book Festival, November 12, 2009.

Epilogue

p. 223 **If Royal had learned:** Joe Fitschen, "About Royal," address at Royal Robbins Memorial, Modesto, March 12, 2018, p. 1.

Bibliography

Since many of the articles cited here appear in three of the same publications, they are indicated by the following abbreviations: *AAJ* = *American Alpine Journal*; *SCB* = *Sierra Club Bulletin*; and *SUM* = *Summit Magazine*. Note also that the only works by Royal Robbins himself cited in the bibliography are two unpublished pieces. Everything else, including works that informed the research for this book, can be found in Select Works by Royal Robbins below.

Films

Brown, Roger C., director. *Sentinel: The West Face.* Summit Films, 1963.
Lowell, Josh; Mortimer, Peter; Rosen, Nick; directors. *Valley Uprising.* Sender Films, 2014.

Books

Accidents in North American Mountaineering. New York: American Alpine Club, 1986.
Achey, Jeff, Dudley Chelton, and Bob Godfrey. *Climb! The History of Rock Climbing in Colorado.* Seattle: Mountaineers Books, 2002.
Ament, Pat. *Royal Robbins: Spirit of the Age.* Mechanicsburg, PA: Stackpole Books, 1998.
———. *Wizards of Rock: A History of Free Climbing in America.* Berkeley, CA: Wilderness Press, 2002.
Arce, Gary. *Defying Gravity: High Adventure on Yosemite's Walls.* Berkeley, CA: Wilderness Press, 1995.

Chouinard, Yvon. *Some Stories: Lessons from the Edge of Business and Sport.* Ventura, CA: Patagonia, 2019.

Clark, Paul, and Eric Redd. *Sierra Club Oral History: South Sierrans III.* Sierra Club, 1980.

Denny, Glen. *Valley Walls: A Memoir of Living and Climbing in Yosemite.* Yosemite, CA: Yosemite Conservancy, 2016.

Duane, Daniel. *El Capitan: Historical Feats and Radical Routes.* San Francisco: Chronicle Books, 2000.

Fitschen, Joe. *Going Up: Tales Told along the Road to El Capitan.* Berkeley, CA: Heyday Books, 2012.

Franklin, Jonathan. *A Wild Idea.* New York: Harper Collins, 2021.

Frison-Roche, Roger. *First on the Rope.* Janet Adam Smith, trans. New York: Prentice Hall, 1949.

Harding, Warren. *Downward Bound: A Mad! Guide to Rock Climbing.* New York: Prentice Hall, 1975.

Henderson, Kenneth. *Handbook of North American Mountaineering.* Boston: Houghton-Mifflin, 1942.

Hill, Lynn, with Greg Child. *Climbing Free.* New York: WW Norton, 1993.

I Remember Yosemite: Yosemite National Park Oral History Project. El Portal, CA: National Park Service, 2008.

Jeffers, Robinson. "Shine, Perishing Republic." *Roan Stallion, Tamar, and Other Poems.* New York: Boni and Liveright, 1925.

Jones, Chris. *Climbing in North America.* Berkeley, CA: For the American Alpine Club by University of California Press, 1976.

King, Clarence. *Mountaineering in the Sierra Nevada.* New York: Scribner's, 1902.

Meyers, George. *Yosemite Climber.* London: Diadem Books; Modesto: Robbins Mountain Letters, 1979.

Miller, Lauren DeLaunay, ed. *Valley of Giants.* Seattle: Mountaineers Books, 2022.

Patey, Tom. *One Man's Mountains.* London: Canongate, 1997.

Perrin, James. *The Villain: A Portrait of Don Whillans.* Seattle: Mountaineers Books, 2005.

Pippin, Donald. *A Pocketful of Wry: An Impresario's Life in San Francisco and the History of the Pocket Opera, 1950s–2001.* Berkeley: Oral History Center, The Bancroft Library, University of California, 2001.

Robbins, Royal Shannon. *Outlines of Ancient and Modern History.* Philadelphia: William J Haversley, 1875.

Roper, Steve. *Camp 4: Recollections of a Yosemite Rock Climber.* Seattle: Mountaineers Books, 1994.

Rowell, Galen A., ed. *The Vertical World of Yosemite.* Berkeley, CA: Wilderness Press, 1974.

Messner, Reinhold, Domenico Rudatis, and Vittorio Varale. *Sesto Grado.* Milano, Italy: Longanesi, 1971.

Sherman, John. *Stone Crusade: A Historical Guide to Bouldering in America.* Golden, CO: American Alpine Club, 1994.

Tenderini, Mirella. *Gary Hemming: The Beatnik of the Alps.* Glasgow: Ernest Press, 1995.

Terhune, Albert Payson. *Lad, a Dog.* New York: E. Dutton and Company, 1919.
The Sierra Club: A Handbook. San Francisco: Sierra Club, 1947.
Ullman, James Ramsey. *High Conquest.* Philadelphia: J.B. Lippincott, 1941.
Watts, Alan. *Rock Climbing in Smith Rock State Park.* Guilford, CT: Falcon Guides,
    1999.
Wilson, Ken, ed. *Hard Rock.* London: Granada, 1971.

Articles

Chapter 1: Ride the Trail in Style

Brooks, Janet Rae. "Flush with Success." *Salt Lake City Tribune*, November 14, 2000,
    p. 29.
Harley, Steven. "Where Westerns Were in the Saddle." *Los Angeles Times*, February
    13, 2011. latimes.com/local/la-xpm-2011-feb-13-la-me-then-20110213-story
    .html.
Notices, *Mansfield News.* Mansfield, Ohio, November 30, 1938.
Salter, James. "Victory or Death." *Esquire.* May 1985, p. 196.

Chapter 2: Anarchy and Aimlessness

"Barbara Lilley." *Sierra Club Leaders, L-R*, angeles.sierraclub.org/about/chapter
    _history/great_leaders/leaders_l_r. Last accessed December 22, 2021.
Crime Report, *Hollywood Citizen-News*, February 17, 1945, p. 3.
Crime Report, *Hollywood Citizen-News*, April 7, 1950, p. 2.
Currie, Scott. "Don Wilson: A Retrospective." *International Society for Neuroethology
    Newsletter*, March 2011, p. 9.
Gallwas, Jerry, to John C. Preston, April 12, 1954, Yosemite Central Files, Mountain
    Climbing 1957–1969, L3423-L48.
Johnson, Christopher E. "Born with Steel Spoons in Their Mouths: Sierra Club High
    Trippers and Wilderness Use, 1930–1941." *Clio* 14 (2004): pp. 89–110.
Mendenhall, John, and Ruth Mendenhall. "Forty Years of Sierra Club Mountaineering
    Leadership, 1938–1978. South Sierrans III." *Sierra Club Oral History*, interviews by
    Paul Clark and Eric Redd, Sierra Club, 1980, p. 15.
O'Neill, Megan. "Lynn Newcomb Dead at 91." *Los Angeles Times*, September 6, 2011.
    latimes.com/socal/glendale-news-press/news/education/tn-gnp-0907-newcomb
    -story.html. Last accessed December 21, 2021.
Sparks, Steve. "Fred Martin—June 9th, 2011." Accessed at avalleylife.wordpress
    .com/category/list-of-interviews/fred-martin.

Chapter 3: Rotten Lucky Bastards

Berry, Bill. "Tahoe City and Pasadena Skiers Win at Edelweiss." *Sacramento Bee*,
    February 9, 1953.
Burton, Hal. "They Risk Their Lives for Fun." *The Saturday Evening Post*, Vol. 228, No.
    35, February 25, 1956, pp. 34–35, 99, 101–102.
"Climbers Conquer East-Shoulder of Half-Dome." *Daily Facts*, Redland, CA, July 30,
    1957, p. 1.

Grossman, Steve, with Jerry Gallwas. "Mark Powell." Obituary, *AAJ*, 2021, p. 216.

"N.W. Face Half Dome." *Mugelnoos*, Number 271, July 14, 1955, p. 3.

"Seedings Announced for National Junior Ski Fest." *Salt Lake City Deseret News and Telegram*, March 6, 1953, B3; "Junior Downhill Order." *Salt Lake City Deseret News and Telegram*, March 11, 1953.

Sherrick, Mike. "The Northwest Face of Half Dome." *SCB*, November 1958, pp. 43, 9, 19–23.

"Ski Racing." *Los Angeles Times*, January 13, 1953, p. 52.

"Three Climb Half-Dome's East Slope." *Bakersfield Californian*, July 30, 1957, p. 3.

Van DeGrift, Ethel. "New Snowfall Raises Spirits of Local Skiers." *Los Angeles Times*, February 24, 1953, p. 56.

Vogel, Bea. Interview by John Rawlings, August 20, 1997. Stanford Alpine Club Oral History Interviews. Department of Special Collections and University Archives, Stanford University Libraries, Stanford, CA, Box 1, Folder 13.

Whitman, Walt. "Song of Myself," (1892 Version). Accessed at: poetryfoundation.org /poems/45477/song-of-myself-1892-version.

Wilts, Chuck. "Hardest North Face Yet?" *Mugelnoos*, Number 295, July 11, 1957, p. 1.

Chapter 4: The Big Daddy

"Athletes and Observers of Fourteen Nations Are Competing and Watching the Trial Events at Squaw Valley." *Healdsburg Tribune, Enterprise and Scimitar*, Healdsburg, CA, February 26, 1959, p. 1.

"Climbers Face Gruelling Test on El Capitan." *Los Angeles Times*, Southland Edition, September 9, 1960, p. 1.

"Climbers Near Mid-Point on El Capitan." *Los Angeles Times*, Southland Edition, September 11, 1960, p. 1.

"El Capitan Climb." *Los Angeles Times*, November 13, 1960.

Fitschen, Joe. "The Northwest Face of Half Dome." *SCB*, October 1960, p. 60.

"4 Veteran Climbers Begin Ascent of El Capitan." *Los Angeles Times*, September 8, 1960, p. 60.

Harding, Warren. "We Conquered El Capitan." *Argosy*, April 1959, Number 23, pp. 23–26, 104–106.

Pett, Saul. "The San Francisco Beatnik Colony Is Really Out of This World, Man." *Courier-Journal*, Louisville, KY, p. 53.

Rowell, Galen; Steck, Allen; Wilson, Ken. "Interview with Royal Robbins." Originally printed in *Mountain*, November 1971. Reprinted and cited in Rowell, Galen A., ed., *The Vertical World of Yosemite*, Berkeley, CA: Wilderness Press, 1974, p. 185.

"Ski Trails." *Los Angeles Times*, Southland Edition, February 14, 1958.

Chapter 5: Poste Restante, Chamonix

Chouinard, Yvon. "Modern Yosemite Climbing." *AAJ*, 1963, p. 325.

"Climbers Conquer El Capitan Face." *The Miami Herald*, November 1962, p. 11.

Cooper, Ed. "Direct Southwest Face of Yosemite Valley's El Capitan." *AAJ,* 1963, p. 340.

Crofut, Doris. "Tuxedo Man Scales Rugged Yosemite Cliff After Thanksgiving Dinner of Cold Stew." *The Rockland Independent*, December 6, 1962, p. 27.

Fitschen, Joe. *Going On, Yosemite, Chapter Two, the Gunks, Winter, Spring 1961–62*, accessed at: joefitschen.com/uncategorized/going-on-chapter-2.
Harlin, John, II. "Eigerwand." *AAJ*, 1963, p. 374.
———. "Petit Dru West Face Direttissima." *AAJ*, 1966, p. 88.
Kendall, Henry W. "The Walker Spur of the Grandes Jorasses." *AAJ*, 1963, p. 376.
Kennedy, John F. "Moon Speech." Rice Stadium, September 12, 1962. Accessed at er.jsc.nasa.gov/seh/ricetalk.htm.
Macdonald, Allen. "The Realm of the Overhang." *SCB*, December 1962, Volume 47, Number 9, p. 5.
"Other Yosemite Ascents." *AAJ*, 1961, p. 371.

Chapter 6: We've Got Nothing Else But Climbing
Ament, Pat. "Royal Robbins, 1935–2017." Accessed at publications.americanalpine club.org/articles/13201214749.
Denny, Glen. Interviewed by Jim McCarthy, Jim Aikman, Ellen Lapham. *AAC Video Inspiration Project*, San Francisco, May 20, 2016, p. 18.
McCarthy, James P. "The Southeast Face of Proboscis." *AAJ,*1964, p. 60.
McCarthy, Jim. Interviewed by John Heilprin and Pete Takeda. AAC Video Inspiration Project, Estes Park, CO, October 2, 2017. unpaginated.
McCracken, Richard K. "Mount Hooker's North Face." *AAJ*, 1965, p. 348.
Ream, Rich. "Alpenbock Climbing Club." *AAJ*, 1965, p. 482.
Ryan, Paul G. "My Complicated First Yosemite Rock Climb." Accessed at paulgryan .substack.com/p/my-first-yosemite-rock-climb#:~:text=My%20complicated%20 first%20Yosemite%20rock%20climb.

Chapter 7: When the Saints Come Marching In
Amatt, John. "The North Face Direct of Søndre Trolltind." *AAJ*, 1968, p. 1.
Chouinard, Yvon."Muir Wall, El Capitan." *AAJ*, 1966, p. 47.
"Deux Américains Réussissent Une Grande Premiére Dans L'aiguille du Dru." *Le Monde*, August 16, 1965.
Gray, Dennis. "Big in the UK . . . Royal Robbins, Jeff Lowe and Warren Harding." February 2019. Accessed at footlesscrow.blogspot.com/2019/02/big-in-uk-royal -robbins-jeff-lowe-and.html.
"Leysin: Le Club Vagabond, Comment Est Organisé Ce Club et les Réactions des Gens de la Region." *Carrefour*, March 22, 1967. Accessed at rts.ch/archives/tv /information/carrefour/3455779-carrefour-220367.html.
Rand, Abby. "Leysin: For the Young and Frugal." *Ski Magazine*, January 1971, p. 96.

Chapter 8: To Engrave My Initials on the Face Forever
Chouinard, Yvon. "The North Wall of Mount Edith Cavell." *AAJ*, 1962, pp. 54–56.
Conley, Spencer. "A Rock Climbing First." *Oakland Tribune*, May 7, 1969, p. 40.
———. "Yosemite Chiller, Man vs. El Capitan." *Oakland Tribune*, May 16, 1968, p. 15.
Drummond, Edwin. "Out of the Mid-day Sun: Lost Arrow Chimney." *SUM*, 15, Number 3, April 1969, p. 23.
———. "White Elephant, White Whale." *Ascent*, Volume 1, Number 3, May 1969, p. 29.

Haan, Peter. "Royal Robbins: 'This Importing Business Is a Real Can of Worms.'"
     November 27, 2009. Accessed at supertopo.com/climbers-forum/1022257
     /Royal-Robbins-This-importing-business-is-a-real-can-of-worms.
Hudson, John. "The North Face of Mount Geikie." *AAJ*, 1968, p. 62.
Robbins, Elizabeth. "Nutcracker." *Alpinist*, March 1, 2000. Accessed at alpinist.com
     /doc/ALP23/first-ascent-nutcracker-liz-robbins.
Rowell, Galen. "Rescue on the South Face of Half Dome." Cited in Rowell, Galen A.,
     ed., *The Vertical World of Yosemite*, Berkeley, CA: Wilderness Press, 1974.
Wiessner, Fritz. "The UIAA Classification System." *AAJ*, 1969, p. 365.
"Yosemite Climbers Nearing Record on El Capitan Wall." *Oakland Tribune*, September
     6, 1968, p. 2.

Chapter 9: What Is Acceptable and What Is Not

Chouinard, Yvon. "Modern Yosemite Climbing." *AAJ*, 1963, p. 326.
Denny, Glen. "Washington Column—The Prow." *Ascent*, Number 1, Volume 4, May
     1967, p. 45.
"El Capitan Climb for Publicity." *San Francisco Examiner*, December 13, 1970, p. 13.
Fitschen, Joe. *Going On.* Chapter 11, Cathedral Spires, Alaska, January 11, 2021.
     Accessed at joefitschen.com/uncategorized/going-on-chapter-11#more-418.
Harding, Warren. "Reflections of a Broken Down Climber." *Ascent*, Number 5, July
     1971, p. 34.
Herbert, TM. "Comments on the Two Ascents of the Wall of the Early Morning Light."
     AAJ, 1971, p. 361.
Jones, Chris. "The Future." *Mountain*, Number 4, July 1969, p. 25.
Kroger, Chuck. "El Capitan—Heart Route." *Climbing*, Number 5, January 1971, p. 9.
Millikan, Richard G. C., and David S. Roberts. "Kichatna Spire." *AAJ*, 1967, p. 278.
"Rescue Move Looms for Challengers of El Capitan." *Sacramento Bee*, November 12,
     1970, p. 37.
"Robbins Coming Down." *The Colorado Springs Gazette Telegraph*, October 13, 1969,
     p. 1.
Rowell, Galen. "An Elegy for Yosemite." *Climbing*, May/June 1971, p. 11.
Wilson, Ken. Editorial. *Mountain*, May 1971.

Chapter 10: There Is Only One Eminence

Bourjaily, Vance. "Different Points of View." *New York Times*, August 5, 1979, p. 3.
Bridwell, Jim. "Brave New World." *Mountain*, Number 31, 1973, p. 26.
Haan, Peter. "The Salathé Wall Solo." *AAJ*, 1972, p. 74.
Paumgarten, Nick. "The Last Book." *New Yorker*, April 15, 2013. Accessed at
     newyorker.com/magazine/2013/04/15/the-last-book.
Robbins, Royal. "Personal Birth Story." Unpublished.
———. "The Tory." Unpublished, unfinished article, January 31, 1972.
Robinson, Doug. "The Whole Natural Art of Protection." *Chouinard Catalogue*, 1972,
     p. 24.
Salter, James. Notes on *The Eiger Sanction*, 1975, Box 24, Folder 3.

Chapter 11: Rivers and God

Blum, Deborah. "Boaters, Wild Water Fans at Odds Over River Use." *Modesto Bee and News Herald*, February 12, 1984, p. 3.

Casey, Kurt, and Fields Marshall. "History of First Descents." Accessed at riversofchile.com/history-of-first-descents.

Clark, Brian. "High Fashion." *Sacramento Bee*, January 24, 1986, p. 110.

Fraser, Christa. "High Peaks and Deep Canyons." *Adventure Sports Journal*, October 20, 2009. Accessed at adventuresportsjournal.com/flashback-high -peaks-and-deep-canyons-by-kayak.

Johanson, Matt. "Robbins, Royal, 'The Best Medicine.'" *Adventure Sports Journal*, June 1, 2011. Accessed at adventuresportsjournal.com/royal-robbins-the- best-medicine.

Reg Lake, ed. "Triple Crown Soundtrack." No date.

Williams, Tyler. "The Triple Crown." *Men's Journal*. Accessed at mensjournal.com /adventure/from-the-mag-the-triple-crown.

Chapter 12: A Mountaineer Is Always Free

Brooks, Janet Rae. "Flush with Success." *Salt Lake City Tribune*, November 14, 2000, C3.

"Competition Climbing." *Alpine Journal*, 1994, p. 157.

Moran, Tim. "Robbins, Royal Brand Called a Good Fit." *Modesto Bee*, October 4, 2003, p. A-16.

Robbins, Damon. Cited in "1935–2017: Big Wall Pioneer and World Explorer Royal Robbins Remembered." Accessed at alpinist.com/doc/web17w/newswire -royal-robbins-obituary.

Rowland, Marijke. "Outdoor Clothing Maker Plans to Expand in Modesto." *Modesto Bee*, March 20, 1999, p. I 3.72.

Epilogue

Ament, Pat. "Royal Robbins, 1935–2017." Accessed at publications.americanalpine club.org/articles/13201214749.

Branch, John. "Royal Robbins, Conscience of Rock Climbers, Dies at 82." *New York Times*, March 15, 2017. Accessed at nytimes.com/2017/03/15/sports/royal -robbins-dead-mountain-climber.html.

Langer, Emily. "Royal Robbins, Celebrated Rock Climber Who Left No Trace of His Ascents, Dies at 82." *Washington Post*. Accessed at washingtonpost.com/sports /royal-robbins-celebrated-rock-climber-who-left-no-trace-of-his-ascents-dies-at -82/2017/03/16/25d041b8-09a0-11e7-93dc-00f9bdd74ed1_story.html.

Select Works by Royal Robbins

The following list is a select compilation of the written works of Royal Robbins, including books as well as magazine and journal articles. In lieu of listing certain of these works in the bibliography, they are grouped here instead, to gather Royal's published writings all in one place. Since Royal wrote so frequently for the same publications, this list uses the following abbreviations: *AAJ* = *American Alpine Journal; SCB* = *Sierra Club Bulletin;* and *SUM* = *Summit Magazine.*

Books

Advanced Rockcraft. Glendale, CA: La Siesta Press, 1973.
Basic Rockcraft. San Francisco: La Siesta Press, 1971.
Fail Falling: My Life (Vol. 2). City of Industry, CA: Pink Moment Press, 2010.
The Golden Age: My Life (Vol. 3). City of Industry, CA: Royal Robbins Adventures, 2012.
To Be Brave: My Life (Vol. 1). Ojai, CA: Pink Moment Press, 2009.

Articles

"A Final Tribute." *The Climbing Cartoons of Sheridan Anderson.* Joe Kelsey; Schenectady, New York: High Peaks Press and Richard DuMais, 1989, pp. 141–142.
"Alone on the John Muir Wall, El Capitan." *AAJ*, 1969, pp. 319–322.

"An Excursion in Scotland." *The Scottish Mountaineering Club Journal,* 1969, pp. 139–144.

"Arcturus—A New Route on Half Dome." *SUM,* April 1971, pp. 4–7.

"Arcturus, Northwest Face of Half Dome." *AAJ,* 1971, pp. 358–359.

"A New Route on the Petit Dru." *AAJ,* 1963, p. 375.

"An Excursion to Scotland." *Scottish Mountaineering Club Journal,* 1969, p. 139.

"A Real Bloodsucker." *Mugelnoos,* July 9, 1959.

"A Review of Downward Bound." *Mountain Gazette,* May 1975.

"A Visit to Britain." *SUM,* June 1968, pp. 73–75.

"Boulder Gorge, Yosemite." *AAJ,* 1968, pp. 140–141.

"Californians in Alaska." *AAJ,* 1970, pp. 58–62

"Charles Marshall Pratt, 1939–2000." *AAJ,* 2001, p. 460.

"Cirque of the Towers Traverse." *AAJ,* 1965, p. 423.

"Climbing El Capitan." *SCB,* December 1960, pp. 47–55.

"Climbing with a French Accent." *Mugelnoos,* Sept. 13, 1962, p. 3.

"Cutting Canadian Capers." *SUM,* October 1968, p. 14.

"El Cap Commentary." *Mountain,* January 1973, pp. 22–32.

"El Capitan: The Dihedral Wall." *AAJ,* 1965, pp. 414–415.

"El Capitan, First Continuous Ascent." *Mugelnoos,* October 13, 1960.

"Foreword." *Mirrors in the Cliffs.* Perrin, Jim, ed.; Diadem Books, 1983, pp. 13–15.

"Foreword." *Beyond The Vertical.* Kor, Layton; Colorado: Bob Alpine House, 1983, pp. 7–9.

"Foreword." *First Descents—In Search of Wild Rivers.* John Lazenby and Cameron O'Connor, eds. Birmingham, AL: Menasha Ridge Press, pp. ix–x.

"Fractured Laws of Logic." Letters to the Editor, *Climbing,* February–March, 1991, p. 12.

"Fun Climbing in Yosemite." *Mugelnoos,* October, 1959.

"Gary Hemming." *Mountain,* 6 (November 1969), p. 9.

"Grand Sentinel." *AAJ,* 1968, pp. 77–80.

"Half Dome—A Direct Ascent of the Northwest Face." *SUM,* April 1964, pp. 2–7.

"Half Dome, Direct North Face." *AAJ,* 1964, pp. 177–178.

"Half Dome—The Hard Way." *SCB,* Vol. 42, No. 10, December 1957, pp. 12–13.

"Happenings in the Valley." *SUM,* December 1967, pp. 26–27.

"In Cold Blood, West Face of Sentinel Rock." *AAJ,* 1971, pp. 359–360.

"Incident on Half Dome." *SUM,* January–February 1969, pp. 2–5.

"International Climbers in Yosemite." *SUM,* Vol. 12, No. 1, January–February 1966, p. 29.

"Introduction." *Robbins Mountain Letters,* catalogue, 1976.

"Longs Peak, The Diamond." *AAJ,* 1964, pp. 195–196.

"Manure Pile Buttress: Nutcracker," *AAJ,* 1968, p. 142.

"Middle Teton, North Face." *AAJ,* 1961, p. 367.

"Mountaineering Notes." *SCB,* October 1961, p. 52.

"New Climbs in The Grand Tetons." SCB, Vol. 46, No. 8, October 1961, pp. 53–54.

"North Wall of Sentinel Rock." *SUM,* Vol. 9, No. 3, March 1963, pp. 8–11.

"Nutcracker, Manure Pile Buttress, Yosemite." *AAJ,* 1968, pp. 141–143.

"Nuts to You." *SUM*, Vol. 13, No. 4, May 1967, pp. 2–7.

"On Technique." *SUM*, Vol. 15, No. 3, April 1969, pp. 24–27.

Review of *Direttissima*, Peter Gilman and Dougal Haston (New York: Harper and Row, 1966); *AAJ*, 1967, p. 246.

"Royal Arches Direct." *SCB*, Vol. 46, No. 8, October 1961, pp. 56–57.

"Sierra Traverse." *First Descents—In Search of Wild Rivers.* Cameron O'Connor and John Lazenby, eds.; Birmingham, AL: Menasha Ridge Press, 1989, pp. 61–67.

"Scree." *SUM*, Vol. 16, No. 6, July–August 1970, pp. 36–37.

"Solo Ascent of El Capitan." *SUM*, Vol. 15, No. 2, March 1969, pp. 12–17.

"Summary of Yosemite Climbing." *SUM*, Vol. 13, No. 2, March 1967, pp. 20–21.

"Talus of Yosemite." *SUM*, Vol. 14, No. 5, June 1968, p. 33.

"The East Wall of Upper Yosemite Falls." *AAJ*, 1964, pp. 75–78.

"The El Capitan Climb." *SUM*, Vol. 16, No. 10, December 1970, pp. 30–31.

"The Magnificent Maverick." *SUM*, Vol. 11, No. 4, December 1970, p. 14.

"The North America Wall." *AAJ*, 1965, pp. 331–338.

"The North America Wall." *SUM*, Vol. 11, No. 4, May–June 1965, pp. 2–9.

"The North West Face of Half Dome." *Mugelnoos*, September 1957, p. 4.

"The Northwest Face of the Higher Cathedral Spire." *SCB*, October 1961, pp. 58–59.

"The North Face of Lower Cathedral Rock." *SCB*, October 1961, pp. 57–58.

"The Pinecrest Climb—In Email Newsletter." November 7, 2004.

"The Prow." *SUM*, Vol. 16, No. 6, July–August 1970, pp. 2–7.

"The Prow, Washington Column." *AAJ*, 1970, p. 124.

"The Salathé Wall." *AAJ*, 1963, p. 332.

"The West Face," *Ascent*, Vol. 1, No. 2, May 1968, pp. 2–4.

"The West Face—El Capitan." *AAJ*, 1968, pp. 73–76.

"Three Early Influences." *Alpine Journal*, 2005, p. 231.

"Time for a Change." *SUM*, November 1968, pp. 2–5.

"Tis-sa-ack."*AAJ*, 1970, p. 78.

"Tis-sa-ack."*Ascent*, Vol. 1, No. 4, May 1970, pp. 14–19.

"Vandals in the Temple." *Rock and Ice*, November/December 1990, p. 45.

"Yosemite Climbers Nearing Record on El Capitan Wall." *Oakland Tribune*, September 6, 1968, p. 2.

"Yosemite Climbing." *SUM*, Vol. 12, No. 6, July–August 1966, p. 22.

"Yosemite's Higher Cathedral Spire." *SUM*, January 1, 1962, pp. 10–13.

"Yosemite Notes." *SUM*, Vol. 16, No. 5, June 1970, pp. 36–37.

"Yosemite Notes." *SUM*, Vol. 16, No. 6, July–August 1972, p. 40.

"Yosemite Notes." *SUM*, Vol. 16, No. 9, November 1970, pp. 33–34.

"Yosemite Renaissance." *SUM*, Vol. 17, No. 9, November–December 1971, p. 31.

Peter Hoang

About the Author

David Smart has climbed in North America, Canada, and Europe for nearly five decades. He is the author of *Emilio Comici: Angel of the Dolomites*, winner of the Boardman Tasker Award for Mountain Literature; *Paul Preuss: Lord of the Abyss*, winner of the Banff Mountain Film and Book Festival's Climbing Literature Award; two novels; and a memoir, *A Youth Wasted Climbing*, shortlisted for a Banff award. In addition, he holds holds the H. Adams Carter Literary Award from the American Alpine Club and the Summit of Excellence Award from the Banff Mountain Film and Book Festival.

Smart is the founding editor and editorial director of *Gripped* climbing magazine and three other magazines. An active route developer in the Rockies and northern Ontario, he lives in Toronto.

MOUNTAINEERS BOOKS, including its two imprints, Skipstone and Braided River, is a leading publisher of quality outdoor recreation, sustainability, and conservation titles. As a 501(c)(3) nonprofit, we are committed to supporting the environmental and educational goals of our organization by providing expert information on human-powered adventure, sustainable practices at home and on the trail, and preservation of wilderness.

Our publications are made possible through the generosity of donors, and through sales of 700 titles on outdoor recreation, sustainable lifestyle, and conservation. To donate, purchase books, or learn more, visit us online:

MOUNTAINEERS BOOKS
1001 SW Klickitat Way, Suite 201 • Seattle, WA 98134
800-553-4453 • mbooks@mountaineersbooks.org
www.mountaineersbooks.org

An independent nonprofit publisher since 1960

YOU MAY ALSO LIKE

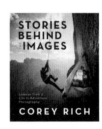

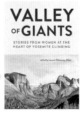